The Body, Dance and Cultural Theory

Also by Helen Thomas

Dance, Gender and Culture (ed.)
Dance, Modernity and Culture
Dance in the City (ed.)

The Body, Dance and Cultural Theory

HELEN THOMAS

palgrave
macmillan

First published 2003 by
PALGRAVE MACMILLAN
Houndmills, Basingstoke, Hampshire RG21 6XS and
175 Fifth Avenue, New York, N.Y. 10010
Companies and representatives throughout the world

PALGRAVE MACMILLAN is the global academic imprint of the Palgrave
Macmillan divison of St. Martin's Press, LLC and of Palgrave Macmillan Ltd.
Macmillan® is a registered trademark in the United States, United Kingdom
and other countries. Palgrave is a registered trademark in the European
Union and other countries.

ISBN 0–333–72431–3 hardback
ISBN 0–333–72432–1 paperback

This book is printed on paper suitable for recycling and made from fully
managed and sustained forest sources.

A catalogue record for this book is available from the British Library.

Library of Congress Cataloging-in-Publication Data

Thomas, Helen, 1947–
    The body, dance, and cultural theory / Helen Thomas.
       p. cm.
    Includes bibliographical references (p.) and index.
    ISBN 0–333–72431–3 (hbk.)   ISBN 0–333–72432–1 (pbk.)
      1. Dance—Social aspects. 2. Dance—Anthropological aspects.
    3. Body, Human—Social aspects.   I. Title.
    GV1588.6.T44 2003
    306.4'84—dc21   2003042928

10 9 8 7 6 5 4 3 2 1
12 11 10 09 08 07 06 05 04 03

Printed in China

To Paul and David

Contents

PART II DANCE, THE BODY AND
CULTURAL THEORY

Acknowledgements

I would like to thank the following people for their invaluable help, guidance and support in the development and the fine-tuning of this book. I wrote the first half of the book while I was Head of Department and had a severe bout of RSI. I would like to thank Goldsmiths College for enabling me to have the support of a research assistant over a period of two years to stop me using the computer. As the research assistant, Jamilah Ahmed, who was then my PhD student, sat silently and patiently at the computer, sometimes for hours, waiting for the words to come out of my mouth so that she could word process them, I became acutely aware that writing is an embodied activity. I learnt a great deal about writing/working with Jamilah and I am extremely grateful to her for the time and effort she put into this book and other research projects over those difficult, and sometimes hilariously funny, times. Gay Morris read and commented on Chapters 1–6. I thank her for the criticisms, corrections and suggestions, many of which I took on board in the final draft. Through Gay's efforts, I also learnt more about the differences between UK English and US English. Thanks also to Don Slater and Stacey Prickett, who read and commented on Chapters 1–3 and 4 respectively. Stacey also tried out some of the material in her MA ballet course. Bryan Turner reviewed the manuscript and made some very helpful suggestions to fine-tune it. Paul Thomas proof-read the whole manuscript from a non-sociological point of view, correcting my grammar on the way, for which I am extremely grateful. I also thank my editor, Catherine Gray, for her insightful comments on the first draft of four of the chapters and for making the final process run smoothly and quickly. Despite all this expert advice and assistance, I am only too aware that in the final analysis, the responsibility for the work lies firmly with me.

Helen Thomas

Introduction

The study of the body in society has been a major focus of social and cultural analysis since the late 1980s. The body is generally the primary means of expression and representation in western social and theatrical dance. Given this, one might suppose that social and cultural analysts, whose interests centred on the relations between the body and culture, might have afforded dance more than a passing glance in their deliberations. Few social or cultural theorists of the body have been drawn to address dance systematically as a discursive or situated aesthetic practice, to generate insights into, for example, the politics of sexual and/or racial and/or class differences as they are traced through representations of the body and inscribed in bodily practices. These concerns have preoccupied social and cultural critics in the past twenty or so years.[1]

This has not been the case with other artistic and cultural fields such as art, literature, film or the mass media, whose products and discourses surrounding the body have been used as source materials for the analysis of difference and representation (for example, Pollock, 1988; Mulvey, 1989; Gaines and Herzog, 1990; Goldstein, 1991; Nead, 1992; Phelan, 1993; Gamman and Makinen, 1994; Gilman, 1995; Wolff, 1995; Betterton, 1996; Foster, 1996; Curti, 1998). The journal *Body & Society*, established in 1995, has seldom contained research articles that feature the word dance in the title. Having said this, the publication of a number of multidisciplinary collections and single-authored texts on dance since 1990 (for example, Cowan, 1990; Novack, 1990; Ness, 1992; Thomas, 1993a, 1997; Browning, 1995; Foster, 1995, 1996b; Goellner and Murphy, 1995; Koritz, 1995; Desmond, 1997, 2001; Malbon, 1999; Pini, 2001) points to the fact that there is an emergent interest in dance within the margins of the more established academic disciplines such as sociology, anthropology, cultural studies and literary theory. This, in part, is due to the increasing blurring of the boundaries between academic disciplines that has taken place since around the mid-1980s, in response to what was labelled as a 'series of crises in representation' (Boyne and Rattansi, 1990). But this emergent interest may also have something to do with the fact that the majority of the aforementioned authors and editors have trained in two disciplines, one of which was dance.

The study of dance as a significant movement system in its own right, from a formalist (aesthetic) or a contextual perspective, is a relatively new area of scholarship compared with other more established academic disciplines, such as sociology or cultural studies. But the boundaries of dance scholarship are also being eroded, through the impact of the challenges posed to the unity of theory and method by feminist, post-modernist and poststructuralist thought. Recent dance scholarship has been influenced increasingly by the shifts and swings that have befallen other disciplines. The problematic of the body in connection with issues involving representation and difference has become a key area of inter-est for a number of 'dance studies' writers (for example, Franko, 1993, 1995; Burt, 1995, 1998; Daly, 1995; Koritz, 1995; Morris, 1996a, 2001; Cooper Albright, 1997; Desmond, 1997, 2001; Briginshaw, 2001). Just as there appears to be an emergent interest in dance as a topic of inquiry from several social and cultural critics, so there is a burgeoning interest among dance scholars in the themes and issues that have preoccupied more traditional disciplines in recent years.

The major aim of this book is to harness the interest in the body in social and cultural analysis to the concern with the body in dance studies; to examine, by means of a case study approach, a variety of ways (by no means complete or inclusive) of looking at dance as a social and/or artistic bodily practice. The book draws on a range of perspec-tives that have engaged social and cultural critics: feminism, semiotics, poststructuralism and postmodernism. In so doing, it indicates the strengths and weaknesses of these approaches. In turn, the book aims to contribute to contemporary debates in social and cultural criticism concerning the construction and production of difference and repre-sentation that emerged through a series of theoretical and methodolog-ical interventions and that fostered the interest in the study of the body in recent years.

The original intention was to start with dance case studies and work outwards to the social and cultural analysis of the body. This proved too unwieldy and presumed some background knowledge of the study of dance and of the body. Moreover, the fact that dance studies is relatively young in research terms means that it does not have quite the range of case study material to draw on as other more established disciplines.

In the end, I chose to start with the problem of the body in social and cultural theory and from there move outwards towards questions associated with conducting ethnographic research and then on to the particular dance case studies. The book is in two parts: the first addresses the body in social and cultural theory and the second is directed towards dance and the body and cultural theory. There is a gradual shift of focus from a consideration of the body in society in Part I, 'Cultural Bodies', to the body in dance in Part II, 'Dance, the Body and Cultural Theory'. The intention is that dance becomes a means of reflecting on the problems associated with the ways in which the body has been conceptualised generally in social and cultural theory, which are addressed in Part I. At the same time, I hope to show that dance offers cultural and social criticism a rich and relatively uncharted terrain for studying cultural bodies.

Chapter 1 centres on an examination of approaches to the body before it became a major area of interest in the 1980s. The chapter offers a brief and selective chronology of the uneven development of the study of the body in anthropology and sociology. It also sets out the terms, shifts and nuances of the debate between two major perspectives on the body: social constructionism and foundationalism. This involves a consideration of the separation between the mind and the body in the predominant tradition of western social thought and the privileging of the former over the latter.

In Chapter 2, the 'story' of the body in social and cultural studies directs attention to debates within feminism and poststructuralism that have had a significant impact on the area of study. The chapter does have a historical dimension. The main aim, however, is to elaborate on the triumph of social constructionist over foundationalist approaches and the consequence of this for social analysis, which, to a large extent, sustained and supported the mind/body dichotomy inscribed in the western humanist tradition. The chapter also addresses recent attempts to develop a more corporeal approach to the study of the body, which involves the construct of embodiment. Chapters 1 and 2 need to be treated together, as the intention is to assemble a picture of certain key concerns that have predominated in social and cultural approaches to the body, historically and thematically.

Chapter 3 builds on the first two chapters by redirecting questions of theory towards the problems associated with conducting qualitative research, particularly ethnography. This involves an exploration of postmodern and feminist interventions in ethnography which questioned hitherto taken-for-granted assumptions regarding the use of ethnographic methods. The discussion directs attention towards the contention that ethnography is an embodied activity and that the ethnographic field is an embodied social and physical space. The embodied character of ethnographic research has not been particularly highlighted in anthropology. This is where dance anthropology comes into the analytic frame. Dance anthropologists have drawn attention to the embodied nature of dance ethnography. Two dance case studies are drawn upon to consider the questions they raise regarding ethnographic research and the study of the body. Dance, it is argued, as a topic and resource for research, offers the possibility of overcoming the mind/body dualisms that have haunted much of the work on the body. This chapter functions as the connecting cog between Part I and Part II.

The shift in the focus of the book towards dance, the body and cultural theory is established in Part II, through the four case study chapters. Chapter 4 centres on an examination of specific dance forms and practices. The aim, here, is to counter the lack of attention given to the moving body in social and cultural studies. It offers a close examination of the prioritising of the senses of sight in ballet and touch in contact improvisation from the performers' and spectators' perspectives. In so doing, it explores and highlights some of the dualisms in western culture. The chapter considers the notion that 'bodies have histories', which emerged in Chapter 2, by addressing the problems associated with reconstructing dances from the modern dance tradition on contemporary dancing bodies.

Dance as a performance art, unlike other art forms, such as painting, literature and sculpture, does not leave behind it a record of its presence in the form of an object. Drama and music are also performance arts but performances are based on interpretations of a writer's script or a composer's score. If we want to know what a particular dance looked like, dance scholars and interested parties generally have to resort to descriptions in history books, the odd still picture or comments from dance critics. There has been a growing concern to preserve and restore past dances which were created by early modern dance choreographers in the 1930s, as a consequence of developments in film and video technology and dance notation. Chapter 5 addresses the problems associated with attempts to preserve and reconstruct dances from the past for audiences and dancers of today. In so doing, it examines issues of authenticity in music and dance and technical reproduction.

Chapter 6 draws on a range of case studies on social and theatrical dance to examine questions of representations of race, sexuality and particularly gender in dance. The first part of the chapter centres on a discussion of four ethnographic studies involving social dancing, which highlight the ways in which the body in the dances under consideration is marked by race and sexuality. The second section examines the ways in which representations of women and sexuality in dance have been analysed in recent studies in dance history. The influence of feminist theory on approaches to dance history is also explored. One of the implications to be drawn from all the case studies discussed in this chapter is that dance has the potential to disrupt or transgress the dominant social order. This leads to a discussion of the often unquestioned linking of dance with liberation or resistance and, by extension, the feminine, in certain dance studies approaches and contemporary cultural criticism.

The final case study in Chapter 7 is contemporary club culture or rave culture in the context of youth cultures. This includes a critical assessment of the cultural theories and observations which commentators have drawn on to explain the emergence, rapid expansion and subsequent segmentation of rave culture. The chapter also incorporates a brief discussion of the influential subcultural theories of 'resistance' and 'style' that emerged from the pioneering work of the Birmingham Centre of Contemporary Cultural Studies. The importance of dancing in rave did not feature strongly in the accounts of rave culture in the early 1990s. That is, cultural commentators of rave seldom asked what clubbers actually did when they were out clubbing. The codes and practices of dancing in the context of clubbing events have been addressed in several recently published studies. The final section of this chapter centres on a discussion of three particular case studies of rave and post-rave culture, which gives consideration to the ways in which the authors critique traditional subcultural analysis of youth cultures and postmodern approaches to rave, which emerged in the early 1990s. The studies show how subjectivities are embodied. One of the key ways in which subjectivities and intersubjectivities are articulated in club culture is through dancing and, as such, the practices of clubbing, which involve an embodied understanding, require careful attention.

Part I

Cultural Bodies

Chapter 1

The Body in Culture: Before the Body Project

Introduction

I shall begin this initial discussion of developments in approaches to the study of the body in contemporary western culture with an anecdotal account which I hope will point to recent shifts in discourses of, and around, the body.

In the late 1980s and early 1990s, I gave a series of lectures on the sociology of the body for an MA programme in the Sociology Department at Goldsmiths. These lectures developed and grew over time with the inclusion of new material. Although the interest in culture in sociological discourse, which became known as the 'cultural turn' in sociology, was gathering force by this time, the inclusion of the body in course programmes was still relatively new. One of the most disconcerting features of giving these sessions was the regularity with which this talk about the body in society seemed to provoke strong responses and unusual bodily behaviour in some of the students. That is, unusual bodily behaviour for what, in the context of other lecture courses, was an orderly lecture format with groups of mature and interested students. On one memorable occasion, when I was in full flow, a student seated behind a desk in the left-hand corner in the front row stood up suddenly and, without saying a word, stomped straight across the room passing directly in front of me, and exited stage right out the door. To all intents and purposes he did not appear to be going for a natural break. He returned some time later, retracing his pathway across the room in front of me to his desk, as if I were simply not there. Meanwhile, another student was questioning, in what I could only perceive to be a verbally accusative manner, what he considered to be the impossibility of the body being a 'natural' symbol. Yet another student, who was seated towards the back right-hand corner of the room (the top right-hand diagonal is a powerful position on the stage), rose

9

to his feet to point out the futility of studying the body in society in the first place, with extended forearm and finger pointing in rhythm with his speech. This student, I seem to remember, also walked out of the lecture and came back in again. These kinds of responses, which were uncommon in the context of the more traditional aspects of sociology I routinely lectured on, appeared to be the norm in the annual sessions on the body in society and culture.[1]

There are some unspoken but generally acknowledged ground rules of acceptable behaviour associated with giving or attending a formal academic lecture, just as there are cultural conventions for 'proper' audience behaviour, although these may vary according to cultural context. The traditional 'lecture' generally takes place in an ordered, bounded public space in which the teacher or lecturer routinely speaks from the front of the room, with the students in front of him or her, sitting in tiers or behind rows of desks, listening and making notes. In terms of interpersonal spatial arrangements, the lecturer is the one who moves, sometimes more or less, while the students remain relatively still in their place. Generally speaking, the hierarchical relationship works in such a way that students can interrupt the proceedings to comment or ask questions if they are invited to do so by the lecturer. To some extent, this is because the unspoken lecturer/student relation in the standard lecture setting is founded on the notion of a one-way communication process from the individual lecturer to the assembled student body, although occasional low-level whispers between neighbouring students are commonplace and acceptable. Any teacher who has tried to break out of the formal lecture mould and encouraged students to communicate publicly across the invisible spatial divide that exists between teacher and students in this setting will understand how difficult this usually is to achieve. The student who speaks out publicly, almost, as it were, separates him/herself from the group. As likely as not, he or she becomes the object of the gaze for the lecturer and the other students who turn their bodies towards the speaker and this, I suggest, contributes to the difficulty of speaking out. Moreover, it is often the case that other students do not like it when a student does engage the lecturer because it interrupts the communication flow from the teacher to the rest of the student body.[2]

What is interesting about the lectures on the body discussed above is that the unspoken rules for appropriate behaviour in the lecture space were disrupted, and were made visible and unstable by the intrusion of bodies and voices into, and across, spaces that are generally treated as 'sacred'. As these bodily behaviours disordered the sacred spaces, the rule-bound character of the spaces was revealed. It was not only the rules that were made visible; the individual bodies were also thrust into visibility in an environment in which they are usually in a collective frame.

In certain respects, these bodily interruptions reminded me of going to see performances of Merce Cunningham's dance company in the late 1960s when they first began to perform in London on a regular basis. It almost became 'business as usual' for certain members of the audience to stomp out of the auditorium mid-performance, outraged by what they considered to be Cunningham's avant-garde 'not dance' style of choreography to the accompaniment of John Cage's 'not music' compositions. Cunningham was committed to pushing the boundaries of dance art as far as he could and no doubt expected these outbursts of audience indignation.

I, as lecturer/performer, was getting near to the point where I dreaded giving these lectures on the body because of the effect they seemed to have on the students, and on the interaction with the body–subject who was standing out in front doing most of the talking. Over the years, as audiences became more familiar with the Cunningham/Cage aesthetic, and the work gained in status, fewer and fewer people walked out of the auditorium during a Cunningham performance. Similarly, a few years down the line, this 'body work' lecture block came to be received with much more ease and engagement by subsequent generations of students.

Although the body had been a marginal topic in mainstream academic discourse, it turned into a veritable industry in the 1990s. In effect, it became a 'body project' (Shilling, 1993) generating conferences, numerous book publications and articles with the body in the title, and even an academic journal devoted to exploring the relations between the body and society. From being previously resistant to this kind of work, sociology students now came to sign up in droves for courses with the body and/or culture in the title. Even my courses or sessions on the Sociology of Dance began to lose the totally feminised appeal that such course content had held for several years, and increasingly began to attract interested male students. My anecdotal evidence reflects recent shifts in the fortunes of the study of the body within social and cultural studies which, it has been argued, have resulted from the influences of feminism, postmodernism, the concern with health (prompted by HIV and AIDS), the environment and consumerism in late modernity.

In this chapter and the one that follows, I hope to build up a picture of certain key concerns that have predominated in social and cultural approaches to the body. It is not my intention to provide a comprehensive overview of developments in the study of the body. There are a number of recent texts that offer sustained accounts and critiques of the developments and debates on the body in different areas of the social sciences and humanities (see, for example, Turner, 1984, 1992; Ussher, 1989; Featherstone *et al.*, 1991; Shilling, 1993; Csordas, 1994a; Seymour, 1998; Williams and Bendelow, 1998; Burkitt, 1999; Weiss and Haber, 1999). Chapters 1 and 2 will lay the groundwork for certain recurrent themes within the social sciences and humanities that will be taken up and explored in relation to dance, as a topic and resource of cultural inquiry, in the succeeding case study chapters. In western theatre dance and social dance forms, the moving body is the primary mode of expression and representation. Theories of the body, as I will show in the dance case study chapters, have also become important in the field of dance studies in recent years, particularly in regard to gender representations and difference. A number of dance scholars have also become concerned to show how an attention to dance and dancing can contribute to social and cultural analysis of the body, as well as criticisms of the ways in which the body has been conceptualised in social and cultural studies. As will become clear in Part II, the activity of dance or dancing has not held a major interest for social and cultural critics, which is surprising, given the growth of academic interest in the body and culture. In order to begin to understand this neglect and in part remedy it, it is first necessary to contextualise recent approaches to the study of the body in terms of a 'pre-history' of the body in the traditions of sociology and anthropology.

This chapter continues by focusing on considerations of the body in the social sciences prior to the turn to culture and the body in these areas. The aim is to show how these contributed to the subsequent dominance of social constructionist approaches in contemporary social and cultural studies. The term 'social constructionism', as Chris Shilling has noted, 'is an umbrella term to denote those views which suggest that the body is somehow shaped, constrained and even invented by society' (1993, p. 72). The body, for social constructionists, to a greater or lesser degree, is a social entity. As such, they argue that analysing the body as a biological or natural phenomenon cannot generate adequate explanations. Naturalistic approaches view the body as a pre-social, biological entity. Observable differences between individuals, groups and cultures, from the perspective of naturalism, are biologically determined and not socially constructed. In naturalistic approaches, the body is the foundation upon which the social is built.

Social constructionist approaches privilege the symbolic, textual or discursive aspects of the body over and above, and often to the exclusion of, foundational, physical and experiential elements, which are also available in the history of the body. In so doing, as I hope to show, social constructionist approaches have helped to sustain the dualisms inherent in the western humanist tradition of thought. Although this is largely a 'historical' discussion, contemporary developments are also brought into the frame, where relevant.

Before the body project

Although the body as topic and resource for social and cultural analyses has blossomed in the years leading up to the new millennium, it would be a mistake to think that hitherto it had been entirely absent in all areas of the social sciences. It can be argued that the subject of the body as a topic of inquiry *in its own right*, until quite recently, had been largely ignored by sociology, although, as Shilling (1993) has argued, it can be seen to be lurking underneath the surface of the discourses. Having said this, sociology has paid scant attention to the singularly most apparent fact of human life, which is that human beings *have* bodies that are both physically delimiting and enabling and that, to a certain extent, they *are* bodies (Turner, 1984). It is, after all, through our bodies that we feel, see, smell, touch, think, speak and experience the world. In part, the failure of sociology to address the body directly is a result of its overriding concern to separate and privilege the social over the natural world and the individual. The founders of sociology in the late nineteenth century sought to demarcate the domain of sociology from other more established social and natural sciences, in order to establish sociology as a scientific discipline in its own right. At the heart of the classical tradition of sociology there lies a rigid separation of the social from the biological and psychological, with the former assuming prime importance. The domination of social aspects over physical and psychological elements in the classical tradition, for the most part, has formed the basis of modern sociology (see Thomas, 1998a, pp. 110–12). In so doing, it has reinforced the culture/nature, mind/body dualisms inherent in the liberal humanist tradition of thought. As Paul Hirst and Penny Woolley have noted:

> Sociologists have, on the whole, energetically denied the importance of genetic, physical and individual psychological factors in human social life. In so doing they have reinforced and theorized a traditional cultural opposition between nature and culture. Social relations can even be seen as a *denial* of nature. (1982, p. 22)

As Bryan Turner (1991) has indicated, there are other related reasons why classical European sociology did not give rise to a coherent sociology of the body. Classical theorists like Max Weber, Émile Durkheim, Georg Simmel and Ferdinand Tönnies were concerned to define and understand the character of industrial urban societies rather than the differences between human beings in terms of social evolution. Their concern was centred on the 'problem of social order'. That is, they wanted to know how it was possible for societies to survive and maintain a degree of social order in the face of the rapidly changing economic and political structures, in what was often viewed as an increasingly alien social environment. Classical sociology was also concerned to understand the character of industrial capitalism and the kind of social action that it was founded upon. The construct of social action that resulted from this modern social formation, particularly from the point of view of German sociology, as Turner (1991) argues, was one instrumental reason. That is, social action came to be viewed in terms of the most efficient means to achieve a given end. This model of rational action, in effect, became the yardstick for measuring all other forms of action. The question of the ontological status of the social actors, according to Turner, was overshadowed by this rational means–ends model, which served to formulate the key notions of the social actor: agency, choice and goals.

Further, Turner argues, the key thinkers in the classical tradition were concerned to map the historical development of the shift from feudalism to capitalism, and to understand the causes and effects of changing social structures. Consequently, the central problematic of what is nature, which, as we shall see, helped to mould anthropology, remained quiet, although implicated, in sociology. Simon Williams and Gillian Bendelow (1998, p. 23), whilst agreeing to some extent with Turner, have recently argued that the body is recoverable through a careful 'critical re-reading' of the sociological classics in 'corporeal terms', in light of the insights generated through the turn to the body in late modernity. Thus, for example, in Weber's (1976 [1904–5]) analysis of the pivotal role of the Protestant ethic in the development of modern capitalism, through Puritanism's emphasis on hard work for its own sake and the denial of all things of the flesh, the ascetic body is already and always implicated. In a poignant discussion towards the end of his text, Weber warns us that the ghost of the Protestant ethic that haunts modern capitalism, rationalisation, is in danger of penetrating into every corner of everyday life, with a resultant dehumanising effect. 'The Puritans', he tells us, 'wanted to work in a calling;

we are forced to do so' (p. 181).[3] The process of rationalisation, for Weber, entails 'a disenchantment of the world'.

Similarly, the construct of human (bodily) labour is central to Marx's philosophical anthropology, which he addressed in the 1844 *Economic and Philosophical Manuscripts* (1959). It is through the engagement of human labour that men (*sic*) differentiate themselves from nature and become social beings, transforming the natural world and themselves in the process. Moreover, capitalist societies, according to Marx, require continual production and reproduction of bodies in order to survive, which means that 'bodies become both the *means* and *object* of human labour' (Williams and Bendelow, 1998, p. 11). Having said this, Marx was overwhelmingly concerned with developing and demonstrating his historical materialist analysis of the capitalist mode of production with a view to projecting its demise, as opposed to focusing on the 'sensual emotional aspects of human beings' (1959, p. 12). Weber, too, was ultimately concerned with the social structure of modern capitalism and with generating a value-free sociology. His ruminations on the sorry ramifications of asceticism on modern capitalism are brought to an abrupt halt with the recognition that he is straying into 'the world of judgement and faith' (1976, p. 182), which, he declares, is of no interest to the task at hand. The real task is to trace the 'fact and direction' (p. 183) of the influence of Protestantism on modern capitalism. Thus, although there may be a history of the body in classical sociology waiting to be excavated, other factors, including the 'spectre of biologism' (Williams and Bendelow, 1998, p. 13) and the emphasis on instrumental action (Turner, 1991), as discussed above, were significant causes of the relative neglect of the body in sociology.

While classical sociology ultimately neglected to place the body at the centre of its agenda, it has been a focus of anthropological attention, to a greater or lesser extent, since the late nineteenth century (see Polhemus (1975) for a detailed discussion of the various phases of development in the anthropology of the body). A brief discussion of the reasons behind the emergence of the body as a site of investigation in the discourses of anthropology will shed further light on the dualistic character of sociology and the triumph of social constructionist approaches to the body in the social sciences. In turn, this will facilitate an understanding of recent challenges to sociology that were prompted by the rise of new developments within the academy and cultural changes in late modernity. These challenges subsequently opened up the pathway for the emergence of the body project.

In its early phase of development in the nineteenth century, anthropology directed its attention towards a consideration of the universal state of humanity. That is, it directed attention towards asking questions about the nature or essence (ontology) of man (*sic*). Philosophical anthropology, within the context of European colonialism and cultural imperialism, had to consider what human beings had in common (the universals) in relation to wide-ranging observable differences between cultures. Not surprisingly, as Turner (1991, p. 1) indicates, 'the ontological centrality of human embodiment emerged as a site of universality'. Because all human beings are and have bodies, certain requirements must be satisfied in order for the species to survive. 'The fact of human embodiment' led to a consideration of what were the minimum requisite social and cultural conditions for the maintenance and continuation of the species. Despite the wide-ranging observable differences between cultures, human beings at root were deemed to share certain common characteristics which made possible the survival of the species. The body, in part, as Turner suggests, provided one answer to the problematic question of social relativism and thus became a significant issue in the initial stages of anthropology.

Moreover, the body in pre-modern societies played a pivotal role in the rites of passage from one social status to another. Because the body constituted a more universal site for public symbolisation through ritual, it became a significant focus for the anthropological gaze. This is not to imply that the centrality of the body is only to be found in the societies of the 'other'. As Horace Miner's 1956 paper on 'Body Ritual among the Nacirema' ('American' spelt backwards) clearly showed, body rituals were central to the rapidly expanding consumer culture of the most dominant western market society in the postwar era. In this context, individuals conducted the many rituals enacted on the body on a daily basis in the privacy of the bathroom 'shrine', as opposed to public ceremonies. Further, in contemporary consumer culture, dress, demeanour and cosmetics are important markers of lifestyle and social class. Consequently, women are constantly being invited to transform themselves by doing something to their bodies. This notwithstanding, the public signification of the body as a marker of the individual's status, age, family, sex and tribal affiliation is more clearly symbolised in pre-modern societies, and anthropology in the nineteenth century started out by focusing on these sites.

The incorporation of evolutionary theory and, particularly, social Darwinism into anthropology also contributed to the interest in the body, although its influence in the development of the discipline was largely of a negative kind. Charles Darwin's (1969) study of *The Expression of the Emotions in Man and Animals*, first published in 1872, argued that bodily expression is either innate or biologically determined and that it is cross-culturally universal. Responses to Darwin's thesis led to the development of a culture/nature debate within anthropology that centred on the issue of whether bodily expression is culturally relative or universal (Polhemus, 1975). The followers of social Darwinism, being interested in the natural, non-social aspects of behaviour, adopted the universalist position as a means of verifying their proposition. Cultural anthropologists, such as Kroeber (1952), Hall (1969), and La Barre (1978), being interested in the cultural aspects of human behaviour, have tended to adopt the cultural relativist position that bodily expressions varied from culture to culture.

This culture/nature debate developed into a second related debate, namely the learnt versus the innate character of bodily expression, or the nurture/nature dichotomy, with the cultural anthropologists again championing the nurture side of the argument (see Bateson and Mead, 1942; Hall, 1969; Efron, 1972; Birdwhistell, 1973). Neo-Darwinists (Eibl-Eibesfeldt, 1972; Ekman, 1977), unsurprisingly, rejected the nurture argument. On the basis of evidence drawn from comparative studies of animals and humans, they argued that there is a high degree of association and consistency across cultures between primary (natural) effects such as anger and fear and the facial gestures that express them. Accordingly, the neo-Darwinists argued, these facial expressions are natural and not subject to cultural learning.

The notion of the 'human animal' exemplified in the naturalistic approach to the body has had an impact on and, to a certain extent, has reinforced contemporary popular perceptions of the body as the biological basis upon which the individual and culture are built (see Fast, 1970; Morris, 1979). This view also finds expression in the recent development of sociobiology (see Hirst and Woolley, 1982, pp. 66–89). The dominance of the cultural strand in anthropology, in comparison with the marginal development of physical anthropology, however, has meant that the key theoretical trends in anthropology, like sociology, have addressed the cultural side of the nature/culture divide (Turner, 1991).

The American cultural anthropologists and ethnographers mentioned above were so busy doing battle with the students of animal behaviour that they failed to develop a more comprehensive theoretical approach to the study of the body (Polhemus, 1975). As the discussion in Chapter 2 will demonstrate, a significant exception to this is to be found in the work of Erving Goffman (1971, 1972, 1979). There was, nevertheless, a small but consistent tradition, which developed out of the European Durkheimian school of thought and which sought to examine the relations between the body and society, in terms of 'body symbolism' (see Needham, 1973; Polhemus, 1975; Thomas, 1998a). Writers such as Robert Hertz in 1909, Marcel Mauss in 1934 and much later Mary Douglas in the 1960s and 1970s considered the 'social' aspects of body expression in order to illustrate the rules and the categories that are constituted through the 'social body', or society.

The body as symbol

Durkheim, as suggested earlier, attempted to demonstrate the power of the 'social order' over institutions and individuals. Society, for Durkheim, constituted a reality in its own right. He sought to reveal how society shaped the individual in its own image by examining a range of social phenomena including the division of labour, suicide, and knowledge and beliefs. Durkheim did not specifically examine the relation of the body to society in any detail, except to indicate that it was located on the profane side of the sacred/profane religious dualism (Williams and Bendelow, 1998). Durkheim (1976 [1915]) argued that 'primitive' religious thought was characterised by the polar opposition between the sacred and the profane. The sacred embodied all that is good and pure while the profane represented all that is harmful to the sacred, the common and impure. Objects categorised under the sacred were elevated in the eyes of society, while those categorised under the profane were lowered and despised. The categories, rules and rituals surrounding the sacred and profane in primitive religions were established by consensus and maintained by coercion, according to Durkheim. That is, they were socially generated, not natural facts of existence. The sacred, in order to maintain its purity, had to be protected from outside forces and thus was surrounded by rituals to maintain its distinction and to ward off potential danger. The sacred/profane opposition affected the ways in which social groups treated the body. While the soul, for example, was viewed as sacred, the body was viewed as 'essentially profane' (see Williams and Bendelow, 1998, pp. 13–14). Durkheim, as indicated above, did not develop this in any depth. Rather, it was his views on the social construction of knowledge and beliefs, which he addressed in *The Elementary Forms of Religious Life* (1976 [1915]), which provided the impetus for this particular social constructionist tradition of the body. From the examination of aboriginal Australian and native American-Indian 'primitive' belief systems,

Durkheim argued that the basis of knowledge and belief in the cosmos in primitive systems of thought was constituted from within society itself as opposed to external social forces. Thus, primitive systems of belief and knowledge, for Durkheim, were socially constructed. Durkheim did not apply his findings to 'modern' industrial social systems because of his adherence to a dichotomous model of 'us' (modern)/ 'them' (primitive), and his belief in the objectivity of (modern) science (Douglas, 1975b). That is to say, he envisioned that modern societies were completely different from primitive societies. He also believed that while primitive systems of thought were socially determined, modern systems of thought were objective because they were based on science. Regardless, if these two beliefs are removed from the picture, the theoretical import of the analysis remains. This is particularly the case if the tables are turned round and contemporary western systems of thought and practices are examined in the same light as those of the traditionally perceived 'primitive others' (Douglas, 1975b), as Horace Miner (1956) demonstrated in his 'Nacirema' essay which was mentioned earlier. On first reading, the Nacirema tribe appear to be engaged in a strange set of ritual bodily practices that are far removed from 'modern' western market societies. On close inspection it turns out that the 'sacred shrine', where a myriad of body purification rituals take place, is nothing more than the bathroom, and the 'charm-box', in front of which the rituals are performed, is just the medicine cabinet. Miner's essay not only called into question the objectivity of anthropological accounts of societies of the 'other', it also begged the question as to whether the divide between 'us' and 'them' is as great as it is usually perceived (Douglas, 1975b). From this vantage point, forms of knowledge (traditional and modern) may be viewed as being generated from and organised within the social realm and enacted through a whole variety of everyday practices and experiences. That is, knowledge, 'ours' and 'theirs', and that includes bodily knowledge, is socially constructed.

Hertz, Mauss and latterly Douglas sought to apply Durkheim's ideas on the social construction of knowledge to the study of the body. In essence, they argued that the ways in which the body is viewed and treated in society reflect the rules and values inscribed in the social order. The characteristics of the 'natural' untamed body are given a symbolic loading by society, and societal members treat those, in turn, as natural or non-social. The human body in this approach is viewed as a microcosm of society, upon which order and symbolic values are imposed and in turn are rendered as 'natural' or non-social. This follows Durkheim's view of the individual as a microcosm of society.

So powerful is the social over the individual that the individual, without knowing it, is constrained to act in certain ways by the system's rules and categories. The body, in this view, is a symbol of society, which can be examined for the purposes of gaining a greater understanding of the social system in question. Hertz (1973 [1909]) turned his attention to the study of left/right body symbolism arguing that there was a tendency towards the primacy of the right hand in 'primitive' religious belief systems. The right hand was accorded a privileged status because it was categorised as sacred, while the left was despised because it was affiliated with the profane. This, in turn, generated much debate within the French school of anthropology as to whether the right hand was indeed revered and valued over the left throughout non-western cultures (see Needham, 1973).

Mauss (1973 [1934]), on the other hand, examined everyday 'techniques of the body' such as running, sleeping and walking, arguing that these so-called 'natural' bodily behaviours are learnt through formal and informal educational processes within a given culture. The concern with bodily techniques reemerged many years later in Pierre Bourdieu's ideas on bodily hexis and habitus, in Foucault's work on technologies of the body and in Goffman's analysis of everyday bodily behaviour in public places, which will be addressed more fully in the next chapter. Other researchers have used Mauss's work as a starting point for developing the sociology of emotions (Lyon, 1997), and for comparing and contrasting dialectical analysis in anthropology stemming from the neo-Kantian tradition of thought with the descriptive approach offered by Mauss (Hunter and Saunders, 1995).

Hertz and Mauss particularly stated that they were concerned to incorporate the 'natural' aspects of the body into their accounts. Hertz argued that biological considerations should be included in the study of the body in society. Mauss argued that the analysis of bodily techniques should involve physical and psychological elements as well as the social. Thus, they recognised the importance of including what Turner (1992) has termed a 'foundationalist' approach to the body, which takes account of the fact that we have, and to a certain extent are, bodies. Foundationalism, in Turner's sense, is linked to naturalism inasmuch as it recognises that the body is a biological organism. But foundationalism is more inclusive than most naturalist approaches because it also takes in the view that human beings experience the world through their bodies (Shilling, 1993). Naturalistic viewpoints generally do not factor in this idea of the 'lived experience' of the body into their accounts. In the last resort, Hertz's and Mauss's overwhelming adherence to the social constructionism inscribed in the Durkheimian paradigm rendered redundant any significant exploration of the phenomenal (lived) body. As a consequence, they reinforced the culture/nature dichotomy discussed earlier in this chapter.

Douglas's work built on and extended the approach taken by Hertz and Mauss, in particular, by maintaining that the body is always treated as an image of society. The symbolism worked out on the human body, according to Douglas, is one of the most direct areas of human experiences:

> The body is a model that can stand for any bounded system. Its boundaries can represent any boundaries that are threatened or precarious. The body is a complex structure. The function of its different parts and their relation afford a source of symbols for other complex structures. (Douglas, 1970, p. 138)

The 'powers' and 'dangers' that the social system generates, Douglas argues, are reproduced in the human body. The margins and boundaries of the social system, she maintains, are particularly vulnerable to attack from outside forces that could destabilise the society. Douglas (1970) examines cultural attitudes to bodily waste, such as nail parings, hair loss, faeces and so on. She argues that the social system's concern to maintain itself in its boundaries is reflected in the care taken to maintain the boundaries and margins of the body, through associated ritual cleanliness. We come to know our society through the rules and rituals surrounding the body and the prevailing societal attitudes towards it. Therefore, the sociologist or anthropologist can learn much about the society under consideration by paying close attention to the attitudes, perceptions and practices associated with the body. In this way, the body becomes a legitimate site for social investigation.

Turner (1992) has suggested that Douglas's work is more concerned with the symbolism of 'risk' than with the body symbolism as such. Thus, as Douglas demonstrates in *Purity and Danger* (1970), societies at risk or at times of crisis will symbolically shroud the boundaries of the body with rituals and sanctions to preserve it and to prevent unwanted foreign matter from polluting or defiling it. With individuals increasingly being exposed to danger through environmental hazards and technological developments generated by global systems, it is not so astonishing, as Shilling (1993) has commented, that the body has become a project for pressure groups and individuals living in contemporary 'risk societies' (Beck, 1992). Environmental scientists and consumer groups, for example, have expressed concerns over the possible long-term dangers to bodily health, particularly to growing bodies, resulting from the increasing use of chemicals and pesticides in food growing and production.

In an attempt to get away from the culture/nature and the west/rest hierarchies in sociology and anthropology, Douglas (1973, 1975b) developed her analysis of the relation between 'two bodies' (the physical body and the social body). The central concern, here, is to provide a method for the analysis of ritual and body symbolism that would enable comparisons to be made between social groups who share the same social environment. She does this by adopting and modifying Basil Bernstein's (1971) influential (Durkheimian-inspired) theory of linguistic 'speech codes' and Mauss's concept of the body as an image of society. She proposes a modified structuralist approach and argues that there 'is a natural tendency' to represent situations of a certain kind 'in an appropriate bodily style' (1973, p. 97). She takes up the universalism inherent in the structuralist position by maintaining that the body is a 'natural symbol' because it is symbolised in all societies, to a greater or lesser extent. Her concern is not to delineate the features or common attitudes towards the body across cultures, as a structuralist approach such as that of Lévi-Strauss (1978) would advocate. Rather, attention is directed to analysing the ways in which particular cultures symbolise the body at a given moment in time. This is a consequence of her (Durkheimian) view that the 'social body constrains the way the physical body is perceived' (1973, p. 97). Douglas maintains that there is a reciprocal process of communication between the social body and the physical body and that the 'physical experience of the body' is 'always modified by the social categories through which it is known' (ibid., p. 64). She suggests that as the 'natural' expression of the body is culturally encoded and determined, so the 'social dimension' has to be treated seriously. This is an elaboration of the cultural relativist stance proposed in *Purity and Danger*, in which she argued that 'there is no such thing as absolute dirt', it is rather 'a matter of disorder', which 'exists in the eye of the beholder' (1970, p. 12).

Although Douglas begins from the proposition that there is a 'natural body', the focus of inquiry is overwhelmingly directed towards understanding the social formation that is mirrored in the ways in which the body is symbolised and perceived. As a result, according to Shilling (1993, p. 73), Douglas runs the risk of collapsing the ways in which individuals routinely experience, understand and perceive their bodies 'into the propositions and the categories made available by the social body'. That is, the phenomenal, experiencing body is in danger of becoming a blank slate upon which society stamps its image. Shilling points out that although Douglas's work has been influential in the social constructionist approach to the body in anthropology, sociologists for the most part have drawn on other sources to develop their social constructionist approaches, which are founded on an anti-foundationalist stance towards the body (Turner, 1992). However, it should be noted that poststructuralist feminists, such as Julia Kristeva, Judith Butler and Elizabeth Grosz, have drawn on and/or have developed aspects of Douglas's work on the body. Her ideas on the dangers located in the boundaries and margins of a social system (Butler, 1990a), and her construct of bodily disorder and dirt (Kristeva, 1982; Grosz, 1994), formulated in *Purity and Danger* (1970), have been particularly important.

As the body project began to get under way in the 1980s, Douglas's 'two bodies model' multiplied to take account of different aspects of the body in relation to the world. Nancy Scheper-Hughes and Margaret Lock (1987), for example, proposed a 'three bodies' typology: the individual, social and political. The individual body refers to the lived subjective experience of the body, while the social body, much like Douglas's, refers to the ways in which the body is used in systems of representation as a symbol of nature, culture and society (Csordas, 1994b). The body politic, echoing Foucault, refers to the regulation and control of bodies. John O'Neill (1985) proposed a 'five bodies' model which added the world's body, consumer body and the medical body to the political and social bodies. O'Neill starts from the proposition that 'human embodiment functions to create the most fundamental bond between self and society' (1985, p. 23). The world's body, for O'Neill, relates to the human proclivity to anthropomorphise the cosmos, which means to give it a human shape, a tendency that he sees to be everywhere in retreat in the modern world. The social body, conceptualised in Durkheimian terms, centres on the 'interrelationship between our two bodies – the communicative and the physical' (p. 49). The body politic refers to the recurring ways in which the human body has constituted a 'symbolic expression' of the political community's 'beliefs concerning the sources, sustenance and potential threats to the orderly conduct of its members' (p. 67). The consumerist body refers to the creation and commodification of new bodily needs generated by a consumer-oriented culture in which the use of goods stand as markers of self-identity. The notion of medical bodies refers to the medicalisation of the body whereby, with the development of new technologies, more and more aspects of the body come under the scrutiny of the medical gaze.

It was Turner's 1984 study of *The Body and Society*, which examined the production of bodies in relation to changes in the system of production, that perhaps made a more significant impact on the development of the sociology of the body. Turner took as his starting point the Hobbesean problem of order, which focused on the issue of the regulation of bodies in society, as a means of generating a typology of 'bodily order' that operates from the level of society to the individual. In order to overcome some of the limitations of this approach, Turner proposed to rework Hobbes's classic problem of social order. Turner employs Foucault's (1984) distinction between 'the regulations of the population and the discipline of the body' to create his 'neo-Hobbesean' framework. He also draws on Featherstone's (1991a [1982]) distinction between 'the interior of the body as an environment and the exterior of the body' (Turner, 1984, p. 91), through which the individual presents him/ herself to the outside world. Turner proposes that there are four related elements to the Hobbesean problem of order. At the population level, there is the problem of control of reproduction through time and 'regulation in space'. At the individual level, there is 'the restraint of desire as an interior body problem and the representation of bodies in social space', which relates to the outer 'surface of the body' (ibid.). Following the systems theorist Talcott Parsons (1951), Turner argues that all social systems have to 'solve these four sub-problems'. These distinctions are then used as tools for 'formulating a general theory of the body and for locating theories of the body' (Turner, 1984, p. 91). Turner's work, as suggested above, stands as an important landmark in the 'exhumation of the body' (Seymour, 1998, p. 8) in sociology. His unearthing of the role of the body in sociology in the sociological tradition was important to the subsequent development of the body project.

The body as a topic of social research was beginning to raise its head elsewhere in the late 1960s and early 1970s in connection with studies of non-verbal communication, and Douglas (1975a), in part, was responding to this, particularly in her essay 'Do Dogs Laugh?' Hall's (1955, 1969) proxemics (the study of interpersonal spatial relations and the use of public and private space within cultures) and Birdwhistell's (1953, 1973) kinesics (the study of everyday movement as a separate channel of communication within the context of culture) exemplified this emergent concern with non-verbal communication. This US-based work, which began to develop in the 1950s, involved multidisciplinary teams of researchers and in many ways grew out of the interest in communications theory at that time. Its primary aim was to develop a serious 'scientific' approach to the topic.

Non-verbal communication

In a review of Birdwhistell's *Kinesics in Context*, which was first published in 1970, Laurie Taylor wrote:

> Time is running out for those who make social capital out of their knowledge of body language. 'Your words are saying "no" but the tilt and angle of your eye says "yes" ', type of thing is losing its novelty after all those popular magazine accounts and telly demonstrations. (1971, p. 467)

Birdwhistell's (1953, 1973) work on kinesics can be seen as a sustained attempt to lift the topic of 'body language' out of popular magazine and television accounts, with the psychological reductionism it had suffered from, and afford it a status worthy of systematic investigation from a behaviourist science framework. He developed a methodology and notational system for analysing everyday movement in micro-social contexts. Birdwhistell (1973) examined other notational systems, such as that developed by the choreographer and dance theorist Rudolf Laban, in the 1920s. Labanotation or kinetography Laban, as it is known,[4] continues to develop and has been used for many years to notate a range of dance styles and choreographic forms, as will be discussed in Chapters 4 and 5.[5] While Birdwhistell agreed that Labanotation was useful for notating movement in certain contexts, he decided not to adopt it for the study of kinesics because it was 'designed as a method for choreography' (1973, p. 257).

Most historical maps of the study of the body today pay scant attention to this developmental work that began in the early 1950s and continued through to the 1970s (see, for example, Birdwhistell, 1953; Hall, 1955; Scheflen, 1964). I suspect that this is partly because the dominant schemas that informed kinesics, American structural linguistics, communication theory and behaviourism were already coming under attack for their positivist biases through critical developments in European social thought in the late 1960s (see Bernstein, 1971; Walsh, 1972; Kristeva, 1978 [1969]). As a consequence, it ended up in the twilight zone. Nevertheless, this work generated discussion and research interest at the time, particularly in micro studies of social order and in social psychology (see, for example, Goffman, 1972; Laver and Hutcheson, 1972; Benthall and Polhemus, 1975; Argyle, 1975; Henley, 1977). Some dance researchers have also recognised the importance of this work in putting body movement onto the academic agenda (see Thomas, 1986; Daly, 1988).

The 'systems' approach that Birdwhistell proposed was developed in the USA by a multidisciplinary team of linguists, psychiatrists and anthropologists. In this framework, body movement is treated as a 'learnt form of communication, which is patterned within a culture and which can be broken down to an ordered system of isolable elements' (Birdwhistell, 1973, p. xi). Communication within the systems framework is viewed as a multichannel process involving language, body motion and smell, through which interactants in any given situation continually contribute by sending messages. It is also through this multichannel process that they make sense of the situation at hand. This approach rejects the common-sense idea that language is the central message system or that it is the only channel of meaning. Neither does body movement simply duplicate what is being communicated through the linguistic channel. That is, there is not necessarily a goodness of fit between speech and gesture. Body movement does not always follow or punctuate speech patterns. Body motion, for Birdwhistell, is a separate channel of communication that stands in a structural relation to the other channels. He steers away from the thorny problem of using the term 'body language' to counter claims that kinesics is a form of 'pseudolinguistics', and to preserve the notion that body motion is a separate channel of communication (1973, p. xiii). At the same time, the work of American structural linguistics (the Sapir–Wharf–Bloomfield school), which had developed a highly technical and rigorous approach to the analysis of everyday speech, forms the basis of Birdwhistell's methodology. This school of linguistics was heavily criticised by a new generation of socio-linguists for concentrating on the minutiae of speech patterns and for failing to relate language to the structure of social relations (Bernstein, 1971; Poole, 1975). That is, this school failed to take into account the social context in which language is used and performed. Thus, although Birdwhistell stresses that body motion does not simply follow speech, he uses the techniques of descriptive structural linguistics as models on which to 'develop a methodology which would exhaustively analyse the communicative behaviour of the body' (1973, p. xiii).

Birdwhistell attempts to analyse the degree of structuration between the channels as they are observed and recorded within a given social context. Drawing on Goffman's (1959) insights into the 'neglected situation', Birdwhistell emphasises that analysis must be carried out in relation to the total social context in which it occurs. In this way, the analysis of the speech and the body movement should not be taken out of the context of the social interaction. The construct of social context that he employs, which is drawn from 'territoriality' studies in animal psychology (ethology), is entirely behavioural. The contexts of human social relations are not viewed as qualitatively different from those of animals. This is because 'society' in Birdwhistell's kinesics, as formulated in the ethological studies he draws on, is theorised as an essential condition for the maturation and environmental adaptation of humans and animals. Hall's (1955, 1969) study of proxemics also draws heavily on ethological studies. In the final analysis, two technicist frameworks, ethology and American structural linguistics, inform Birdwhistell's kinesics. Ultimately, questions of cultural signification are subsumed under the demands of this 'objectivist' approach to socio-cultural occurrences.

Julia Kristeva's (1978 [1969]) critique of Birdwhistell's kinesics gave early warning of shifts in European social thought made possible through developments in semiotics, Marxism and psychoanalysis that would reverberate through the social sciences and the humanities on both sides of the Atlantic in a few short years. These developments, in turn, would contribute to the 'crises in representation' (Boyne and Rattansi, 1990) which befell the social sciences and the humanities in the late 1980s. In her essay, Kristeva (1978, p. 280) praises Birdwhistell's kinesic analysis as 'the first endeavour to study the gestural code as a system autonomous from speech, although approachable through it'. She considers it 'significant' that Birdwhistell sought to develop a 'scriptural' terminology as opposed to a 'vocal' terminology by using terms like 'kinesic markers' because they are not 'derivative of spoken language'. She argues that Birdwhistell's approach is so bound up with positivistic assumptions concerning communication, the message and the human subject embedded in western thought that ultimately it can not free itself from the domination of language. It remains locked into an ideology of exchange. Part of the problem is that Birdwhistell's kinesics is 'dominated' by the demands of positivist sociology. The major terms that Birdwhistell employs, such as 'subject', 'perception', 'human being' and the 'truth' of a message or communication, Kristeva argues, are being called into question by developments in linguistics, semiotics and psychoanalysis. Birdwhistell's approach is founded on 'a philosophy of communication' which is based on 'the intellectual domination of language' and a society based on exchange.

In order to escape the ideology of exchange, Kristeva suggests, it is necessary to move away from the 'philosophy of communication'. Kristeva's proposed remedy is to view gesturality as a 'semiotic text', which is 'in the process of production'; that is, as a 'signifying practice'. Taking gesturality seriously as a signifying practice, according to Kristeva, is a better way forward because it opens the possibility of not

being 'blocked by the closed structures of language', by focusing on the
signifying processes of bodily action. As will become evident in
Chapters 3, 4, 5 and 6, dance scholars frequently bemoan the fact that
despite the growth of interest in the study of 'the body' in academia in
recent years, the moving dancing body has warranted little attention.
Kristeva's theory of signifying practices, as will be shown in Chapter 6,
was the starting point for Ann Daly's (1992, 1995) analysis of the
'feminist practice' of the early modern dancer Isadora Duncan.

International conferences such as the 1972 Institute of Contemporary
Arts (ICA) programme, 'The Body as a Medium of Expression'
(see Benthall and Polhemus, 1975), also sought to advance research in
the study of the body, recognising that hitherto little serious work had
been done in this field in comparison with the field of verbal language.
Jonathan Benthall (1975, p. 7), with his feet set firmly in the social
constructionist camp, suggested that the dominance of the study of
verbal language to the 'neglect of the expressive resources of the body'
is a consequence of the logocentricity of industrialism, the triumph of
reason over experience and mind over body (see Thomas, 1995).
Hence, there was a concern to move away from the term 'non-verbal'
communication, which could be seen as a 'logocentric manoeuvre'
(Benthall, 1975, p. 7), in favour of human bodily expression.

The 1975 annual Association of Social Anthropologists (ASA) conference on 'The Anthropology of the Body' (see Blacking, 1977, p. vi)
sought to address the key debates in the 'use of the body as a nonverbal
medium of expression' in different cultural contexts such as dance,
gesture, posture and so on. The intention was to take the discussion
further than the ICA conference, to 'break down the dichotomies
between body and mind, emotion and reason, nonverbal and verbal'
(ibid., p. vi) in the analysis of cultures. The human body was perceived
to be 'the link between nature and culture in all human activities'
(p. 5). Thus, there was an attempt to build on the insights offered by
anthropologists such as Mauss and Douglas, but also to pay attention to
foundational aspects of the human body within the context of culture.
In so doing, the conference agenda foreshadowed more recent critiques
of the predominance of anti-foundational or discursive approaches
to the body over foundationalist or phenomenological approaches
(see Turner, 1992; Csordas, 1993; Shilling, 1993; Seymour, 1998).

The foundationalist stance offered in the edited collection (Blacking,
1977) based on the ASA conference was in line with the neo-Darwinist
views on non-verbal communication discussed above, which had been
roundly criticised by Ted Polhemus (1975) for producing simplistic

positivistic accounts. In order to bring the phenomenal body back into the discussion of a sociology or anthropology of the body, it is not necessary to resort to the incorporation of reductionist biological models, which, as Turner (1992) points out, are rooted in nineteenth-century positivism. Turner, as indicated earlier, argues that sociological approaches to the body need to take into account the fact that humans not only *have* bodies, but also *are* bodies. Sociological approaches to the body rightly address the ways in which the body exists in the world; that is, how it is represented or symbolised by society. But this is only attending to one aspect of the body. It would also be legitimate to ask what it is like to *be* a body in the world. Turner (1992, p. 41) suggests that the insights offered by philosophical anthropology and phenomenology concerning the distinction in the German language between *Leib* and *Körper*, the subjective, lived 'experiential body' and the objective, instrumental 'institutionalised body', provide greater potential as a corrective to the oversubscription of anti-foundationalist approaches to the body. The 'double nature of human beings', according to Turner,

> expresses the ambiguity of human embodiment as both personal and impersonal, objective and subjective, social and natural ... it precisely indicates the weakness of the Cartesian legacy in sociology, which has almost exclusively treated the human body as *Körper*, rather than both simultaneously *Körper* and *Leib*. In approaching the body as an objective and impersonal structure, sociology has by implication relegated the body to the environmental conditions of social action. (1992, pp. 41–2)

The phenomenology of Paul Schilder (1950 [1935]) and Maurice Merleau-Ponty (1962) has had an impact on recent developments in psychoanalytic approaches (see Weiss, 1999) and sociological approaches to the body (see Turner, 1984, 1992). In his study of body image, Schilder argued that *Körper* and *Leib* could not be separated, as there is a unity between the outer representational body and the subjective experiential body. Merleau-Ponty also rejected the Cartesian mind/body dualism and insisted that the body and the psyche are inextricably connected. For Merleau-Ponty (1962), human beings are embodied subjectivities and any analysis of the relation of the self to the world has to begin from the fundamental fact that we are embodied. The body is not simply a house for the mind, rather it is through our lived experience of our bodies that we perceive of, are informed by and interact with the world. Phenomenology has informed the work of several philosophers inquiring into the nature and aesthetics of western theatre dance (Langer, 1942, 1953; Sheets-Johnstone, 1979 [1967],

1984; Fraleigh, 1991). This work is situated within the tradition of philosophy of art. Although Merleau-Ponty's work was rooted in the realm of philosophical inquiry, it has been a source of inspiration in recent years for a number of writers attempting to overcome the dualistic approaches to the study of the body in society (see Turner, 1992; Crossley, 1994, 1995a, b, 1996a, b; Csordas, 1994b; Grosz, 1994; Jung, 1996). The import of phenomenology as a corrective to biological reductionism on the one hand, and to the neglect of the lived body in social constructionism on the other, will be taken up in the next chapter.

The point of the preceding discussion was to indicate that there was evidence of an emergent interest in the 'social aspects' of body in the 1960s and 1970s, prior to the explosion in the 1990s. I also wanted to show that certain themes, which are central to current debates, were beginning to be generated or implied earlier. Polhemus's (1978) reader, *Social Aspects of the Human Body*, is further evidence of this. Harold Garfinkel's 1967 ethnomethodological ethnographic study of Agnes, an 'intersexed' person, is an early example of 'passing' (Garfinkel, 1984). This study is also significant in regard to the key issues of the relation between perceptions of the inner/outer body, nature/culture, sex/gender and power/knowledge. These questions will be examined more fully in the following chapter and will be taken up further in connection with the body in dance and gender representations in dance, in Chapters 4 and 6.

Garfinkel's study of 'Passing and the Managed Achievement of Sex Status in an "Intersexed" Person' sets out to reveal how 'societies exercise close controls over the ways in which the sex composition of their own populations are constituted and changed' (1984 [1967], p. 116).

In 1958, Agnes was a white 19-year-old, who had been brought up as a boy, had developed secondary female characteristics at puberty and was now living and working successfully as a 'woman'. In order to pass for a woman, Agnes had to study and learn what a woman does in minute detail. Whereas 'natural women' ordinarily take their femaleness for granted as a fact of life, Agnes, having been brought up as a boy, had to consciously construct herself as a woman in order to pass for one. Mauss (1973) and Birdwhistell (1973) have argued that the learning of bodily techniques is particularly evident in gendered behaviour. While women do not routinely have to think about how to sit, move, stand and carry their bodies like a 'woman', Agnes did.

Agnes wanted to have, and subsequently did have, an operation to remove the male genitals from her body and create female genitals in their place. She was referred to a doctor at the Neuropsychiatric Institute, University of California, where studies were being conducted on individuals who were classified as male or female at birth but who had subsequently developed severe anatomical anomalies normally associated with the other sex, which rendered them 'intersexed'. This case was one of a series that Garfinkel studied in collaboration with medical colleagues at the University of California. In order to be eligible for the operation, Agnes had to convince the doctors (and Garfinkel) that she was not a transsexual, and that she had not taken female hormones. That is, the 'experts' had to be sure that the development of Agnes's female characteristics were a result of natural, pathological failures in her 'male sex makeup'. Despite the presence of the penis from birth, Agnes insisted that she had always felt like a woman inside. Before the operation Agnes was very proud of her well-formed breasts, citing their presence as evidence of her femaleness. But she viewed the presence of the penis as a 'freak of nature'. That is, although it was part of her anatomy, its presence was contrary to her embodied female sense of self.

So successful was Agnes's passing that she was treated by the doctors and Garfinkel as having a rare disorder called 'testicular feminization syndrome' (Garfinkel, 1984, p. 285) and was therefore able to have the operation. Indeed, Agnes had learnt the art of behaving like a woman so well that Garfinkel commented that she appeared very feminine and on occasions seemed to be more female than a 'natural female'. Leaving aside for the moment Garfinkel's heterosexist notions of the trappings of femininity, it is clear from the discussion that Agnes's perception of her own body was measured by how she considered a 'natural' woman would look upon it, or how a heterosexual man would look upon a 'real' woman. Agnes insisted on having a very ample vagina constructed. The large breasts and the ample vagina indicated 'true' femaleness to Agnes. There could be no doubt regarding the sex of a person who possessed these characteristics. After the operation Agnes felt that she had finally become the natural woman she always thought herself to be. That is, her inner/outer body was consistent with the image of a real woman as others perceived it and with the woman that Agnes stressed she had felt herself to be in her inner body prior to the operation. Thus, the outer appearing body was now at one with the lived body. Occasionally, there was evidence of a nagging doubt at the back of Agnes's mind in case a 'real' heterosexual man could detect that her vagina was not natural but surgically constructed.

Some five years after the operation, Agnes shocked the experts by calmly announcing that she had indeed taken female hormones. Thus,

Agnes had passed herself off to the 'scientific' experts as a biologically defective male who had developed female characteristics, even though this was not the case. Agnes had so successfully negotiated the rules of femininity laid down in her own culture that she passed not only *for* a woman but *as* a woman.

Garfinkel's study raised issues concerning nature and culture in regard to medical and lay conceptions of sex and gender, and it pointed to the ways in which gendered behaviours are learnt, negotiated and produced within the context of culture. It also suggested, contrary to common-sense perceptions, that the body and sexuality are not fixed 'natural' entities but are unfinished and unstable. As such, it foreshadowed emergent debates in second-wave feminism concerning the distinction between sex and gender and the social construction of femininity and masculinity (see Gatens, 1996). Moreover, it resonated with more recent poststructuralist feminist critiques of 'compulsory heterosexuality' and gender as 'performative' (Butler, 1990a, 1993; Brooks, 1997). At the same time, the body work that Agnes had to put in to pass as a 'natural' woman points to the corporeal construction of subjectivity. This arguably contrasts with the 'overdetermination of the subject by discourse and social process in Butler's work' (Boyne, 1999, pp. 221–2) and in other discursive approaches, which will be discussed in the next chapter. Moreover, the medical identification of Agnes as a 'biologically defective male' prior to the operation seems to support Luce Irigaray's subsequent critique of western philosophical and psychoanalytic discourse for interpreting sexual difference 'as though it were only one sex, and that sex is male' (Irigaray, cited in Gatens, 1996, p. viii). That is, the male becomes the yardstick by which sexuality is measured.

It should be clear from the preceding discussion that although the body has not necessarily been a central focus of research in sociology and anthropology, it has not been quite as absent as is sometimes supposed. Moreover, certain recurrent themes that pervaded the 'prehistory' of the body, as we shall see in the next chapter, are also evident in a range of different theoretical frameworks that became central to the body project. These recurrent themes concern the problem of the dualisms in western social thought. This chapter has tried to do two things: first, to provide a brief and selective chronology of the uneven development of the study of the body in anthropology and sociology, and, second, to lay out the terms, shifts and nuances of the debate between social constructionist and foundationalist approaches to the body. The next chapter moves the story of the body in social and cultural studies into debates in feminism and poststructuralism. Although there is a historical dimension to that discussion too, the main thrust of the chapter is directed towards an elaboration of the triumph of social constructionism and anti-essentialism over foundationalism, along with a consideration of recent attempts to develop a more corporeal approach to the study of the body, which takes account of embodiment.

Chapter 2

The Body in Culture:
The Body Project

Introduction

This chapter begins by indicating the ways in which feminism and certain aspects of poststructuralism have impacted on the development of the study of the body in social and cultural theory. Feminists and poststructuralists (in very broad terms) have been critical of and attempted to overcome the problems of dualism inscribed in the western humanist tradition of thought. As discussed later in this chapter, they too may be criticised for contributing further to the dominance of the socially constructed body in social and cultural theory and, therefore, perpetuating the mind/body distinction embedded in Cartesian dualist thought. The chapter concludes by focusing on Nick Crossley's (1995a) merging of two seemingly different approaches to the body. Crossley appropriates the phenomenological framework of Merleau-Ponty, whose attempts to surmount the mind/body dualism in Cartesian thinking were alluded to in the previous chapter, and combines it with a rereading of Goffman's (1972) analysis of routine everyday bodily behaviour in public places.

Bodies of difference

There is little doubt that the impact of feminist challenges in the 1970s and 1980s to the dominant (patriarchal) discourses embedded in western social thought has contributed much to the current concern with the body in social and cultural studies. Although all societies, as far as we know, seem to draw strong lines of demarcation between what it is to be male or female, the ways in which sexual difference is perceived and organised, as Sherry Ortner (1974) has pointed out, vary from culture to culture and are often quite contradictory. Second-wave feminists noted that women were almost universally accorded a lower status compared with men. Despite adopting different epistemological positions, feminists were generally united in their aims to understand and counter the unequal position of women in society. Thus, they began to question if these perceived hierarchical differences between the two sexes were due to natural (biological) differences or cultural (socially constructed) influences. Consequently, the ramifications of perceptions of women's bodies for social relations loomed large in second-wave feminist debates on the unequal position of women in western cultures.

The sharp distinction between the constructs of nature and culture in regard to men and women in western social thought and cultural practices constituted a major critical focus of feminist debate. In terms of the binary opposition between nature and culture central to the western humanist tradition, women have repeatedly been situated on the nature side of the divide, based on their capacities for reproduction and mothering. Women's and men's biological differences have been used repeatedly to explain differences in their respective roles in social life, sometimes with positive connotations, but more often with negative implications. The 'biology as destiny' viewpoint reasons that it is women's reproductive capacities that make them fit for the private sphere (home) and in turn limit their entry into the public sphere (work, politics). This reasoning has been invoked by populist sociobiologists, as discussed in the previous chapter, as well as a range of social thinkers from Aristotle to Durkheim, to shore up existent social inequalities between men and women (Sydie, 1987).

The assumption that women are closer to nature was taken up, or at least assumed, by feminists who positioned themselves in different theoretical camps: particularly existential, liberal and radical feminists (Gatens, 1996). Some, such as Simone de Beauvoir (1972 [1949]) and Shulamith Firestone (1970), considered that biology placed limitations on women and that in order to achieve equality with men, women had to transcend their bodies or forever be trapped in their 'immanence'. Other feminists viewed the positioning of women with nature in a more positive light. Writers such as Susan Griffin (1978) and Mary Daly (1978), for example, called for a celebration of the female body, which, they maintained, had been continually undermined and devalued through patriarchy's separation from and hatred of nature and by extension, women. Others, from a socialist feminist perspective, such as Michèle Barrett (1988) and Ann Oakley (1974), argued for a distinction to be drawn between the categories of sex and gender.

Oakley's influential study, *Sex, Gender and Society* (1974), set out to demonstrate that there is no universally agreed correspondence regarding biological differences between males and females and the ways in which these are interpreted within different cultures. She argued that the meanings ascribed to the biological attributes of male and female and masculine or feminine behaviours vary considerably from society to society and thus there is no natural unbroken link between the biological categories of male and female and cultural constructions of masculinity and femininity. As a result of this, Oakley reasoned that the ways in which femininity and masculinity are constructed and passed down in a given culture are at least as important to notions of what it is to *be* a man or a woman as are the kind of genitalia possessed. As such, she argued, it is necessary to make a distinction between sex and gender. Hence, sex came to refer to 'biological differences between male and female', while gender came to be seen 'as a matter of culture' (1974, p. 16).

Feminists in general, despite their different ideological positions, have been concerned not only to analyse the position of women in society, but also to change it. Proponents viewed the focus on gender as opposed to sexual difference as a remedy to 'the dangers of biological reductionism'. It was also seen as an attack on the incipient sexism encapsulated in the binary oppositions of male/female, culture/nature, reason/emotion, active/passive embedded in the western tradition of thought. Although not all feminists adopted the sex/gender distinction, it was central to feminist theorising from the 1970s to the mid-1980s. A fierce debate arose within academic feminism between so-called essentialists (primarily radical feminists), who saw sexual difference as an important factor in women's oppression, and those labelled as social constructionists (Marxist or socialist feminists, feminists of equality), who directed attention towards the social determinants of gender identity (Gatens, 1996). Social constructionism held more sway in Anglo-American feminism and as a consequence, the majority of feminist studies addressed the ideological or cultural trappings of femininity and masculinity and their ramifications for women in contemporary western culture. Feminist intervention into the 'tyranny of slenderness' that pervades western consumer culture's representations of women is a case in point.

In the 1970s, a hitherto little-known 'wasting disease', anorexia nervosa, which was first diagnosed in the 1870s, entered into the popular and medical imagination, prompted by media and medical reports that there had been a dramatic increase in recent years in the number of reported cases. Anorexia came to be viewed as an epidemic afflicting white, intelligent adolescent girls from middle-class backgrounds. There was a rapid increase in research into eating disorders from biomedical and psychological perspectives. In the biomedical model, eating disorders were explained in terms of a disorder of biological processes of the individual anorectic. Anorexia, from this perspective, was seen to have an organic cause such as a hormonal imbalance or some other malfunction. Although it was recognised that stress can cause a change in the chemical balance of the body, psychological or social causes were not treated as central to the condition. From the psychological viewpoint, eating disorders were generally viewed as a pathological response to a crisis in development in adolescence: a fear of growing up or the 'good girl' oscillating between rebellion and compliance, for example. While the family was sometimes implicated in the cause and treatment of the 'disease', wider cultural issues were not considered important. Feminist writers such as Susie Orbach (1978, 1986) and Kim Chernin (1981, 1986) explored women's obsessions with weight and dieting by examining anorexic and bulimic practices within the wider context of consumer-oriented culture. From a psychosocial perspective, they argued that the changing role of women in contemporary consumer culture constituted a principal arena of conflict in the lives of western women and that this played a large part in the observed increases in eating disorders among young women. Contrary to the dominant biomedical and psychological approaches, Orbach argued that compulsive eating is rooted in the social inequality of women. Thus, fat for Orbach 'is a social disease and fat is a feminist issue' (Orbach, 1978, p. 18); the cure, in keeping with ideas that emerged in 1970s feminist approaches, lay in 'consciousness raising'.

The body as a site for political struggle, as Susan Bordo (1993) has pointed out, was a key feature in second-wave feminism, which provided an important starting point for examining and undercutting dominant unquestioned attitudes towards the enslavement of women to their bodies and the beauty ideal. Bordo also notes that those engaging in recent scholarship on the body often overlook this fact, and leap

> straight from Marx to Foucault, effacing the intellectual role played by the social movements of the sixties (both black power and women's liberation) in awakening consciousness of the body as 'an instrument of power'. (1993, p. 16)

But it is not only in the study of the body that feminist interventions have been erased or overlooked. As we shall see in the following chapter, feminist critiques of the traditional tropes of anthropology in the late 1960s and 1970s have also been ignored or overlooked, particularly by those researchers who came to celebrate the critique of traditional ethnographic writing in postmodern ethnography in the late 1980s. The proponents of postmodernism failed to notice that a number of criticisms of traditional anthropology accredited to what came to be called the 'new ethnography' had been made by feminist ethnographers sometime before. Nonetheless, the 'reading' of women's bodies that emerged from this early feminist work came to be viewed as rather one-dimensional by the mid-1980s because it failed to appreciate the differences that race, class, gender, ethnicity and so forth make to the 'determination of meaning' (Bordo, 1993, p. 24). For example, despite the fact that feminist accounts of anorexic or bulimic practices brought the realm of 'culture' into the centre of the debate, their descriptions and analysis, according to Éva Székely (1988), were still problematic. As with the dominant biomedical and psychological models, the 'tyranny of the pursuit of slenderness' in these feminist approaches is treated as an illness or a disease and women are viewed as simply responding passively to psychosocial influences. Feminists like Chernin and Orbach, Székely argues, incorporated aspects of the dominant clinical approaches into their analysis without fully recognising the problems of reductionism, dualism and determinism inherent in those models. Further, patriarchal explanations of the relentless pursuit of slenderness such as those offered by Orbach and Chernin were insufficient because not only are women viewed as victims, but men and women are also categorised as an amorphous mass. As such, they could not adequately address class, ethnic or cultural differences. Why, for example, do not all women fall prey to the global conditions (patriarchy) that prevent women from developing healthy attitudes towards the body? As will be discussed in Chapter 4, there is evidence to suggest that the incidence of eating disorders is comparatively high in professional theatre dance in the west where the pressures to conform to the aesthetic ideal of a super-slim, prepubescent dancing body, particularly in ballet, are high. In researching young women dancers (Thomas, 1993b) in London, for example, and these were not professional dancers, although some did indeed become members of contemporary dance companies in the UK, I found that all the interviewees, apart from one young woman, were obsessed by what they ate, their body shape and image. However, they would not have been categorised as anorexic, by any means. Thus, these kinds of approaches came to be criticised for offering an all too unitary view of women's (and men's) experiences, despite the concern to account for and offer a solution to the particular social and cultural conditions of women's oppression (see MacSween, 1993). As Bordo (1993, p. 63) points out, the culturalist/feminist approach 'altered the clinical terrain' and helped to reveal that the obsession with slenderness is in fact '*overdetermined*' and 'freighted with multiple meanings' (ibid., p. 67). Nonetheless, Bordo argues for a shift away from the oppressor/ oppressed model using the insights of writers such as Foucault on power/knowledge.

The sex/gender distinction also came to be critically reassessed through the influence of theories of sexual difference in French psychoanalytic feminism, which developed the notion of 'writing the body' (Chanter, 1999), which will be discussed further in the chapter on dance and difference. Moreover, although the sex/gender distinction initially seemed to offer a challenge to the body/mind dualism in western humanist thought, it increasingly came to be viewed by a new generation of anti-essentialist feminists, influenced by poststructuralism, postmodernism and postcolonialism, as operating within and reinforcing the dualistic thinking it sought to counter.[1]

By focusing on gender differences, feminists, once more, were privileging *Körper* over *Leib*, according to phenomenologically inclined feminists such as Székely (1988). The body and the psyche, in effect, according to Moira Gatens (1996), became 'passive *tabulae rasae*' in gender theory. Even Barrett (1988), looking back with some Foucauldian insight, came to recognise that perhaps gender feminists, herself included, had overlooked some key problems with the model. In taking the biological male/female distinction as a given, for example, as poststructuralist and postmodernist feminists have pointed out, gender feminists had failed to consider the possibility that the biological is also socially constituted and inscribed with meaning (Gatens, 1996). This moves the idea of social constructionism into the realms of a more radical, discursive, anti-essentialist perspective. Once the determination of sex as a fact of 'nature' is called into question, then sex and sexuality may be treated as moveable feasts: no longer as truths or facts but as 'fictions' that operate as 'truths'. Sexual difference, in this light, like gender, is no longer treated as a biological issue but as a historical one. One question that might arise from this is to ask how the taken-for-granted biological model of sexual difference was produced in scientific discourses in the first instance and, further, what interests and practices did it support.

Bodies of discourse

Thomas Laqueur's (1987) influential reading of the radical reinterpretation of sexual difference in the scientific discourses of reproductive biology, which became established in the late eighteenth century, points to the idea that biological difference is a matter of representation, which facilitated a variety of social and political discourses. The body, according to Laqueur's argument, is not a natural fact of existence, rather, it 'is made' in history. From ancient times to the eighteenth century, men and women were not defined in terms of biological difference. Rather, they were conceptualised in terms of a single model, based on sameness. The female body was treated as an inverted and inferior version of the male. In this hierarchical model of 'homologues', 'it was claimed that women had no truly unique parts, only lesser ones' (Gallagher and Laqueur, 1987, p. viii). The hierarchical model was gradually replaced in the late eighteenth century by a reproductive biological model that stressed sexual difference based on 'incommensurability'. That is, in physical and moral terms women and men came to be defined in terms of difference. The male became the standard by which the female is measured and judged and, as Emily Martin has argued in *The Woman in the Body* (1987), this remains the case in contemporary western culture.

Laqueur argues that the paradigmatic shift to the model of sexual difference was not simply a result of a scientific revolution in the sense proposed by Thomas Kuhn (1962). The theory of homologues had remained dominant despite the fact that differences between the sexes were known 'since the beginning of time': as Laqueur (1987, p. 3) says, 'the one gives birth, the other does not, to state the obvious'. The dualistic model of male and female bodies, according to Laqueur, served to solve certain emergent issues in the social and political discourses of the eighteenth and nineteenth centuries. Laqueur argues that the model did not simply assist a single ideological cause but could be drawn upon by both radicals and reactionaries to legitimate their views.

With the establishment of the binary opposition model, women increasingly came to be associated with their reproductive biology. The essence of woman, in other words, came to be located in her sexually differentiated body. She, that is, woman, became more sexually embodied. At the same time, she was also increasingly viewed as having an absence of sexual feelings. Thus, as Laqueur argues, although it was deemed normal for women to be ruled by their reproductive organs, it was also construed as abnormal for them to have strong sexual feelings. Although the Victorian woman was denied sexual feelings, she was at the same time viewed as being wholly sexually determined through her reproductive cycle. As Williams and Bendelow (1998) have pointed out, while middle-class Victorian women were considered to be under the grip of their uterus by the medical profession, they were also portrayed in literary terms, rather like hothouse flowers, as being in need of male protection and control.

It was not only in biology that differences between the female and the male body came to prominence in the eighteenth century. As Lona Schiebinger (1987) demonstrates, it was during this period that anatomists began to view the anatomical structure of the female body as essentially different from that of the male, which resulted in the skeletal frame taking on distinctive qualities of femininity and masculinity. The 'ideal' woman's frame was constructed with a wide pelvis, a small neck, a narrow ribcage and a small skull. The female skeleton was shown to be childlike and thus unfit to take up the tasks of 'men'. The small skull and wide pelvis were used as evidence that women were (in nature) unsuitable for intellectual labour, particularly science. Despite the anatomists' claims to objectivity and truth, Schiebinger shows that their representations were imbued with cultural overtones to legitimate emergent distinctions between; the public/private spheres, culture/nature and reason/unreason. In contemporary medical textbooks, as Williams and Bendelow (1998) have indicated, men continue to be the yardstick with which women are measured and compared, with their anatomy being described in terms such as ' "smaller", "feebler", "weaker", "less well developed", to demonstrate how women differ from men' (p. 115). The perceived differences between men and women in terms of their physical strengths and capabilities, as will be discussed in Chapters 4 and 6, have also informed the training of dancers and choreography, in the tradition of classical ballet in particular. Iris Young's 1980 classic phenomenological study, 'Throwing Like a Girl', strongly suggested that these kinds of 'naturalist' representations are not simply textual but are worked through at the level of bodily practices.

Young's (1998a [1980]) study draws on Merleau-Ponty's notion of the body–subject but invests it with gender by incorporating elements of de Beauvoir's theory of femininity within patriarchy. She also expands and develops Mauss's construct of body techniques. Young compares and contrasts the differences between men's and women's body movement practices, which, she suggests, are usefully revealed in the ways that men and women typically throw and catch a ball. Drawing on the work of Merleau-Ponty, Young sees that 'it is the ordinary purposeful actions as a whole towards things in its environment that initially defines the relation of the subject to the world' (1998a, p. 261). She also draws on 'de Beauvoir's account of women's existence in patriarchal society as defined by a tension between immanence and transcendence' (ibid.); that is, the tension between woman as 'other', as 'a mere object' and as an autonomous subjectivity. However, de Beauvoir did not address the 'situatedness of the woman's actual bodily movement' in relation to 'its surroundings and the world', according to Young. As a consequence, she tended to view woman's anatomy and physiology as partly responsible for 'women's unfree status' (p. 260). It is precisely this bodily situatedness that Young's study addresses. She notes that women are more hesitant and reactive in going for and catching a ball than men and that, unlike men, they tend not to put their whole body behind the action of throwing. They are also less likely to direct their action in a particular spatial direction. Young, like Mauss, suggests that training is an important factor in women's body techniques, but she also considers that the tendency for women to objectify themselves (through the male gaze) contributes to the inhibitions of women's embodiment and their spatial orientations:

> As lived bodies we [women] are not open and unambiguous transcendencies that move out to master a world that belongs to us, a world constituted by our own intentions and projections. (p. 269)

Women, according to Young, 'are anchored in their immanence' (ibid.). The explanation of the limitations of women's embodiment does not lie in notions of a female essence or in anatomy and physiology. Rather, she argues, the causes 'are rooted in the particular *situation* of women as conditioned by their sexist oppression in contemporary society' (ibid.).

The problem with this analysis is that it treats women as victims who are physically disabled by a sexist society. Men, once again, are constituted as the marker and measure against which women's actions are considered. Also, young women's lived experiences of their body movement today are likely to be very different from those of older women, such as Young, who grew up in the middle of the twentieth century. In another essay, reflecting on this study some twenty years later, Young (1998b) readily admits to these limitations. Moreover, she suggests that the model of action employed in her earlier essay is problematic because it is instrumental, which she now sees is a consequence of uncritically adopting phenomenology's notion of purposeful action. The concern with instrumental action (the most efficient means to achieve a given end), as discussed in the previous chapter, was one of the major reasons that prevented sociology from placing the body at the centre of its analysis. The philosophical method of phenomenology, on the other hand, as formulated by Husserl (1965), was defined as the 'first philosophy', which, in contrast to naturalism, positivism and historicism, sought to investigate the realms of subjective consciousness. Its proponents viewed phenomenology as a movement away from positivism's instrumentalist concerns. The notion of 'intentionality', which relates to the idea of the individual as a subject of will, and which is central to phenomenological theorising, bears a certain resemblance to instrumental action. Young also suggests that her earlier study accepted uncritically 'the opposition between immanence and transcendence', and 'the necessary unity of the acting subject' (1998b, p. 289). She proposes that another project might look at 'specifically feminine forms of movement' that are goal- or work-related but cannot be easily collected under the 'unifying instrumental model of action' (p. 298). This might involve the practice of multitasking, which is often associated with women.

Despite these acknowledged limitations, Young stands by her initial paper. She argues that the 'structure and assumptions' that underpin her earlier work still seem to resonate with women's contexts and 'human possibilities'. She envisages a more 'plural and engaged' approach to studying women's embodiment, one which is not unidirectional or mutually exclusive, but plural and synchronic. Despite this, she maintains that the motivation behind the earlier study remains useful today. In the final analysis, she suggests, all accounts are partial and the partiality needs to be recognised and accepted as such.

What Young's critique of her earlier work shows is just how difficult it is to not get caught up unwittingly in dualistic models of men and women. Her study, in effect, points to the fact that while some practices and representations do change over time, such as women's relation to their bodies in action, others continue in the background although they appear to be out of the picture. Sandor Gilman's (1992) insightful study of nineteenth-century iconography confirms this view. Gilman's study shows how the bodies of the prostitute and the black Hottentot female come to stand as icons of an aberrant sexuality, and he also reveals how these negative images, of black female sexuality in particular, still shape perceptions in contemporary popular culture. This is despite the fact that 'contemporary thinking about black female bodies', as bell hooks (1992, p. 63) has noted, 'does not attempt to read the body as a sign of "natural" inferiority'.[2]

John Perpener's revelatory study (2001) of the careers of eight African American concert dance pioneers from the 1920s to the 1940s shows how deep-seated ideas about the 'Negro' body and the 'Negro' entertainer had consequences for the way the dancers, male and female, were perceived by dance critics of the day. This, in turn, he argues, contributed to these African American concert dancers being written out of the canonical development of mainstream American modern dance history. Perpener's study builds on Lynne Emery's (1988 [1972]) landmark historical survey of black dance in the USA. With the exception perhaps of Katherine Dunham and Pearl Primus, African American concert dance pioneers were ignored by mainstream critics, mentioned only in passing, and/or viewed as lacking in importance, when considered next to the developments and artistic achievements of mainstream concert dance artists like Martha Graham or Doris Humphrey. Perpener shows how racialist ideas inherent in American culture, centred on the black body, fed into liberal humanist approaches to dance criticism. This resulted in certain black concert dance artists, such as Edna Guy, Pearl Primus and Talley Beatty, being criticised and their efforts downplayed for displaying an over-concern with (aesthetic) 'American-European' dance technique, instead of performing the 'natural' movement characteristic of *the* 'Negro dance'. They should, instead, go back to their Africanist heritage to develop their *own* dance form. When they did just that, however, black concert dance artists were considered to be lacking in serious artistry, or accused of being overly sensuous. The excavations of dance historians like Perpener (see also Burt, 1998; DeFrantz, 2002) have led to a reevaluation of the ways in which black bodies have been racialised in and erased from dance cultural history. The issue of erasure or race emerges again in Chapter 6 in a different context: the national dances of Cuba, Brazil and Argentina.

The work on the history and representations of the human body, exemplified by writers such as Laqueur (1987), Gilman (1992) and others, has had a significant impact on social research on the body, 'by demonstrating that human bodies have been invested with a wide range of shifting and unstable meanings' (Shilling, 1993, p. 74). This work has also been used to support those who take an anti-foundationalist or anti-essentialist stance towards the body. As Gallagher and Laqueur (1987) point out, Foucault's anti-essentialist discursive approach has been crucial to the recent rethinking of the body in society.

Technologies of power

Foucault's work has had an enormous impact on poststructuralist and feminist critiques of mind/body dualism. Foucault adopts a radical anti-humanist stance, which is highly critical of universalistic claims to truth. As opposed to considering if human nature exists, Foucault, as Paul Rabinow (1986b, p. 4) shows, historicises such questions and instead asks 'how has the concept of human nature functioned in our society?' Thus, his attention is directed towards asking 'how' questions as opposed to 'why' questions. Social phenomenology, stemming from the work of Schutz (1967), is also concerned with 'how' questions rather than 'why' questions. However, its focus is directed towards an understanding of the processes through which we come to make sense of the world, to unpack the processes of our common-sense thinking. Social phenomenology, despite its critique of positivism, remains within the parameters of the liberal humanist tradition. Foucault's aim in his historical studies, on the other hand, is 'to discover the relations of specific scientific disciplines and particular social practices' (Rabinow, 1986b, p. 5) and, through an examination of their various modes and practices, to 'unmask' their so-called neutrality in order to challenge them.

Foucault seeks to understand the actual workings of power in society, which appear to be 'neutral and independent' (Rabinow, 1986b, p. 6). He argues that the 'will to knowledge' that is the hallmark of liberal humanism, underscored by the key notions of reason and freedom, has not cast light on how 'power' functions in western societies. The problem at the heart of Foucault's concerns, as Rabinow argues, is that of the subject, which is central to the discourses and practices in modern western culture. Knowledge and power, for Foucault, are inextricably linked and cannot be separated. His aim is not to analyse power in itself or to develop a causal analysis, but rather to 'create a history of the different modes by which, in our culture, human beings are made subjects' (Foucault, cited in Rabinow, 1986b, p. 7).

The body, as Rabinow (1986b) demonstrates, is central to Foucault's critique of history and to his key concern with subjectivity. Foucault's interest with the body, according to McNay (1992), makes its first appearance in his 1971 essay on 'Nietzsche, Genealogy, History' (1986), in which he critiques the traditional tropes of history and develops his approach through an elaboration of Nietzsche's genealogical method. The body is the starting point for Foucault's notion of 'effective history':

> The body is molded by a great many distinct regimes; it is broken down by the rhythms of work, rest, and holidays, it is poisoned by food or values, through eating habits or moral laws; it constructs resistances. 'Effective history' differs from traditional history in being without constraints. Nothing in man – not even his body – is sufficiently stable to

serve as the basis for self-recognition or for understanding other men. The traditional devices for constructing a comprehensive view of history and for retracing the past as a patient and continuous development must be systematically dismantled. (1986, pp. 87–8)

The body, for Foucault, then, is an unfinished, unstable entity, which is produced through a range of discourses and practices and is productive in 'constructing resistances'. In the first volume of *The History of Sexuality* (1984), Foucault stresses that his approach to the history of the body is not one that only takes account of the meanings and values that have been bestowed upon it through the development of 'the modern technologies of power' (p. 152). Rather, his concern is with a ' "history of bodies" and the manner in which what is most material and vital in them has been invested' (ibid.). Thus, Foucault is directing attention towards the material body. The body is the principal target of power/knowledge relations, transmitted through discourse, and Foucault directs his genealogical analysis towards the transformation of the body in history. For example, the rise of modernity was accompanied by shifts in discourses that produced a profound impact on the construction of the modern subject. The 'target' and object of discourse shifted away from 'the body as flesh' to 'the mind' and the characterisation of the body as machine in classical Cartesian thinking. The construct of 'the mindful body', as Shilling has noted, 'is defined through its possession of consciousness, intentions and language' (1993, p. 76). In contrast to more traditional societies where the body is controlled by brute force, the body of the subject in modernity becomes caught up in a range of practices that control, constrain and objectify it through strategies of surveillance. This shift in the discourses surrounding the body in modernity is the subject of Foucault's *Discipline and Punish* (1977) and *The Birth of the Clinic* (1973).

In *Discipline and Punish*, for example, Foucault shows that under the monarchical regime 'the body was a highly visible target of penal repression' (Shilling, 1993, p. 76) and that those who seriously offended against the body politic had their punishment meted out on their physical bodies. In seventeenth-century society, as Foucault notes, the king's body was essential to the functioning of the repressive regime of power. The king's body, according to Foucault, 'wasn't a metaphor, but a political reality' (1980, p. 55). The king's body *was* the body politic. In the nineteenth century, it is 'the body of society' that becomes the guiding principle and it is 'this social body which needs to be protected' (ibid.). The tools of scientific management were brought into the penal system in the nineteenth century to control those individuals who offended against the social body by keeping their bodies under constant surveillance within the confines of the institutional space of the prison. The model for this form of surveillance was exemplified by Jeremy Bentham's architectural Panoptican device.

The principle of the Panoptican is an outer circular building consisting of individual cells each of which has two windows, one facing out, the other facing in towards a central watchtower, which has windows looking out to the outer circle of cells. An overseer in the central tower can see the prisoners in their individual cells, but the prisoners cannot see the overseer or any of the other inmates. The idea behind this surveillance device is that the individual prisoners would control their behaviour because they would know that, at any time, they could be being watched. The system also included a mechanism for the controllers to be observed by their superiors, and thus prisoners and controllers were subject to the all-seeing 'eye of power'. Foucault (1980) shows that the concern with disciplining bodies through a central system of observation began to take shape in other architectural projects such as military schools, hospitals and factories in the late eighteenth century. Thus, technologies of surveillance were designed to control the intentions of the subjects under the gaze, in a range of key institutional spaces.

The body is subject to similar transformations in Foucault's (1984) analysis of sexuality. The Christian confessional, in which the priest functioned as an intermediary between the individual sinner and God, occupied the key site in which sexuality was formulated and inscribed (Shilling, 1993). The 'priest', as Shilling (ibid., p. 76) notes, 'was concerned with people's sexual *activities* and the dominant sexual discourses were concerned with the body as flesh'. After the Reformation the focus began to shift towards *intentions* as well as practices, and increasingly the concern with sex began to shift away from the body as flesh and towards the mind of the speaking subject. Just as the prisoner in the modern penal system was captured by light, in contrast to the 'principle of the dungeon' (Foucault, 1980, p. 147), so sexuality 'was driven out of hiding and constrained to lead a discursive life' (Foucault, 1984, p. 33). Sex, far from being repressed in the nineteenth century, 'was put into discourse' (ibid., p. 11), and Foucault's intention is to locate 'the regime of power–knowledge–pleasure that sustains human discourse in the modern world' (ibid.). Thus, sex was subjugated to a proliferation of discourse, particularly through science where there was a drive to search for the 'truth' of sex. As we have seen, this was partly evidenced by the shift in the discourse of anatomy and biology in the late eighteenth century. As discourses on sex proliferated in the nineteenth century, so four different types of sexual subjects were targeted and classified through the mechanisms of power/knowledge: the 'hysterical woman', the 'masturbating child', the 'Malthusian couple' and the 'perverse adult'. These four discursive figures represented a change in the 'scope of the discourse' on sex 'away from the individual body' towards a focus on the 'reproductive fitness of the *social body*' (Shilling, 1993, p. 77). As a consequence of the dominance of these figures, Shilling (ibid.) points out, the ' "legitimate heterosexual couple" tended to function as the norm, classifying other people's and other forms of sexuality as deviant'.

Foucault's historical analysis shows that from the eighteenth century, as governments become increasingly interested in people's welfare and growth of the population, so 'a new regime of power takes hold' (Rabinow, 1986b, p. 17), which he terms 'bio-power'. With bio-power, human beings as a species come into focus as the object of attention and intervention. The human body also becomes an object of control and manipulation. The aim of the disciplinary technologies in schools, factories, prisons and hospitals is to produce a 'docile body that may be subjected, used, transformed and improved' (Foucault, 1980, p. 198). These disciplinary technologies, which forged useful, productive, regulated bodies through training and control of space, preceded modern capitalism and, according to Foucault, were 'prerequisites for its success' (Rabinow, 1986b, p. 18). Contemporary consumer capitalism has given rise to a 'new mode of investment' in the body, in which emphasis is placed less on the regulation of bodies 'by repression' and more on 'control by stimulation'.

Foucault's anti-humanist, anti-essentialist analysis of the discursive body has had a major impact on the work of researchers across social and cultural studies who seek to examine the body from a social constructionist perspective and the technologies of the self it facilitates. Certain strands of feminism, in particular, as indicated earlier, have used this discursive approach to criticise the notion that the natural body is the basis on which identity and difference are forged. Feminists have also drawn on his work to support their claims that the body is an unfinished entity and that gendered identities are not stable, fixed or static but are produced through discursive practices. The biological body, in Foucault's analysis, is also discursively fashioned, historically contingent and constituted through power/knowledge relations. Some feminists have used this approach to argue their case for excluding the biological as an area in its own right (Shilling, 1993). For Butler (1990a), for example, sex is a discursive effect of gender.

It is precisely the concern with 'compulsory heterosexuality' (characterised by the 'Malthusian couple' cited earlier) that Butler (1990a, 1993) and 'queer' theorists who draw on her ideas have highlighted and challenged in the last decade (see Fraser's (2000) incisive discussion on this). I will expand on this trajectory a little by first returning to the case of Agnes, which was discussed in the previous chapter. In her speech acts, Agnes reiterated that she was in essence a 'real' woman and the doctors too, until Agnes revealed otherwise, were convinced that she had not wilfully transgressed the normative boundaries of the binary sexual divide by taking female hormones. Neither Agnes nor the doctors sought to 'trouble' gender. Agnes's sense of what a real woman's body should look like and how a woman should behave was also shot through with a 1960s stereotypical heterosexual normativity. Garfinkel (1984), however, did perhaps see an element of 'drag' in Agnes's behaviour when he mentioned, almost in passing, that she seemed to be more like a woman than a 'natural' woman. Was Agnes performing gender or was gender simply performing her? That is, could her gendered utterances (in speech and gesture) be construed as acts of resistance or transgression or did they remain within the bounds of gender performativity? 'Performance' acts, in Butler's (1993) view, potentially critique and subvert the fixity of the normative heterosexual economy. Performativity, on the other hand, 'consists of a reiteration of norms which precede, constrain and exceed the performer' (ibid., p. 234). Butler (1990a, p. 137) indicates that the cultural practice of 'drag' might offer the possibility of subverting the 'expressive model of gender' and the notion of a true gender identity (although, as we shall see in Chapter 6, she argues that it can also shore up the 'truth-regime' of gender). Although she does not in any way discuss dance as a practice that can do this kind of work, choreographers in the 1980s and 1990s, like Mark Morris and Bill T. Jones among others, presented works that set out to 'trouble' the truth-regime of gender identification and desire. Both Morris and Jones, who is black and HIV positive, have openly discussed their homosexuality in the press and in their work. In an essay, entitled 'Styles of the Flesh', Gay Morris (1996b) brings Butler's ideas on performativity to bear on Mark Morris's multifaceted treatment of gender in *Dido and Aeneas* (1989) and *The Hard Nut* (1991). In the former, as Morris points out, the choreographer 'performed the central female roles of Dido and the Sorceress, using his own body as a site of gender instability to examine sexual desire' (1996b, p. 141). In the latter (a Morris make-over of the ballet *Nutcracker*), he uses his company members 'to create a proliferation of gender identities'. Gay Morris argues that these two dances 'offer the kind of theatricalized critique of gender Butler envisions' (ibid.), while building on this through dance acts. In *The Hard Nut*, for example, Mark Morris enables us to query (or 'queer') gender performativity through 'cross-dressing and movement':

> We see a 'girl' who looks like a 'boy', but still looks like a 'girl', moving like a 'boy', and we are struck by a series of jolts that constantly refocus our attention on the instability and performative aspect of gender. (p. 151)

Despite the potential of Foucault's discursive body for feminism, writers such as McNay (1992, 1999), point to certain limitations in his approach. To begin with, despite his interest in the body, Foucault's approach to the disciplined body has been criticised for being 'gender blind', and thus continues in a long line of social theory that ignores women as subjects. His analysis of 'undifferentiated' individuals as 'docile bodies' leaves little room for differences in experience and individuality, and as a result, as McNay (1992, p. 47) argues, women (and men) end up as passive, silent subjects. Many feminists have been at pains to counter such a view of women. Moreover, Foucault's (1984, p. 142) notion that there 'are no power relations without resistances' is difficult to locate in the face of the universal regulation of bodies through power/knowledge/discourse. However, McNay (1992) considers that Foucault's later work on the technologies of the self in his final two volumes on the history of sexuality, at least to a certain extent, holds more potential for feminism. This is because unlike other poststructuralist or postmodernist approaches, such as that of Derrida or Baudrillard:

> The exploration of the identity proposed by Foucault is not simply an endless dispersal of the subject, or a celebration of heterogeneity *qua* heterogeneity, but is linked to the overall political aim of increasing individual autonomy, understood as a humanizing quality of social existence. (McNay, 1992, p. 193)

Despite Foucault's attempt to develop a 'history of bodies', 'the body' in this anti-essentialist analysis, according to Shilling (1993), ultimately disappears because it is wholly constituted as an effect of power/ knowledge; as it is brought into discourse so it disappears as a material phenomenon. 'It is present as an item of discussion, but is absent as an object of analysis' (p. 81). In the end, it is not the body that requires examining in Foucault's work; rather it is discourse that calls for examination.

Other developments in social theory, such as the analysis of class, status and consumption, have also led to a reconsideration of the role of the body in society. In Pierre Bourdieu's (1993) concept of habitus, for example, which is outlined below, the body is treated as more than a social construction. That is, it is not like a set of clothes that you can put on or take off at will. The bodies of 'agents' are marked by the distinctions of class, gender and race. The heightened focus on the body in consumer culture, as Foucault's insightful quotation below suggests, has positive and negative ramifications for the way in which the body is viewed and treated within western societies.

'Get undressed – but be slim, good-looking and tanned!' (Foucault, 1980, p. 57)

The heightened concern with bodily appearance and preservation is evidenced by the vast amount of cosmetics, diet and exercise products that are marketed, bought and sold in the rapidly expanding western consumerist cultures, which have increasingly ageing populations (Featherstone, 1991a). Consumer culture was given a considerable boost in the 1970s and 1980s through the establishment of the New Right with its 'free to choose' radical liberal ideology of the market. Postmodern theories in the 1980s stressed the collapsing of the traditional binaries between high art and popular culture and the 'aestheticisation of everyday life' in a world in which experience is simulated through the 'evil demon of images' (Baudrillard, 1987). Postmodernists pointed to an epochal shift from a modern society based on production to a postmodern society founded on consumption in which the consumerist 'body/self has become primarily a performing self of appearance, display and impression management' (Csordas, 1994b, p. 2). As Douglas (1975a) has argued, the relationship between society and the body is not a simple one-way top/down process from the social or political body to the physical body. Rather, there is a reciprocal relation between the bodies, so that each informs (and transforms) the other. The current preoccupation with the body, as Foucault's analysis suggests, is also closely linked to biopolitics and the care of the self. Mike Featherstone (1991a), in his 'consumerist body' thesis (Lyon and Barbalet, 1994, p. 51), sees that consumer culture tunes into the preoccupation with the body and entices the consumer to take various measures to prevent, or, at the very least, ward off the inevitable onslaught of bodily decay. This, according to Featherstone, is accomplished through mobilising the idea of the body as an instrument of pleasure and self-preservation. Thus, there is a shift from the purposeful 'useful' labouring body to that of the representing body.

Images of the beautiful body, as Berger noted in *Ways of Seeing* (1972), stress the importance of 'the look' and of bodily surveillance, which, as a number of feminists argued (see, for example, Betterton, 1987; Parker and Pollock, 1987), have traditionally impacted more on women than on men. The politics of the 'gaze' not only reach into the corners of cultural texts (Mulvey, 1989), they are also evidenced in a whole variety of ways in everyday life (Coward, 1984; Bordo, 1990b). The promotion and encouragement of exercise, for example, which is visible in a consumerist 'gym culture', is heavily gendered in terms of exercise spaces and equipment, and acceptable degrees of muscularity (Johnston, 1998). While men are encouraged to work on strengthening their muscles, women are encouraged to achieve a toned look, in which muscle definition does not transgress the normative codes of the binary divide between femininity and masculinity (Schultze, 1990). In Chapters 4 and 6, we will consider the ways in which modern dance and postmodern dance have attempted to transcend the traditional codes of gender representation and difference.

The added value attached to the current concern with disciplining the body, according to Featherstone (1991a), is not locatable in terms of the ideals of greater spiritual development, as in monastic or religious life. In contemporary consumer culture the concepts of discipline and hedonism are no longer viewed as binary opposites. Rather, the disciplined body can be seen as a prerequisite for releasing the potential for individual expressivity and for achieving sexual pleasure. Nor, according to Featherstone, is it entirely on the grounds of better health. Health improvement, though, becomes an artefact of the time and labour spent on the body. More importantly, in contemporary consumer culture the prize for the disciplined body in terms of diet, exercise and cosmetics is locatable in the notion of a more attractive physical appearance and thus a more marketable self. Contemporary consumption forges a link between the 'body, self and culture' (Falk, 1994, p. 7). The body, self and culture in post-traditional societies are not givens, as Anthony Giddens (1991) points out. In contemporary societies, risk and uncertainty are key features. We can no longer derive a sense of our self from our traditional place in the social order (class, status, gender). Instead, our self-identity is constituted through a 'reflexively organised endeavour'. The body, according to Giddens, or the regulation of it, is key to the maintenance of our sense of self, our narrative of self-identity. The traditional perception of the body as 'a "given", the often inconvenient and inadequate seat of the self' has been altered by 'the increasing invasion of the body by abstract systems'

(1991, p. 218) in contemporary high or late modern societies. 'The body, like the self, becomes a site of interaction, appropriation and reappropriation', which is 'fully available to be "worked upon" by high modernity' (ibid.); it is no longer a taken-for-granted natural fact of existence. Giddens suggests that the more uncertain we are about our bodies (and the self), the more we perceive them as being capable of 'being worked upon', to improve and transform them. This notion of the flexible body is a key feature of the consumerist body.

Featherstone suggests that the stress on 'body maintenance and appearance' within consumer-oriented cultures implies two basic categories, the inner body and the outer body:

> The inner body refers to a concern with the health and the optimum functioning of the body that demands maintenance and repair in the face of disease, abuse and the deterioration accompanying the ageing process. The outer body refers to appearance as well as the movement and control of the body within social space. (1991a, p. 171)

Featherstone's construct of the outer body relates to what Douglas called the 'social body', George Herbert Mead (1934) called the 'me', Charles Cooley (1956) termed the 'looking-glass self' and what Turner (1992) referred to as *Körper*. In consumer culture, the care and attention given to the inner body is not principally about maintaining a healthy body as an end in itself. Rather, 'within consumer culture', according to Featherstone, 'the inner and outer body become conjoined' (1991a, p. 173). The management and control of the inner body are primarily directed towards transforming and beautifying the outer body, attempting to make the outer, appearing body more presentable and more re-presentable.

It is important to note that commodification and consumption did not just burst onto the scene in the late twentieth century. Consumer culture has been in evidence since the late eighteenth century. Indeed, as Don Slater's (1997) illuminating analysis shows, the growth of consumer culture has been inextricably entwined with the development of modernity. Notwithstanding this, it may be argued that the basis of consumer culture as we understand it today was being cemented by the 1920s. Developments in Fordist production processes in the initial years of the century (Harvey, 1989), and the introduction of Taylor's scientific management (Braverman, 1974), facilitated a vast increase in the production of goods. At the same time, wage increases and the entry of women into the system of production helped to create a demand for goods (Slater, 1997). This was aided and abetted by the introduction of consumer credit in the USA, which promoted the ethos of 'buy now, pay later' (Featherstone, 1991a). With the expansion of consumer culture, the nineteenth-century work ethic (Weber, 1976), which emphasised hard work and moderation in all things, at least for the working classes, yielded to a language of hedonism that required new needs and wants, couched in a discourse of necessity for the self. The establishment of the new mass media, particularly film (Eckert, 1990) and advertising (Featherstone, 1991a), paved the way by sponsoring the new icons of leisure and the pursuit of pleasure and satisfaction through the new lifestyle. The initial stages of this period of consumer culture took place at a time when the proportion of the workforce engaged in manual labour was beginning to decline and the white-collar sector was expanding, which it has continued to do (Lyon and Barbalet, 1994). The consumerist body in contemporary western societies has supplanted the purposeful, 'useful', labouring body, with the representing body.

The images and concerns surrounding the body in consumer culture, then, are not static or fixed. Rather, they are subject to change and revision. Victorian capitalism sought to conceal the body by clothing the male body in a dark, sober loose-fitting suit suitable for the mental labour that the Victorian middle-class male engaged in. The suit, as John Berger has noted, was the first costume 'to idealise purely *sedentary* power'. It represented, Berger continued, 'The power of the administrator and the conference table' (1980, p. 34). The middle-class female body was concealed by cramming it into corsets and long heavy dresses which, in turn, restricted freedom of movement, and for nineteenth-century dress reformers, constituted a source of female health and hygiene problems. Contemporary consumer capitalism, by contrast, seeks to display the human body in a way that celebrates its so-called natural form. However, and this is important, it is not any old natural form that is celebrated by consumer culture. Rather, the natural body is highly codified, disciplined, worked on and subject to idealisation (Schiebinger, 1987; Nead, 1992). On the one side, as Foucault (1980, p. 57) so astutely pointed out, we have the freedom to take our clothes off, but the other side entails an unfreedom, because the codicil decrees that if we do, we must be 'slim, good-looking and tanned'. The majority of women may no longer wear corsets but there are more ways of containing the body than by using objects to hold it in. Now we use our own muscles to hold our bodies in and diet to flatten the 'bulge' (Bordo, 1990b). If this does not work, then surgery may offer the desired effect. The requisite 'natural' form celebrated by consumer culture is achieved through constant surveillance and control.

Featherstone (1991a) argues that by working on the body, through diet, exercise and/or cosmetics, consumer culture induces people to self-manage their appearance. It entices them to be responsible for how they look. Letting the body go is viewed as a sign of moral slackness. In other words, it is your duty to keep your appearing body in good (idealised) condition, even though your real body is spreading out through middle age, too much food and so on. If in doubt, there are any number of magazine articles and adverts offering the individual advice on how to take control of the body in order to improve its appearance, and thus its inner health.

Although women have been more clearly bound up with the 'look' and the self-looking world of images, consumer culture has increasingly co-opted men into the world of the appearing body in recent years through the promotion of exercise, fashion and cosmetics (Nixon, 1992). Increasingly, according to Featherstone (1991a), the maintenance of a good outer bodily appearance (male or female) in consumer culture is seen as essential for the successful expression of individuality and sexuality. So that, on the one hand, consumer culture encapsulates the ideology of hedonism but, on the other, it suggests that individual pleasure can only be gained through a regime of bodily maintenance. In order for the individual to realise the freedom and pleasure that the body inheres, he or she has to keep it in captivity by governing it and disciplining it. The idealised natural body that consumer culture seeks to reveal finds its expression in, and is realised through, bodily control. Freedom, it seems, can only be achieved through coercion, while self-expression (hedonism) can only be found through duty. An orderly functioning body can only find its expression through the rigorous pursuit of aestheticism. The inner body finds its expression through the outer appearing body, which is maintained by false (or fake) means.

The body in contemporary consumer culture takes on the status of a commodity, which, as this brief discussion has shown, functions on a number of intersecting levels. The consumerist body, for Lyon and Barbalet, is 'significantly passive' (1994, p. 52). In contrast to the labouring, useful body, the consumerist body is 'an object of exchange'. One of the consequences of the consumerist body construct is that it once more stresses representation over embodiment, *Körper* over *Leib*. Whilst recognising that 'the body is [the] subject of and subject to social power',

Lyon and Barbalet argue that the body is not simply passively shaped by society and thus is not extrinsic to the processes of its being shaped:

> Persons do not simply experience their bodies as external objects of their possession or even as an intermediary environment that surrounds their being. Persons experience themselves simultaneously *in* and *as* their bodies. (1994, p. 52)

They seek to develop an approach in which 'the body can be understood simultaneously at an individual and a social level, as an agent as well as an object in the social world' (p. 63). Their conceptualisation of the 'social body' seeks to overcome the limitations of viewing the body as subject or object, as structured or action-oriented, by incorporating the notion of 'active emotion', which they view as simultaneously biological, social and psychological. They argue that 'it is through emotion that the intersection of the individual order and social order may be most clearly seen' (ibid.). The role of emotion in social life, like the body, has lived a shadowy existence in sociology and it too has come out of the shadows in recent years, partly as a result of a reexamination of Elias's work. Although this is an important area, I am not going to explore it here, for reasons of space. The concern to overcome the subject/object, agency/structure polarisations, which are reflected in representations of the body in social and cultural theory, has also been a key theme in Bourdieu's work.

Bourdieu's analysis of the body, developed over many years of theoretical and empirical study, focuses on the multiple commodification of the body in modern cultural formations. His approach has been influential in understanding the heightened role of the body in contemporary western culture (see Featherstone, 1991b; Shilling, 1991; Wacquant, 1995).

The body, for Bourdieu, like Foucault, is an unfinished entity. It is a carrier of symbolic value, which develops in concert with other social forces and is important to the preservation and reproduction of social inequalities. The body in modern society, for Bourdieu, has come to constitute a form of physical capital. The commodification of the body does not only refer to the buying and selling of its labour power under capitalism. It also pertains to the ways in which the body has come to be inscribed and invested with power, status and particular symbolic forms that are crucial to the accumulation of certain resources. Social bodies, then, are not simply written-on pages. Rather, they are produced by acts of labour, which in turn have a bearing on how individuals develop and maintain their physical being. These acts of labour also affect the way people learn how to present their bodies in everyday life through body techniques, dress and style. As the individual's body comes to be formed, it bears the unmistakable marks of his or her social class. The inscription of class on the body is a result of three particular determinants, the social location, the habitus and taste. Social location refers to the material class conditions, the economic, social and cultural, which impinge on the everyday life of individuals and assist in the formation of their bodies. The word 'habitus' refers 'to a habitual or typical condition, state or appearance, particularly of the body' (Jenkins, 1992, p. 74). The word has a long history and can be found in the work of a variety of thinkers such as Durkheim and Mauss, although neither of these gives it a prominent role (Bourdieu, 1990a, p. 12). Bourdieu defines the habitus as follows:

> The habitus, as the word implies, is that which one has acquired, but which has durably become incorporated into the body in the form of permanent dispositions. So the term constantly reminds us that it refers to something historical, linked to individual history, and that it belongs to a genetic mode of thought, as opposed to an essentialist mode of thought (like the notion of competence which is part of the Chomskian lexis). (Bourdieu, 1993, p. 86)

Although the habitus appears to be innate, it is rather like a property or a form of capital, which is embodied. It is important to note that Bourdieu's concept means more than simply habit or bodily techniques and dispositions that are merely reproduced on a mechanical and/or automatic basis. The habitus is reproductive but according to Bourdieu (1993) it is also productive:

> the habitus is a product of conditionings which tends to reproduce the objective logic of those conditionings while transforming it. It is a kind of transforming machine that leads us to 'reproduce' the social conditions of our own production, but in a relatively unpredictable way, in such a way that one cannot move simply and mechanically from knowledge of the conditions of production to knowledge of the products. (Bourdieu, 1993, p. 87)

The third determinant of class on the body is taste. According to Bourdieu, taste 'classifies' and, at the same time, 'classifies the classifier' (1984, p. 6). Bourdieu's much quoted and debated study of the 'social uses of art and culture', *Distinction* (1984), which he describes as a 'sort of ethnography of France' (p. xi), argues that particular patterns of taste, consumption choices and lifestyle habits are linked to particular class positions and occupations. These, in turn, allow the sociologist to 'map out the universe of taste and lifestyle with structured oppositions and finely graded distinctions which operate within a particular society at a given point in history' (Featherstone, 1991b, p. 18). The status of goods as markers of class in capitalist societies changes over time. The continuous supply of new and desirable commodities within consumer capitalism, or the appropriation of goods by those lower down the scale, means that those goods which were once deemed to be markers of the upper classes lose their exclusive status through mass circulation. In order to maintain their distinction from those beneath them on the social ladder and take back their place in the social hierarchy, the upper classes have to invest in new goods. In this context, as Featherstone (ibid.) points out, knowledge becomes crucial: that is, 'knowledge of new goods, their social and cultural value and how to use them appropriately'. Thus, aspiring groups have to learn about the consumption habits and lifestyle of the group they wish to enter into. But the symbolic goods we surround ourselves with classify us and, at the same time, our knowledge of their worth enables us to classify others. Nonetheless, as Bourdieu (1984) points out, this knowledge has to be somehow 'naturalised' through our body style, posture and demeanour, or our bodily 'hexis' as Bourdieu calls it, so as not to betray us as impostors. Thus, the body comes to play a crucial productive and reproductive role in the complex web of relations between class, status and goods.

Transcending the body/mind dualism?

The recent interest in the body, as suggested earlier, is situated within the broad framework of changes in late twentieth-century capitalism. These shifts include: the growth of mass and consumer culture, the politics of identity and difference, the rapid growth of technology, the 'moral panics' associated with the advent of HIV and AIDS, and the concern with the environment and pollution, or biopolitics. The interest in the body has led to a search for new paradigms. Some, as we have seen, have embraced poststructuralism, while others, like Shilling (1993), for example, have argued that the work of the sociologist Norbert Elias is a good place to begin to reevaluate the role of the body in society. Elias's theory of the 'civilising body' (1978 [1939]), although not without problems, according to Shilling, represents a significant improvement on social constructionist viewpoints, in that he seeks to intertwine biological and social factors within the dynamics of historical processes and state formations. Elias's approach is also touched upon in the chapter on the body in dance. But this interest in the body has also led to a reevaluation of earlier work in the field, including Goffman's dramaturgical approach to social life, which was an inspiring force for Bourdieu's work on the body. As Williams and Bendelow

(1998, p. 61) argue, Goffman's work is saturated with a concern to examine corporeal features of social relations:

> whether we are talking about the routine organisation of social interaction or the micro-politics of public order, the relationship between social identity and self identity or symbols of class status and the arrangement between the sexes, Goffman's sociology is anchored in the fundamental problem of human embodiment.

Nick Crossley (1995a) provides a thoughtful reevaluation of Goffman's contribution to the sociology of the body, through a consideration of two key constructs in the 'social theory' of the body, body techniques (from Mauss) and intercorporeality (from Merleau-Ponty). Goffman does not explicitly use these constructs in *Relations in Public* (1972), which is the focus of Crossley's discussion, or, indeed, in any of his other writing. Crossley argues that Goffman does cover the same ground and thus offers insights into the development of these constructs.

Crossley rightly points out that the value of Mauss's work lies in the fact that it demonstrated that the body is an appropriate object for sociological inquiry. Mauss, as argued earlier in the chapter, produced an over-socialised account, which ultimately left no room for individual negotiation, agency or action in terms of the body. Because action in this framework is conditioned by history and learning, it cannot consider the ways in which the individual can transform this knowledge at hand, into the action flow of everyday life. This dualistic approach to the study of the body, as Crossley demonstrates, was partially corrected in the work of Merleau-Ponty who, in *Phenomenology of Perception* (1962) and *The Structure of Behaviour* (1965), discussed how the 'body–subject' transforms the techniques he or she has acquired into constructive action. In these texts, Merleau-Ponty demonstrates that this process is 'co-ordinated' through a perceptual understanding of the context at hand. Familiar bodily techniques, bodily knowledge and so on are accommodated and transformed into action through the assessment of the ongoing situation. Thus, there is a sense of the mind and body coming together in action, which is oriented towards the present context. Although Merleau-Ponty does not develop this perception into a sociological framework, Crossley argues that the idea of embodied action being inextricably intertwined with the subject's perceptual field, the visual, tactile and olfactory channels, can be found in Goffman's work, particularly in *Relations in Public* (1972).

Goffman, unlike Mauss, is not just concerned to demonstrate a close association between different techniques of walking, for example, and different social statuses, genders and classes. He also aims to examine the reproduction and negotiation of these bodily techniques and styles of walking in relation to the situations we encounter in public spaces and places. These contexts, in Goffman's work, are not treated as a by-product of the techniques of walking. Rather, they are viewed as integral to the sociality of walking. Individuals routinely negotiate their bodily behaviour in relation to other individuals in an extra-individualistic (social) manner and, at the same time, they have to attend to the peculiarities of the space/place/environment they are walking in. The exercise of bodily techniques is situated in the social environment that the 'subject–body' is encountering and has to be taken into account if the subject–body is to achieve his or her ends, such as getting to the other side of the street. Thus, action is oriented towards the present and the space the individual is moving: in, with and through. Goffman's idea of the subject–body orienting itself in/with/through the spatial environment forms another link with Merleau-Ponty, who, as Crossley points out, theorised spatiality in regard to embodiment. Interestingly, it also forms a link with Hall's (1969) proxemics and Birdwhistell's (1973) kinesics, but what Goffman does in *Relations in Public* is to remove the problematic behaviourist base that haunted the work of Hall and Birdwhistell, which was discussed in the previous chapter (see Polhemus, 1975; Thomas, 1986).

On the surface, *Relations in Public* considers how we routinely negotiate and navigate our bodies in relation to other bodies and spatial objects in public settings, according to the rules of appropriate bodily behaviour in public places. Our behaviour, as Goffman rightly shows, is highly ritualised despite the 'disenchantment of the world' that Weber predicted would come about through rationalisation. In this way, Goffman's study forms a link with 'Body Rituals of the Nacirema' (Miner, 1956), discussed in the previous chapter, and with the process of the civilising of the body (Elias, 1978).

Goffman considers that the (social) public order is a moral order and as such his approach forms a link with the Durkheimian tradition of body symbolism. Our bodily behaviour in public places, according to Goffman, is rule-governed and, for the most part, we show through our bodily behaviours that we know the rules. If the rules are broken, then some sort of 'excuse-me' has to be put into place, unless of course there is an attempt to subvert the rules. This might explain the bodily interruptions that took place in the lecture on the body, discussed at the beginning of the previous chapter. According to Goffman, if we break the rules, we generally indicate that we usually get them right. By apologising for our momentary lapse of rule-boundedness, we show that we do 'normally' behave in an appropriate fashion. This, in turn, almost in true Durkheimian style, leads us to the idea of the normal and the pathological. A misuse of space/time, looking too long at strangers, for example, not adhering to the rules of walking in public spaces/places in a systematic manner, is likely to lead to charges of abnormality/other/difference and so on. That is, the individual would no longer be able to keep up the typification of normal appearances. Ritualised behaviour, for Goffman, is not fixed but may be modified, transformed and negotiated according to encounters with others and with the environment.

Goffman is aware that there is physical danger in the social/spatial environment, which includes other people. Natural dangers can be held in check through the transformation of the human environment, in the form of buildings, streets and so on and through the management and policing of these public spaces/places. But, according to Goffman, our bodily techniques also have a role to play in anticipating, circumventing or courting possible danger. Goffman adapts the construct of territoriality as defined by animal psychologists into his notion of the 'territories of the self'. There is an invisible bubble around the individual and coming too near to it sets off what Goffman calls 'an early warning system'. The sphere around the individual within which potential sources of danger are to be found is termed by Goffman as the 'Umwelt'. Not only do we have to scan the environment, we also have to scan the other people we encounter. These other people have to be taken into account in our bodily actions in order to circumvent possible dangers. Goffman is at pains to demonstrate that the individual is engaged in a social world, what in phenomenological terms is viewed as an intersubjective world. He suggests that others encountered by the subject–body will also hold a view of what constitutes normal appearance. Hence, others will also be on guard when their 'Umwelt', or immediate area around their body, is in potential danger of being invaded. Thus, action in Goffman's work is not simply a matter of tradition. Rather, embodied action is intercorporeal.

Crossley (1995a) argues that this intercorporeality in Goffman's work is a concrete manifestation of Merleau-Ponty's theory, which challenges the idea inherent in Cartesian thought that the mind is wholly distinct from the body. For Merleau-Ponty, as discussed earlier in the chapter, the mind is not a separate inner world, which is housed in a mechanistic body. There is no substantial difference between mind and body; rather Merleau-Ponty talks in terms of *'behaviour* which is simultaneously meaningful, embodied and intelligent' (cited in

Crossley, 1995a, p. 143). The subjective states of others are available to us through their behaviour, just as our behaviour is also available to them. Subjectivity in Merleau-Ponty's theory, Crossley points out, is not private; rather it is 'publicly available' through behaviour. It is through behaviour that we can understand others and ourselves and not through the hidden unseen properties of mind. We do not simply see an object or a person in our mind's eye, rather we grasp the object through our bodies as it, he or she at the same time grasps us. Thus, the (ap)perceiver and the (ap)perceived are at the same time the (ap)perceived and the (ap)perceiver.[3] By aligning Goffman with Merleau-Ponty, Crossley also seeks to challenge Shilling's (1993) reading of Goffman's approach to the body as dualistic, one that grants precedence to the mind over the body, symbolism over the corporeal. For Shilling, the body in Goffman's work lives a shadowy life, 'as a thing which is represented' (Crossley, 1995a, p. 145). In Crossley's reconfiguration, Goffman emerges as 'a scribe to the corporeal' as opposed to being 'the handmaiden of the Cartesian tradition':

> Reading Goffman in this way has a dual pay off. On the one hand, it allows us to have a corporeal, (non-dualistic) sociology which is sensitive to the meaningfulness of social processes and exchange (without disembodying either). On the other hand, it allows us to operationalise (sociologically) some of Merleau-Ponty's key concepts and to translate his philosophy of embodiment into a sociology and social theory of embodiment. (1995a, p. 145)

Although Merleau-Ponty was not unaware of the implications of his theory for the social sciences (see Merleau-Ponty, 1978), he did not mobilise his concerns into a sociological frame. Crossley argues that it is only in the work of Goffman and his followers that it is possible to see the sociological 'operationalisation' of key constructs such as 'inter-corporeality' and 'intermundane space'.

Thus, in a way we have come back full circle to the concern that Turner (1992) voiced regarding the separation between *Leib* and *Körper* in foundationalist and anti-foundationalist approaches to the body and the privileging of the latter over the former in current social and cultural theory. Recent developments in social and cultural theory, along with changes in the register of late capitalism, have been influential in bringing 'the body' out of the shadows and into the light in academe. But there has been mounting criticism, from a number of quarters, of the dominance of representational or discursive models at the expense of the lived body (see Williams and Bendelow, 1998), which, in the end, shore up the very dualities they seek to undermine through a range of 'isms'. Thomas Csordas (1994b) has argued that representational or discursive approaches to the body, while valuable, need to be complemented by a phenomenological approach, which is concerned with 'somatic modes of attention'. Csordas suggests that dance as a somatic mode of attention, which engages reflexively with the body in movement and stillness, is worth exploring. Not only do we have and are bodies, as Turner (1984) suggests, but our bodies are not generally static. More often than not, however, theories of the body seem to posit a static, immobile body. One of the powerful features of Merleau-Ponty's approach, and Goffman's too, I would suggest, is that there is a strong sense that their body/subjects or subject/bodies are not static but move in time and space or perhaps, more appropriately, in space/time. Dance, as a somatic mode of attention, has been virtually ignored by the academic community, apart from anthropology where the body featured strongly early in the development of the discipline (Ness, 1996). Social and cultural approaches to the body have had a profound impact on the development of dance studies in recent years and there are signs that dance is becoming an area of interest for at least a few social and cultural commentators (see Thomas, 1996). More often than not, these commentators use dance as a metaphor for explaining some other 'social' activity, like the idea of 'performance', for example, or 'incalculable choreographies' (see Foster, 1998). This will be addressed more fully in Chapter 6. As I have argued elsewhere (Thomas, 1995), phenomenological analysis can be a useful tool for examining dance texts because it facilitates a serious consideration of dance movement, at least in the area of western theatre dance (see Sheets-Johnstone, 1979, 1984). But I have also argued that representational or textual methods are useful too, because they afford a serious consideration of the complex sets of relations between the body and society, which dance aesthetics have generally omitted. These approaches do not have to be mutually exclusive, as Csordas (1994b) has pointed out.

This chapter has focused exclusively on the major theoretical issues that have preoccupied social and cultural approaches to the body. Williams and Bendelow (1998), among others, have argued for the need to develop an embodied approach to the study of the body. Much of the work on the body in recent years has been saturated with theory at the expense of empirical investigation, thus continuing the theory/practice divide, although this is beginning to change (see Nast and Pile, 1998). The chapter that follows begins by examining recent concerns that have emerged in the 'ethnographic field'. The second part of the chapter aims to pave the way for an embodied ethnographic approach by attending to the insights offered by dance ethnographers.

Chapter 3

Ethnography Dances Back

Introduction

The aim of this chapter, in line with recent developments in sociology and cultural theory, is to bring ethnography back into the picture through an exploration of some of the central issues to emerge out of postmodern and feminist ethnography. Case studies of dance forms, practices and events will be drawn on with a view to considering the challenges they raise for participant observation studies and for the study of the body. Thus, it will build on the previous chapter by refocusing theory towards the problems associated with conducting empirical research. The discussion will also draw on the 'ethnographic critique of ethnography' within sociology in order to draw out some of the emergent questions that confront the dance ethnographer regarding the nature of description and representation, and explanation and verification. To begin with, it is necessary to give some indication of the extent to which ethnography has been used within the social sciences and cultural studies.

Varieties of ethnography

Over the past thirty or so years, qualitative approaches to studying the social world, such as ethnography, have increasingly moved out of the margins of social research and into the light. In part, this growth in the popularity of qualitative research, according to Martyn Hammersley (1992), may be attributed to the fact that quantitative research methods, which became dominant in the wake of the influence of logical positivism in the 1930s and 1940s, have increasingly come under attack. As Liz Stanley (1990a) has argued, it would be a mistake to think that the 'origins' of ethnography are rooted in a 'contemporary' rejection of quantification. The history of ethnography is complex and it is situated in 'different historical sources' (1990a, p. 619). Although there is no intention, here, of examining the sources in detail, it is worth noting that ethnographic writing has been a feature, to a greater or lesser extent, across many disciplines.

Ethnography has long been the favoured approach in social and cultural anthropology and, until recently, the published ethnographic monograph was considered proof of the author's credentials as an anthropologist. In anthropology, again until recently, ethnography has been treated primarily as a method or technique for collecting data, as opposed to a methodology. Postmodernist and feminist ethnographers, in quite different ways and for different ends, challenged what they saw as the visualist, realist and objectivist frameworks inherent in traditional ethnographic accounts. In so doing, they argued for a more reflexive approach that would facilitate the possibility of the (previously silent or silenced) 'other' to be heard: the voices of members of 'other' cultures for postmodernists and the voices of women for feminists.

Prior to the influence of positivism on the development of survey research and quantitative methods in sociology, social scientists like Henry Mayhew (1861) and Charles Booth (1902–3) used case study material alongside survey methods for researching the conditions of the urban poor in the late nineteenth century. The ethnographic genre in sociology has been influenced significantly by the 'classic' work of the Chicago school of sociology. Under the influence of Robert Park, W.I. Thomas and their pupils, the Chicago sociologists focused on 'urban life', in contrast to the mostly 'exotic' studies of anthropologists around the same period. Rather like the New York Realist painters at the beginning of the century, who were called the 'Ashcan school' because their typical subject matter was the less seemly side of urban life, the Chicago sociologists turned their ethnographic attention to the underside of city life: the hobos, the taxi-dance halls and deviant subcultures. Until recently, the study of the 'underdog' remained by and large a dominant focus of ethnographic study in sociology (Atkinson, 1990). The work of Harold Garfinkel (1984 [1967]) and that of ethnomethodologically oriented ethnographers of the 1970s have also been influential in directing sociology's ethnographic gaze towards understanding how intersubjectivity is negotiated and sustained through the routine mundane practices of everyday life, and thus how social order is produced through social processes.

Ethnography has also been a visible strand running through the studies of popular culture, which have been heavily influenced by the work of the Birmingham Centre for Contemporary Cultural Studies (CCCS). The focus within this framework initially centred on the interpretation of 'deviant' youth subcultures, but later shifted towards a textual analysis of subcultural styles (see for example, Hall and Jefferson, 1976; Willis, 1977, *et al.*, 1990; Hebdige, 1979; Brake, 1985; Thornton, 1995). Cultural critics have since highlighted the need to move away from textual approaches that focus on representation and return to social experience and 'reality' (McGuigan, 1997; McRobbie, 1997; Malbon, 1999; Bennett, 2000; Muggleton, 2000). The main tenets of the CCCS approach to youth subcultures in the 1970s and the critiques of subcultural analysis that emerged in the 1980s and 1990s will be considered further in the context of the development of rave culture in Chapter 7.

Although dance research has a longer history than cultural studies, it has not had such an impact in academe. Nonetheless, dance anthropology, which draws its insights from social and cultural anthropology, has routinely adopted ethnographic methods to examine dance within the context of culture (see Royce, 1980; Spencer, 1985; Kaeppler, 1991; Grau, 1993; Thomas, 1997). There is a further, even less well-known tradition, that emanates from the European tradition of dance ethnology and folklore studies (see Buckland, 1999), where the analyses of dance forms and traditions take precedence over the social and cultural contexts of their performance. Recent studies in dance ethnography (see Cowan, 1990; Novack, 1990, 1993; Sklar, 1991, 1999, 2000; Ness, 1992, 1996, 1997; Gore, 1999) have drawn on postmodernist and feminist insights and critiques of traditional ethnographic approaches.

As this all too brief snapshot shows, there are streams of ethnographic work in a number of areas in social and cultural research such as anthropology, sociology, cultural studies and dance anthropology which have particular and related histories. As such, we need to think in terms of 'ethnographies' rather than the singular 'ethnography' (Stanley, 1990a). Since the 1980s, with the weakening of the boundaries and margins of the disciplines in light of the 'cultural turn' in the social sciences, questions raised in one area of study have increasingly come to be seen as relevant to another. In this way, postmodernist critiques have impacted upon the character of qualitative research within cultural studies, just as postmodernist and, to a lesser extent, feminist ethnographers have challenged the foundations of ethnography within the discipline of anthropology (Clifford and Marcus, 1986; Caplan, 1988; Stacey, 1988; Geertz, 1989; Wolf, 1992; Enslin, 1994). Similarly, the recent 'ethnographic critique of ethnography in sociology' (Brewer, 1994) has drawn on the insights of feminist and postmodernist criticisms, as well as on studies more centrally located in the sociology of science (for further details see Woolgar, 1988; Atkinson, 1990; Hammersley, 1990, 1991; Stanley, 1990b).

In order to reflect upon recent approaches to ethnography and the challenges that they raise, this chapter will not restrict the discussion to one discipline. Indeed, some sociologists, such as Hammersley and Paul Atkinson, prefer to define ethnography in a relatively broad-based manner that involves 'a particular method or set of methods':

> In its most characteristic form it involves the ethnographer participating, overtly or covertly, in people's daily lives for an extended period of time, watching what happens, listening to what is being said, asking questions. (Hammersley and Atkinson, 1995, p. 1)

Hammersley and Atkinson consider that all social researchers, by the very nature of their enterprise, are to a certain extent participant observers. As a consequence of this, they argue, the boundaries and margins of ethnography are more blurred than is sometimes supposed, particularly by the staunch advocates of qualitative inquiry. Hammersley and Atkinson are somewhat critical of what has been termed the 'romantic' movement in ethnography (see Dingwall, 1997, p. 63), and do not wish to make clear distinctions between ethnography and other forms of social research, particularly qualitative inquiry.

Ethnography, as indicated above, may be defined as an in-depth study of a culture, institution and context over a sustained period of time, which is usually longer for anthropologists than sociologists. Ethnographic research employs a range of methods and techniques such as participant observation, interviews, field notes, audio and visual recordings and, in the case of dance, movement analysis. The aims of ethnography, the (far/near) relation between representation and reality and the observer and the observed, are subject to debate and largely depend on the theoretical, political and/or methodological stance of the individual researcher. These issues will be highlighted initially by considering the ways in which postmodernist and feminist debates have contributed to the field. From there, the discussion will move on to consider how dance ethnography is situated within these debates by drawing attention to two case studies in particular (Sklar, 1991; Ness, 1992).

Postmodernism and feminism: 'the awkward relation'

Clifford Geertz's relativist, hermeneutically[1] informed cultural anthropological approach is generally credited with being the catalyst for the postmodern movement in ethnography (Gellner, 1992). The ethnographic enterprise, for Geertz (1975, p. 6), is about doing 'thick description'. That is, the ethnographer's task is to make sense of and provide an interpretation of the diverse life experiences and multiple layers of meanings and structures of cultural events and practices. Ethnography is not about making truth claims from this perspective. On the contrary, this approach challenged the philosophical realism upon which much of ethnography has been founded. Geertz argued that the interpretations of culture that ethnography generates are always based on 'second or third order' constructs and, as such, are interpretations of interpretations. Thus, they are 'fictions' to the extent that they are 'something fashioned' (ibid., p. 15). The break with positivistic conceptions of knowledge, objectivity and fact, according to Geertz (1989), helped to alter the traditional hierarchical relationship between the researcher and the researched. As a consequence, the ethnographic observers were required to ask what precisely they were looking at, and what they were trying to do.

The publication of James Clifford and George Marcus's edited volume *Writing Culture* in 1986 pushed the issues regarding representation, narrative and the character of the authorial voice in traditional anthropological work much further than Geertz, who ultimately resolved that:

> Whatever else ethnography may be … it is above all, a rendering of the actual, a vitality phrased. (1989, p. 143)

The *Writing Culture* collection rejected holistic traditional approaches to anthropology and maintained that the representations of culture that emerged from these perspectives were in fact a result of unequal power relationships which privileged the observer over the observed. The proponents of *Writing Culture* argued for the development of multivocal accounts of representations of culture in which the voices of the 'other', the traditional object of anthropology, could be heard. Thus, they rejected traditional authoritative and 'realist' representations of culture in favour of finding new ways of writing anthropology that could yield some insight into the traditional tropes of anthropology itself and its situated discourse.

This challenge to theories of knowledge and the politics of ethnography both pointed to, and spoke of, a crisis in the field (James *et al.*, 1997). Moreover, the debates that emerged in *Writing Culture* and a subsequent volume by Marcus and Fischer (1986) were also in evidence in other disciplines in relation to modernism and postmodernist strategies. The celebration of this 'new experimental moment in the social sciences' (Marcus and Fischer, 1986) was taken up enthusiastically by some and rejected by others, who saw it either as bourgeois propaganda (that is, the displacement of politics by poetics), or as an exercise in navel-gazing (that is, no need to get out into the field any more). Further, the rejection of the 'grand narrative' of traditional anthropological discourse in the 'new ethnography' in favour of a celebration of a multiplicity of voices was viewed by critics as simply the replacement of one grand narrative for another.

As Steve Woolgar (1988) has noted, proposals for cultural relativism and reflexivity have tended traditionally to lead to heated debates in the social sciences. Peter Winch's (1958) philosophical critique of the western 'objective' canons of rationality in the social sciences, which drew on Wittgenstein's concept of 'language games', provoked much controversy in sociology and anthropology in the late 1960s and early 1970s. The discussions that ensued centred on whether it was possible to understand the constitutive meanings and reasoning of one culture's way of life through the language of another (see Wilson, 1970; Horton, 1971). In the 1970s, phenomenologically influenced sociology advocated a reflexive approach to the study of routine everyday practices and occurrences in relation to specific social contexts. The challenge of phenomenology and ethnomethodology in sociology generated a backlash against the 'reflexivity of accounts' and the relativist stance that it advocated (see Filmer *et al.*, 1972). The more theoretical end of this work (see Sandywell *et al.*, 1975) foreshadowed a shift towards the 'cultural turn' in sociology and the challenge to the dominance of logocentrism in the human sciences exemplified by Jacques Derrida's deconstruction theory, which had a considerable impact in the late 1970s and early 1980s (see Culler, 1983).

Thus, proposals for researcher reflexivity and criticisms of traditional approaches to writing within the new ethnography were not entirely novel. Feminist ethnographers and researchers, for example, questioned the grounds upon which they spoke prior to the emergence of postmodern ethnography (Caplan, 1988; Wolf, 1992). Indeed, many of the issues raised by the new ethnography were addressed, or at least problematised, by feminist researchers. As Pat Caplan (1988) argues, feminism has aimed to break down the dualisms and boundaries that existed between the public and private spheres, nature and culture and theory and practice, as well as between one discipline and another. Feminist scholarship has also challenged the primacy of objectivity in anthropological or indeed sociological accounts, in favour of a version of partial truth which is situated in relation to a researcher's biography, social environment and history.

It is worth noting that, as Margery Wolf (1992) has demonstrated, many of the criticisms that postmodern ethnographers have made regarding the ethnographic process and the practice of accounting for others through the authorial voice of the anthropologist were virtually ignored, and in some cases scorned, when they were raised by feminist anthropologists some years before the emergence of the new ethnography. It is hardly surprising, then, that feminists questioned the complete absence of a feminist voice in Clifford and Marcus's (1986) influential collection *Writing Culture*. In his introductory essay, Clifford acknowledges that as a consequence of feminist interventions in academe, gender now has to be on the ethnographic agenda. Nonetheless, he suggests that feminism has not contributed much in the way of 'innovative textual strategies'. Nevertheless, as Caplan (1988) argues, when feminists began to challenge the grounds upon which anthropology and ethnography were based, they were treated as self-indulgent, whereas when male anthropologists like Clifford and Marcus began to do this, it came to be viewed as 'experimental'. This shift in meaning, and the accompanying rise in status when the challenge comes from men as opposed to women, is not restricted to anthropology, it is evidenced in a range of discourses and practices (see Huyssen, 1986).

The impact of feminist thought is generally considered to have been greater within the discipline of anthropology than other disciplines such as sociology (Stacey and Thorne, 1985). As a result of this, a number of feminists, such as Judith Stacey (1988), for example, started from the proposition that the ethnographic approach was well-suited to the goals of feminist research. Both feminism and ethnography shared a common concern with exploring the experiential and the everyday world and, as such, treated knowledge as being context-bound and interpersonal. In addition, within feminist research the researcher was constituted as an active participant in the research process, and the subjects of research were treated as agents of knowledge. Stacey also assumed that the ethnographic method afforded some power to the subjects of the research, by suggesting that, to a certain extent, they were co-authors of the research. As a consequence, feminist ethnographic research, Stacey believed, offered the possibility of being more attentive to the subjects of the research.

The perceived accord between feminism and ethnography, however, was called into question soon after Stacey (1988) embarked on an ethnographic project. She quickly discovered that this 'romantic' ideal feminist construct of ethnographic research, which aims to attend to the meanings that women give to their lives and thus enable their voices to be heard with a deep sense of respect, could mask other unexplicated forms of exploitation. Stacey became aware that the character of ethnographic research, which relies upon human relations and engagement with others, could place the subjects of research in very real danger of being exploited or manipulated by the ethnographer. Furthermore, doing ethnographic research can place the researcher in a difficult position with regard to how much can be revealed in the name of research and/or confidentiality, and loyalty to the subjects. This interrelation between the researcher and the researched can lead to ethical questions as to what can 'properly' be voiced in the public arena. This may place the researcher in a position of 'inauthenticity', which, in turn, would conflict with feminist principles regarding the relations of researchers to subjects. The discordance between the practice of ethnography and the final product of research can open up further contradictions between feminist principles and ethnographic research, according to Stacey. Although ethnographic research is a collaborative project involving researcher and researched, the researcher in the final analysis is the author and narrator of the ethnography. Thus, as Stacey points out, there is even a danger of exploitation in the very nature of the work that is being carried out and its final product:

> The greater the intimacy, the apparent mutuality of the researcher/researched relationship, the greater the danger. (1988, p. 24)

Nevertheless, Stacey is reluctant to abandon ethnographic principles and suggests that a possible solution to the feminist/ethnographic problematic may be found in postmodern and poststructuralist ethnographies. Within the new self-reflexive ethnography, ethnographic accounts are not representations *of* culture; rather they are (textual) interventions *in* cultures. This idea, to a certain extent, follows on from Geertz's discussion in *Works and Lives* (1989) regarding the 'second-order constructedness' of ethnographic accounts. Stacey considers that the new ethnography, like feminism, rejects naturalistic interpretations of social events and processes. Unlike earlier positivistic accounts, the new ethnography attempts to acknowledge and demonstrate the interpretative voice of the authorial self. By experimenting with different forms of ethnographic representation and writing, it aims to create spaces for different, previously absent voices.

The self-reflexive ethnographic approach that is generated through postmodernism is useful for feminism, according to Stacey (1988), precisely because it calls into question the uncritical celebration of ethnographic methods that have been a feature of feminist research. Marilyn Strathern's (1987) discussion of the 'awkward relationship' between feminism and anthropology offers a word of caution to those feminists who argue for a more fruitful dialogue between feminist research and postmodern ethnography. Unlike Stacey (Stacey and Thorne, 1985) and a number of other feminists, Strathern argues that feminist scholarship has not led to major paradigmatic shifts within the discipline of anthropology. This is in spite of the fact that feminist inquiry has received a more responsive reception within social anthropology, perhaps because of anthropologists' concerns with other societies.

According to Strathern (1987), feminist scholarship and anthropology are not alike. The former, as she points out, is not discipline-bound; rather, it works across disciplines. As such, it cannot be aligned with individual disciplines such as anthropology. The (feminist) gains that have occurred in anthropology, Strathern argues, are locatable within the history of anthropology itself, inasmuch as there was significant female (feminist) imprinting on the discipline since the early days of its inception. Moreover, it has become clear that the position of women in other societies can no longer be taken for granted, and thus has to be attended to within anthropological discourse. In fact, the study of gender has become an area of inquiry within anthropology in its own right. 'The discipline', according to Strathern, 'provides materials for part of the feminist enterprise, namely, the scrutiny of Western constructs' (1987, p. 278).

Strathern suggests that feminist anthropology has been absorbed into the discipline without fundamentally challenging the whole. While recognising that feminist anthropologists have challenged the foundational structure of the discipline by raising questions about male bias, Strathern argues that the major criticisms of the discipline have come from within anthropology, as opposed to from within feminist scholarship. There is a long tradition of radicalisation and renewal within anthropology. The new ethnography, according to Strathern, simply provides the most recent example of the challenge to the tradition from within. Although there are common features between feminist scholarship and the new ethnography, Strathern argues that they challenge the dominant traditions within the disciplines in very different ways. A clear example of this can be found in postmodernism and feminism's shared concern with experience.

Feminism, as Strathern points out, has been concerned to examine the shared experience of women and the appropriation of women's experience by patriarchy. Feminist scholarship has repeatedly shown that women stand as the 'other' in male accounts. As a consequence, feminists were forced to see men as the 'other' in relation to women. In anthropology, by contrast, the aim is to try and remain open to the work and lives of people that one is studying. For example, the new anthropology seeks to include the 'other' in the anthropological account to enable a multiplicity of voices to be heard so that the anthropologist's voice becomes one among many. Thus, the concern becomes to create a relationship with the 'other'. For feminism, on the other hand, according to Strathern:

> There can be no shared experience with persons who stand for the Other. (p. 288)

Feminism proposes that women can begin to discover themselves through a conscious awareness of the 'other' who represses them and through this can come to understand their common past (experiences). The new anthropology, on the other hand, insists that the self can be used as a means of representing the 'other', but the anthropologist can only do this if he or she, in effect, makes a radical break with past knowledge.

The differences between the notion of experience and the relation of the self to the 'other' in feminism and postmodern anthropology could provide a means for opening up a dialogue between the two areas. As Strathern (1987) argues, it would be an 'awkward' dialogue since each has the ability to undermine and 'mock' the other. Strathern concludes that feminism and the new anthropology in the end occupy different worlds. In paradigmatic terms they appear to be irrelevant to each other and accordingly do not offer a challenge, but rather, in Strathern's view, a 'mockery'.

Some feminist scholars have questioned the extreme form of cultural relativism (all accounts are equal) within the new ethnography, arguing that its postmodernist stance has simply substituted the old god-like 'view from nowhere' which was characterised by objectivism and universalism with the 'view from everywhere', characterised by subjectivism and relativism (see Haraway, 1988; Bordo, 1990a). As Susan Bordo (1990a) points out, the view from everywhere, by its very nature, inheres the view from nowhere precisely because it cannot be situated. By adopting the postmodern stance that any account is valid, the new ethnography has the potential to undermine political projects.

Nancy Hartsock (1987), for example, has commented on the fact that the dispersal of power towards a celebration of a multiplicity of voices in postmodernism occurred at the very moment when women and non-western others were beginning to find a voice and to speak from their own subject positions.

It may be argued that the significant challenge to anthropology comes from the undermining or unsettling of the boundaries that have been central to its identity as a discipline in which the self studies the 'other'. Lila Abu-Lughod (1990) suggests that such a challenge is posed not only by feminists but also by a growing number of indigenous anthropologists like Arjun Appadurai (1988) and by those researchers she refers to as 'the halfies'. Halfies are people who live between and across cultures. Both 'halfie' ethnography and feminist ethnography, according to Abu-Lughod, have the potential to disturb or disrupt the boundaries and paradigms of anthropology itself, by demonstrating that we are always a part of and involved in what we study and that we all stand in a definite relationship to it. The new ethnography, by contrast, is unable to escape the 'outsidededness' of its relation to the object of the study, because it sees that all anthropology is predicated upon that premise.

Nonetheless, the de-essentialising of the idea of 'Woman' as a fixed referent, which, in part, resulted from the exchanges between post-modernism and feminism (Nicholson, 1990), has positive features and presents an opportunity for both feminism and ethnography to move on beyond the potential 'mockery' pointed to by Strathern (1987). For Elisabeth Enslin, following Donna Haraway (1988), the very process of intervention 'must be rooted in an epistemology that transcends objec-tivist/relativist dichotomies' (Enslin, 1994, p. 555). That is, feminism needs to generate a theory of knowledge that overcomes the binary divide between objectivism and subjectivism.

The critical reappropriation of vision by feminists, advocated by Haraway, means that feminists have politically and ethically to evalu-ate: 'where to see from, whom to see with, and what to see for' (Enslin, 1994, p. 560). Enslin maintains that feminists and anthropologists must acknowledge that:

> By situating ourselves, our knowledge, and our praxis, we participate in particular conversations, share particular visions, and can be held account-able for seeing and knowing in various spaces of struggle. (Ibid.)

Researchers then, need to take account of the situated character of the processes of representing the 'other', and to see such processes as acts of 'sense making', as opposed to objective and coherent modes of representation. This involves asking questions about narrative and the nature and character of the story being told. In part, as a consequence of the kinds of concerns that *Writing Culture* raised, issues surrounding representation shifted away from the ways in which the worlds of 'the other' are represented and towards the ways in which 'anthropologists' represented others, and indeed themselves, within the narrative of the monograph. As Allison James, Jenny Hockey and Andrew Dawson (1997) have noted, it is but a short step from questioning, or acknowledging the situated character of other people's realities and representations of the world, to acknowledging that those who write the monographs themselves – the fieldworkers – also negotiate reality from their own viewpoint (their biographies, history and situatedness).

The researcher as object

Kirsten Hastrup's (1992) analysis of the process and the ramifications of her autobiography becoming a dramatic representation constitutes a striking example of the researcher finding herself in a position where she becomes an object of representation, in much the same way as the 'other' has been represented in ethnographic studies. Thus, rather than put a society under the microscope, the anthropologist is subjected to the anthropological gaze. Hastrup's analysis, then, develops the aforementioned insights that emerged out of the postmodernist and feminist critiques of the traditional tropes of anthropology. The occasion for the anthropologist putting herself under the microscope resulted from the processes associated with the creation of a theatrical production by the Danish theatre group Odin Teatret entitled *Talabot*. *Talabot* is described as 'a play about the last 40 years of history told through the biography of a woman anthropologist [Hastrup] born in 1948' (Hastrup, 1992, p. 327).

The Odin Teatret group does not work from a precreated text. Rather, the actors actively contribute to the process of the construction of the play from the very beginning, and are guided by the director, Eugenio Barba, in a collective enterprise. Hastrup was interviewed by the director and the actors, and was also asked to write a series of autobiographical pieces about her personal and professional life. In effect, the director and the actors were conducting fieldwork on the anthropologist and the anthropologist was becoming, in turn, the informant and the 'exotic' object of study. As the anthropologist became the object of study, so she felt her 'self' fading away. Hastrup is

particularly concerned to understand and analyse the consequences of
the process of the objectification and representation of the anthropologist and to consider how this very process might enable her to learn
more about the character of being an anthropologist in the world.

Hastrup's moving account of her 'journey out of anthropology' is
based on notes that she made during the process of creating the work
and on later reflections on that process. It also contains an account of
her 'introspective investigation' of her responses to the way the play was
being constructed at various points in its creation. Thus, as Hastrup
points out, the authorial eye is very much in place in this ethnography.
This is in contrast to the standard monograph in which the ethnographer is explicitly there as a fieldworker, but is implicitly absent as the
narrator and author of the ethnographic tale. At the same time, in good
postmodern fashion, the account of the 'lived experience' is rendered in
'story' form.

Seeing herself being played by another woman in the context of the
performance as it was taking shape produced a dramatic effect on
Hastrup. When she saw her character on the stage, it was, of course, no
longer her. The performer was not Kirsten, although at the same time
her life was unfolding before her eyes through the performance:

> The play evoked my biography within the context of world history as sus-
> pended between violence and science. It made me see myself more clearly
> than before. Through the selective fiction of not-me, my reality became
> more focused. (1992, p. 335)

Hastrup notes that when she saw the play, it evoked her reality, albeit
in the shape of a performance. The performance of her life presented a
picture of herself in front of her. The drama of Hastrup's own life was
a part of her and yet, because it was represented outside of herself, it
was not. The performance evoked a reality that was not her, even
although she was deeply engaged by it at the same time.

Hastrup muses that the loss of her self through the representation
of her self in *Talabot* has a close affinity with the loss of the illusion of
the voice of authority in the ethnographic text. The presence of the
ethnographer on the ground as it were, is not enough to ensure that the
'hiddenness' of a culture, or biography, will be brought into the light.
Rather, as Clifford has pointed out (1983), the anthropologist has to
somehow push or prod informants in order for them to give out any
information regarding their culture, or indeed themselves. Hastrup
(1992) suggests that the symbolic violence and the unequal relationship
between the researcher and their collaborator subject can be creative,

if these aspects are recognised. The notion of the self is not one that is fixed or essential, but rather is invented and situated. In turn, this raises the question of authenticity of accounts, in other words, whose voice or voices count?

Following Victor Turner (1974, 1982), Hastrup proceeds to consider the parallels between anthropology and performance. By viewing the object of anthropological study in terms of social drama, the researcher can gain access and insight into a foreign world through the processes of ritual enactment. In this sense the object of the anthropological gaze is used as a practice, as opposed to a conceptual system. The social dramas that unfold before the eyes of the anthropologist can bring about a change and thus reveal a crack in the system or social structure. Moreover, a focus on performance points to the self-reflexivity of the occasion under review. The performances speak to and of the world of the audience, at the same time as presenting or representing another world that is also in process.

Dance ethnography as a situated reflexive bodily practice

Ethnographic research, as Amanda Coffey (1999) has recently commented, is an embodied activity, and the ethnographic field is an embodied social and physical space. Although Hastrup's (1992) account of her movement out of anthropology and into social drama illuminates a range of issues surrounding representation and the ethnographic gaze, what appears to be absent is any discussion of the textual presence of her self as an embodied subject and her relationship to the moving, breathing, performing body/subject who represents and transforms her on stage. While her shifting 'self' is vividly present, it is a rather disembodied self. As demonstrated in Chapter 2, the centrality of the body and embodiment has been the subject of much research in the humanities and the social sciences in recent years. Despite this, the fact remains that there has been little attention paid to the embodied character of the ethnographic enterprise. Sociologists such as Goffman (1959, 1971), for example, as indicated in the previous chapter, have provided vivid ethnographic descriptions of a range of bodily strategies through which the 'self' is presented and negotiated, and the ways in which people routinely negotiate their physical environment. We gain little insight into how the very 'bodily' activities that are involved in the research process, such as observation, interpretation and analysis, impinge upon the experiences of the researcher and/or the embodied others, the researched.

These are the kinds of issues that dance ethnographers like Jane K. Cowan (1990), Novack (1990, 1993), Sklar (1991), Ness (1992) and Barbara Browning (1995), raise by incorporating into the research arena their reflexive self-awareness as experiencing, moving and dancing culture bearers. The consequences of not reflecting on our taken-for-granted routine bodily practices can limit or inhibit our comprehension of the bodily activities of 'others', and this once again emphasises the need to enter the embodied field with some self-knowledge.

Despite recent interest in the study of the body in the social sciences and cultural studies and a concern to seek an adequate account of human embodiment, the human body as a moving agent in time and space is somewhat ignored (Farnell, 1994). Although body movement appears to be fundamental to a great deal of human sociality, it is nevertheless the case that the study of movement has largely been neglected from the point of view of anthropological and general academic discourse. Despite the increased awareness of the relationship between the body, society and culture, the study of movement remains a minority issue. The insights generated through recent approaches to the body could be reframed in terms of issues surrounding the moving body, in order to generate an approach which could perhaps transcend the limits of the mind/body dichotomy inscribed in Cartesian philosophy and provide an antidote to the 'thing'-like character of the body in much social and cultural research (see Chapter 2).

The constructs of gendered performance and performativity (Butler, 1990b) and of choreographing difference (Derrida and McDonald, 1995), have had a significant impact on gender studies and cultural studies in recent years, particularly in regard to representation. Yet, interestingly, these have paid little or no regard to either the enactment of performance or choreography. Indeed, as Susan Foster notes:

> The vast majority of studies implementing the notion of performance have focused on the notion of representations of gender, rather than the orchestrated actions of moving, yet non-speaking bodies. They neglect the body, and yet at the same time use the body to inflect textuality with a new vitality. (1998, p. 27)

These very issues have been addressed by dance scholars and by dance historians:

> dance scholarship has hypothesised for dance the status and capacities of a language-like system. It has recast dance as a cultural practice whose discursive function might be seen as distinct from, yet comparable to language; it has reclassified dance as a system of signs. (Ibid., p. 19)

Foster suggests that perhaps colleagues in other disciplines might learn to look at some of this work in a more systematic and open manner, particularly in relation to feminist studies. This will be explored further in relation to dance and difference in Chapter 6.

While dance scholarship has tended to privilege the study of theatrical dance (high art) over social and popular dance, anthropological studies which include dance have been in evidence for over a century (see Hanna, 1980; Royce, 1980; Kaeppler, 1991; Reed, 1998). Indeed, as Sally Ness notes:

> Dance, as an object of cross-cultural study, has produced a dazzling array of methodological activity. (1996, p. 245)

The 1960s and 1970s saw the emergence of a new generation of American dance anthropologists, who were influenced by the dominant anti-ethnocentric mode of 'researcher objectivity' within cultural anthropology (ibid., p. 252).

Scholars such as Adrienne Kaeppler (1972), Drid Williams (1977) and Judith Lynne Hanna (1980) took their point of departure from the American and British traditions of anthropology (see Kaeppler, 1991; Williams, 1991; Grau, 1993), as opposed to the European tradition of dance scholarship, which has its roots in the folklorist tradition (see Lange, 1980; and Buckland, 1999 for a discussion of this legacy). Although there are a number of overlaps between the two 'schools' (Buckland, 1999), the major difference between the anthropological and the folklorist approach may be characterised in terms of the former's inclination for stressing the contextual aspects of dance and the latter's emphasis on the choreological aspects of dance or the 'end product' (Kaeppler, 1991). The new generation of dance anthropologists, albeit from different theoretical perspectives, sought to uncover the meanings in the various forms of dance under study through the application of communication and linguistic models to the consideration of the structure of human movement (see Thomas, 1986).

Dance ethnographers (Kealiinohomoku, 1970; Youngerman, 1974; Williams, 1977) in the 1970s challenged the commonly held view that dance is a form of natural (essentialist) behaviour which, with its roots in 'primitive' cultures, has developed into a fully fashioned, stylised western theatre dance, commonly regarded as the most advanced 'civilised' form. In so doing, they contested the hierarchical us/them relation of the 'west to the rest', by pointing to the inherent incipient racism and ethnocentrism in viewing dance as a primary feature (natural and ubiquitous) of 'primitive' cultures. As I will show later in Chapter 6, the idea that dance is prelinguistic continues to live on in the work of certain contemporary cultural critics.

Joann Kealiinohomoku (1970), in what is now viewed as a classic paper in dance ethnography, argued that ballet should be treated as a form of ethnic dance. Thus, she dared us to view ourselves with the self-knowledge of how we approach 'other' cultures. In this way, she directed the ethnographer 'at home' to study his or her own dance culture as if it were 'anthropologically strange' (Garfinkel, 1984).

Dance anthropologists, perhaps taking up Kealiinohomoku's (1970) lead, have also turned their anthropological gaze towards their own familiar dance cultures (Novack, 1990, 1993; Koutsouba, 1999; Williams, 1999). It should be noted that the idea that anthropology is largely a discipline which involves using fieldwork methods, such as participant observation, to describe and understand what might be best characterised as the primitive condition, as opposed to the modern, is not entirely accurate. As Daniel Miller (1995) has pointed out, there has always been an interest within anthropology to explore the reflexive responses to and of modern life, although this might have been peripheral in comparison with the larger framework of the discipline.

Dance ethnographers like Kaeppler (1985), Cynthia Novack (1990), Deidre Sklar (1991) and Andrée Grau (1993) embraced the cultural relativism implied in Kealiinohomoku's (1970) argument and adopted a social constructionist view of the relation between dance and culture. With the acknowledgement of cultural relativism, the term 'dance' as a taken-for-granted universal construct was also called into question. Kaeppler (1991, 1999) for example, in her study of dance in Tongan society (1972), argued that the term 'structured movement systems' was more appropriate to describe the movement and choreography of different cultures than the narrowly defined range of body movements in time and space that constitute western 'dance'. Even if the principles that go to make up 'dance' in a given culture can be analysed and described, it is not necessarily the case that these refer to dance alone. Dance may be conceptualised as one part of an integrated theatrical whole. In this case, the theatrical significance of the dance element can only be grasped in relation to the totality. The totality, in this case, in Durkheimian terms, is more than the sum of the parts. The rules that underpin the significant elements of *baratha natyam*, for instance, are not exclusive to the Indian dance form. As Avanthi Meduri reveals in her study of this recently (1930s) reinvented classical tradition of South Asian dance:

The rules that govern Indian dramaturgy are also the principles that define classical dance. Baratha's vision, then, enunciates a total theatre that links all the minutest units of dramatic representations. Each unit, such as dance, can be analysed and described separately, and yet assumes theatrical significance only in the context of the whole dramatic representation. If a minute aspect of the whole is disturbed or exaggerated, the theatre loses its characteristic, significant coherence. (1988, p. 3)

The themes and questions that came to the fore across the range of social and cultural studies (such as gender, sexuality, identity, body, the 'other', self-reflexivity) in the 1980s and 1990s have also found their way into the work of dance and movement ethnographers (Cowan, 1990; Novack, 1990; Sklar, 1991; Grau, 1993; Farnell, 1994). In these recent studies, the dance ethnographer is constituted as a culturally situated embodied individual who has to approach the area of study in a self-reflexive manner (Meduri, 1988, 1996; Novack, 1990, 1993; Sklar, 1991, 1999; Ness, 1992, 1996; Thomas, 1993b, 1997; Browning, 1995). For example, Novack's (1993) analysis of gender in classical ballet skilfully reflects upon her own biography and dance training and brings these to bear on the exploration of a range of unequal power relationships in contemporary culture, showing the ways in which they are structured, symbolised and given visibility in the dancing body. Her analysis of ballet and contact improvisation (Bull [formerly Novack], 1997) will be discussed in some detail in the succeeding chapter through an exploration of the ways in which the senses of vision and touch are differently privileged in three theatrical dance forms.

In order to further examine the relation between dance ethnography and reflexivity, I have chosen to focus on two texts in particular, Deidre Sklar's research paper 'On Dance Ethnography' (1991), and Sally Ness's study of *Body, Movement and Culture* (1992). These texts raise a number of important methodological issues regarding dance ethnography, which I hope to explore.

Dance ethnography, according to Sklar (1991), is quite unique amongst other forms of ethnographic work because it involves necessarily looking at the body and the body's experiences, as opposed to analysing texts, cultural objects or cultural abstractions. Sklar considers that ethnography is a practice whereby the ethnographer seeks to both describe and understand the constitutive features and cultural knowledge of the people being studied. Following Geertz (1975), she suggests that what ethnographers want to find out is how people make meaning in terms of their lives and activities. Sklar considers that an

examination of dance from an ethnographic viewpoint involves treat-
ing dance as a kind of cultural knowledge, a somatic mode of attention
which incorporates mental and emotional aspects, elements of cultural
history and belief systems and values. Cultural knowledge, she argues,
'is embodied in movement, especially the highly stylised and codified
movement we call dance' (1991, p. 6).

Ethnographic descriptions of dance should be situated within the
historical context in which they are performed, and information
concerning the cultural context, the social values, systems of beliefs,
symbolic codes and so on is crucial to the understanding of the dance
event. In other words, Sklar proposes an approach that is similar to
Geertz's (1975) notion of 'thick description'. It is not sufficient to
explain a movement in terms of its codes, that is, *what* it refers to, it is
also important to understand *how* it gets done. This entails that some
attention has to be paid to the movement itself, because from Sklar's
point of view, 'the *way* people move provides a key to the way they
think and feel and to what they know' (1991, p. 6).

As Sklar notes, there are a number of theoretical approaches to the
analysis of movement. Kaeppler (1972), for example, among others,
uses structural analysis and Labanotation,[2] which was alluded to briefly
in Chapter 1, to analyse the movements of Tongan dance.
Kealiinohomoku (1979) on the other hand, examines both the function of dance in culture and movement aesthetics. Williams (1976)
proposes a structural linguistic model for analysing dance and she also
employs Labanotation, which she calls the 'Laban script'. Sklar aims to
integrate movement description into the analysis of culture.

Sklar (1991) demonstrates her approach to 'movement ethnography'
by examining the ritual fiesta of the Tortugas, which takes place once a
year in a small village in southern New Mexico. During this fiesta it is
fairly common for people to state that they can feel the presence of Our
Lady of Guadalupe, the 'dark Virgin' who miraculously appeared three
hundred and fifty years ago in Mexico City. Sklar's intention is to understand this particular feeling and the range of emotions associated with it.

Sklar utilises a qualitative movement analysis as her key methodology,
to analyse the movement in order to assist her understanding of the
religious experience. The movement description itself is the result of a
long analytical process of looking for consistent movement motifs and
patterns, and of making a selection from different kinds of contextual
data drawn from structured and unstructured interviews. As well as
generating a movement observation checklist, Sklar recorded dance
rehearsals on video and studied them in relation to the checklist. She

also observed movement visually and at the same time tried to 'feel with', as she calls it, people moving kinaesthetically. Where possible she participated in the dance fiesta, in order to gain a kind of aesthetic (and kinaesthetic) understanding. This, she claims, enabled her to find (bodily) clues to the sensations of particular movements themselves and to a variety of constructs, social values and social effects that make up the Tortugas fiesta.

Sklar points out that this tripartite process involving movement description, qualitative analysis and her own kinaesthetic awareness of the dance leads her into other directions and considerations outside of the dance, in order to understand the meanings contained in the dance for the performers. She offers an exemplification of this approach through a discussion of a particular dance, the *danzante*, which was danced by eighteen men. The analysis of the movement and choreographic form generated a feeling of 'contained yet driving power' (1991, p. 7), however there was a particular quality of softness and vulnerability in the men's dancing that was difficult to perceive in the dance motifs and patterns. Noting that the men's attention was directed towards an inner-focus as opposed to a concern for the steps themselves, Sklar asked one of the respondents what the men were focusing on. The respondent indicated that in dancing they were focusing on Our Lady of Guadalupe and that dancing was 'the same as dancing with the Virgin' (ibid.). Sklar maintains that if she had not gone beyond the movement and begun talking with the dancers, it would have been impossible for her to know that their dance was a kind of prayer to the Virgin. This revelation still did not account for the softness and gentleness of the movement that she had perceived in the dancers.

The men always danced before an altar upon which was placed a statue of a man kneeling in front of a portrait of Our Lady of Guadalupe. This image represented the original story of the 'dark Virgin' who appeared to Juan Diego on a hilltop, and requested that a church be built on that hilltop in her honour. By attending to the posture and disposition of the sculpture and the myth of the story of the 'dark Virgin', Sklar noted that there was a correspondence between the statue and the 'self-image' of the dancers:

> The humility, devotion, and eagerness to serve that are communicated concretely in the kneeling figure of Juan Diego are also the feelings that motivate the *Danzante* dancers. This is the emotional and contextual subtext of the dance: surrender to the Virgin with humility and devotion. (1991, p. 8)

Thus, movement analysis by itself could not give rise to an understanding of both the content and the form of the dancers' inner-focus; instead conceptual and kinaesthetic frameworks had to be combined. It was also necessary to talk with the dancers in order to understand their observed inner-focus and to move outside the context of the fiesta to comprehend the shared sense of the key image of Our Lady of Guadalupe and its origins.

This multilayered ethnographic approach, according to Sklar, enhances the possibilities for dance research in at least two ways. To begin with:

> An ethnographic examination expands the significance of what we mean when we say 'dance'. (Ibid.)

Further, the ethnographic perspective entails that the researcher is part of the dance event itself and, as noted earlier in the discussion of feminist ethnography, they will be influenced by their own situated knowledge at hand. That is to say, it is not only dances that are rooted in cultural traditions, but dance researchers and ethnographers are also bearers of their cultural traditions and their personal anthropology and these factors need to be integrated into the analysis (Williams, 1976; Farnell, 1999). Sklar, in line with postmodernist and feminist approaches to ethnography discussed earlier, considers that by 'including the researcher as part of the dance event, the ethnographic perspective facilitates self-reflexivity' (ibid.). Through the process of implicating the researcher in the research, the researcher is forced to reflect upon his or her (embodied) self and the researcher/researched relations.

Whilst an ethnographic approach, as Sklar's suggests, may be useful to the analysis of dance, it is also the case that dance can be useful to ethnography. Indeed, as Ness (1992) demonstrates, in some ways being a student of choreography, or a performer, is similar to being an ethnographer, inasmuch as they each require a considerable amount of self-discipline in order to develop their respective areas of work:

> The mastery of a choreographic movement is something very like an ethnographic act, if it is not precisely that, just as the mastery of a cultural role is fundamentally an act of performance. (Ness, 1992, p. 11)

Ness's stunning, choreographically informed ethnographic study centres on an analysis of three different forms of *sinulog* dancing in Cebu City in the Philippines in the 1980s. The sinulogs are 'inspired' and performed in praise of the Santo Niño de Cebu, an image of Jesus as Boy King, the protector of the city deemed to have miraculous powers. The three forms of sinulog are as follows: the *tindera sinulog*, which is a healing ritual; the *troupe sinulog*, which is a formalised, traditional and theatrical dance–drama ritual; and the recently established *parade sinulog*, which is a competitive, large-scale exhibition dance extravaganza. The analysis of these choreographic forms provides a means of interpreting 'the predicament of culture' (Clifford, 1988) in neo-colonial Cebu City, which Ness (1992) describes as a 'border zone', a city caught up in a kind of in-between space between modernity and tradition, and the global and the local.

In a study of early American modern dance, I attempted to show how modern dancers transformed everyday movement into dance movement (Thomas, 1995). Ness's (1992) study begins from an examination of the choreographed movement of the dance sinulogs and deftly shows how these performed embodied practices can speak to, and of, the emergent multivocal symbolism in the routine embodied practices of the everyday life in this urban context. She uses a comparative approach to examine these three movement forms of sinulog to highlight both the emergent symbolism that they share in common and their specificities that speak to other aspects of the experiences of everyday public life in Cebu City.

Ness's analysis shows that the three types of dance sinulog are significantly different in 'design, performance and interpretation' (1992, p. 219). The performances themselves range from individualised choreographed movement to dance dramas with narrative structures and to 'abstract geometric designs' (ibid.). The analysis also demonstrates that different forms of symbolism are at work in the three types of performances and that the dances perform different symbolic functions.

Comparative analysis of the dances (based on Laban Movement Analysis (LMA)[3]), along with participants' and observers' comments on the sinulog variants, revealed a complex set of issues regarding claims to the authenticity of Cebuanic cultural forms and the invention of tradition.[4] The tindera sinulog, for example, despite the low status of the female traders who now performed it, was often referred to as the most original pre-Hispanic influenced local form. It had become the inspiration for the city's promotion of the parade sinulog in the 1980s as 'a symbol of Cebuana regional pride' (Ness, 1992, p. 89). The highly theatricalised troupe sinulog ritual, which developed over many decades, represented the last stages of Spanish colonisation. In contrast to the tindera sinulog, the dancing was masculinised and Hispanicised.[5] Although it was viewed as a showcase of 'national symbolism', the troupe sinulog had become ossified as a form by the 1980s and no longer spoke to the rapidly changing urban contexts of Cebu City. The newest most popular cultural form, the parade sinulog, was disapproved of by the 'elite', while the troupe sinulog (which had emanated from the Spanish elite in the first instance) increasingly came to be seen as the 'authentic' sinulog by these same people. Ness notes that this comparison between the ritual tindera sinulog and the modern parade sinulog often led to an increase in the prestige of the ritual tindera sinulog, which would not have been possible without the development of the parade sinulog.

Despite the perceived differences between the three forms, participants and local observers treated the performances as generally 'the same dance', that is, as variants of a single phenomenon, ' "the" *sinulog*' (Ness, 1992, p. 2). Through an examination of the movement forms and the contexts in which they were performed, Ness found that certain choreographic and contextual features were present to a greater or lesser degree in all three variants. The two most significant choreographic confluences involved, first, the gestural manipulation of symbolic objects, which had the effect of directing the observer's attention to the object being held, and second, a resilient 'bouncy' movement phrase involving 'whole body weight shifts' (1992, p. 202).[6]

From Ness's detailed analysis, this 'bouncy' resilient movement emerges as a significant movement symbol, a crucial 'marker of Cebuana ethnic identity' (1992, p. 54). Although the sinulog could be seen all over the Philippines, it was nevertheless perceived by the city authorities and Ness's informants as something unique and local. When Ness asked her informant (who also performed the sinulog) what it was about the sinulog that made it particularly Cebuanese, she immediately pointed to this bouncy movement and then performed it. The informant also inferred that this resilient movement quality is a characteristic of all Cebuana folk dances. This observed resilient baseline movement, according to Ness, even appears in 'contemporary western-influenced' social dance forms such as disco. Thus, it seems to be a constitutive feature in traditional and non-traditional Cebuana dance practices.

Ness, like Sklar (1991), argues that her skills as a performing student of choreography facilitate a reflexive attention to 'exotic' and everyday movement practices. Her learning process and the act of participating and performing the sinulog afforded her a heightened awareness of the nuances of everyday movement, enabling her to see the links between the two. Examining exotic movement leads to more fully exploring the everyday and as a result the exotic (that is, dance) is rendered ordinary. Attending to the everyday in a different, reflexive sense, for Ness, leads one to be more aware of the rhythms and gestures involved in routine everyday activities, which are generally accomplished with a high degree of inattention. As a result of her 'natural attentiveness' to movement (through years of dance training), Ness is able to identify this resilient 'bouncy' movement in everyday habitual practices such as walking. Hence, it becomes clear that this movement is also integral to everyday Cebuanese 'techniques of the body' (Mauss, 1973), and as such is part of the 'natural attitude' (Schutz, 1967) or bodily 'habitus' (Bourdieu, 1977) of the inhabitants of Cebu City. That is to say, the movement appears so much a part of everyday bodily behaviour that its practitioners are not generally aware of performing it. Ness's analysis further shows that the extent to which this resilient movement has become inscribed in Cebuana culture can be indicated by the fact of its 'incorporation into the vernacular language itself' (1992, p. 55).

The sinulog choreography, for Ness, provides a point of access for understanding the articulation of local 'otherness' in the contemporary urban contexts of neo-colonial Cebu City. Although Ness is at pains to stress that she does not wish to present a homogenised picture of the bodily practices of the inhabitants of Cebu City, the reduction of the dance and everyday movements to particular baseline elements could give rise to such an interpretation. At the same time, she recognises that there 'can be no absolutely objective and completely unproblematic description of another culture's dances' (1992, p. 228), or of one's own for that matter, we might add. The difficulty of translating dance practices into verbal language is a perennial one for dance scholarship and cultural criticism. The question of translation raises its head at intervals and in different contexts in the dance case studies chapters in Part II of this book.

Although understanding dance as a practitioner and/or as an observer may be important to dance ethnography, as Brenda Farnell (1999) points out, it is not enough. It is not possible to effect a direct transfer of knowledge from one culture's dance forms to that of another with the expectation of gaining an understanding of the other culture's dances because, Farnell argues, the conceptual framework and the meanings associated with the dance will be inscribed in the form itself and in the participants' conceptual and physical understandings of it. The ethnographer is required to see movement from the point of view of the 'other' person who is performing it. To this end, the researcher has to ask the performer 'what they thought they were doing' (Farnell, 1999, p. 146). One of the major advantages of using a Laban script to record the movement 'action signs', according to Farnell, is that it begins from the performer's point of view, and as such is not objectivist.

Of course, this implies that the participants/respondents know and/or can say what they are doing. As will be indicated in Chapter 7, several researchers have reported that informants also have great difficulty in translating their experiences of dancing into verbal language (see Malbon, 1999). Farnell's (1994) suggestion further implies that the performer's reply will be taken at face value by the researcher as accurate and authentic. Although Ness also indicates that she asked her informants about what they were doing in their dancing, she did not necessarily take their responses without question or further probing. For example, Ness notes that the tinderas repeatedly said that their dancing was 'just a dance', implying that it was simply part of their tradition and that it did not have any special components; rather, they made it up as they went along. Ness's choreographic analysis, however, revealed that there were elements specific to the tindera sinulog. The resilient baseline movement described above, which was found to be a tacit feature of variable emphasis in all three forms, was not consciously taught, as far as Ness could ascertain from her discussions with performers and teachers. It was so fundamental (inscribed in the habitus) that it remained, for the most part, out of their awareness. This was in contrast to the other key, stylistic element that appeared in all forms, the 'manipulation of hand-held symbols, which was a recognised focus of skill in every case' (1992, p. 223). If Ness had accepted the tinderas' view that their dancing was just dancing without question, the analysis would have been the poorer for it. Instead her comparative analysis of the dances and their relation to everyday movement opens up a complex set of images of Cebu City, drawn out of virtually invisible bodily practices.

I do not wish to imply that employing a movement or choreographic ethnography will reveal the 'true' aspects of 'other' cultures, or indeed of one's own culture. As indicated earlier in this chapter and in Chapter 2, the positivist notion of truth has been thoroughly rejected by most researchers, as has methodological holism. Movement ethnography provides a relatively uncharted and, to a certain extent, 'invisible' (as you see it, so it has gone) 'forest of symbols' (Turner, 1974) to explore the multivocal. Dance as a topic, resource and practice gives a new perspective on cultural symbols and possible interpretations of them. The next chapter continues on this pathway by offering a close examination of two specific dance practices in the western theatrical dance tradition: ballet and contact improvisation. The privileging of the sense of sight in ballet and touch in contact improvisation will highlight the dualisms in western culture, which were discussed in Chapters 1 and 2.

Part II

Dance, the Body and Cultural Theory

Chapter 4

The Body in Dance

Introduction

This chapter is concerned with western dance forms and theatre dancing in particular, in contrast to the dance cultures of 'others'. In order to set the scene for what is to follow, it begins by offering an alternative anecdote to the first 'body story' presented in Chapter 1.

In the early 1980s I taught courses on the sociology of the body and dance to undergraduate and postgraduate dance students in a contemporary dance institution. As indicated in Chapter 1, neither of these topics could be described as operating within the mainstream of sociological or dance discourse during that time. It will be recalled that the talk on the body in particular seemed to provoke some students in sociology to act in atypical ways in the lecture setting in the late 1980s and early 1990s. The responses of the dance students, almost a decade earlier, were quite different. From the start, they were generally fascinated by the body talk, although they found some of the 'sociological' concepts overly theoretical and constantly tried to ground them in 'bodily' practice. As dance students, of course, they were routinely engaged with their bodies in a highly reflexive way, through their daily classes and through performing. Perhaps it was their bodily attentiveness that facilitated their interest and ease in discussing everyday bodily practices as well as dance. As students of dance they would have been exposed to developments in *postmodern dance* in the USA and the rising *new dance* or the independent dance movement in Britain, which challenged the traditionally received notions of dance as a theatre art.

In 1983, I participated in shooting and editing a video that documented the making of a dance work from rehearsals through to performance, which was choreographed by an MA dance student. Mundane everyday movement, like that under consideration in the course I taught, had gained currency in certain quarters of a burgeoning contemporary dance sector. Pedestrian movement was also central to this dance and the dancers rehearsed in coloured sweatshirts and tracksuit bottoms.[1] Twenty years earlier in the same institution, only 'regulation' black leotard and tights with black cardigan could be worn on the dance floor and the task would have been to transform everyday movement into dance movement, not celebrate the former in and of itself.

What was also striking in the lecture/seminar setting with dance students was the fact that these students were very much at ease with both their own bodies and those of their fellow classmates, with whom they often sat in close physical contact. Touching and overlapping bodies were not an uncommon sight. This would have been unusual in a more standard academic context, even among individuals who knew each other quite well. Another striking feature was the fact that although the students would start off sitting on chairs, there was a tendency over the course of the session for rather more than a few to gravitate to the floor. From there they might stretch out their legs in second position and extend and lower the torso forward to the floor in between the legs, stretch out the spine, rotate the shoulders, or generally move about to avoid stiffening up. It was also quite usual for students to peel off or add on various layers of jumpers or scarves during the session.

In contrast to the bodily 'interference' of the sociology students discussed in Chapter 1, the dance students treated their actions as 'business as usual'. That is to say, this was ordinary routine behaviour for these students in a lecture/seminar context. The gravitational pull to the floor, the sporadic 'not-everyday' movements, and the putting on and taking off of items of clothing could be disconcerting for the academic unused to giving lectures/seminars to dance students. The lecture/seminar format, as we have seen, operates on the principle of the mind/body dichotomy, the idea of which is to engage the brain and keep the body under wraps. The uninitiated academic could easily interpret these aforementioned bodily actions as interfering with or countering that aim.

Although I had been a dance student many years before, my first encounter with mobile dance students in a lecture setting was unsettling. I recall thinking that they could not be 'really' listening to what was being said if they were constantly stretching and flexing their bodies and taking off and putting on layers of clothing in a decidedly visible manner. It soon became clear that they were indeed listening with and through their bodies. Their taken-for-granted mode of lecture/seminar behaviour was soon accepted by this teacher too as 'business as usual', unlike the bodily disruptions and eruptions of the sociology students discussed before. It was almost as if the movement memory of the teacher, a habitual form that was lost but not entirely forgotten over the years of becoming an academic, was brought back into play.

Paying attention to dance forms and practices, as the deliberations in the previous chapter on dance ethnography indicated, offers the opportunity of overcoming the mind/body dualisms which have haunted a great deal of the work on the body. Because dance does not exist in a cultural vacuum, but rather is a situated embodied aesthetic practice, it can also highlight and reflect the presence of these very dualisms in the cultural domain. In addition, dance provides a rich set of resources for exploring the 'histories of bodies', by examining technical shifts and transformations of dance styles in relation to the dancing bodies that perform them over a period of time. Furthermore, it provides a site for examining the limitations and extraordinary possibilities of 'the physical body'.

Dance scholarship has taken up enthusiastically the theoretical insights of recent work on the body, particularly poststructuralist and feminist approaches, and has sought to integrate these with the tools of dance analysis, to examine a wide range of dance practices (Foster, 1998). Despite the current preoccupation with the body, social and cultural analysts, as several dance writers have pointed out (Novack, 1990; Thomas, 1995; Foster, 1997; Desmond, 1998), seldom pay attention to dance as a situated aesthetic bodily practice. Exceptionally, a few social and cultural commentators mobilise features of dancing or of dance analysis to instantiate aspects of their theoretical approach to the body (Frank, 1991; Csordas, 1993; Williams and Bendelow, 1998). Close analysis of visceral, kinaesthetic experiences of dancing, from performers' and viewers' perspectives, however, has seldom been undertaken outside the confines of dance scholarship.

The discussion that follows sets in train the work of redressing this situation. It begins by examining the hierarchy of senses involved in two different contemporary dance forms, *classical ballet* and *contact improvisation*. This draws heavily on the content and form of an illuminating analysis by dance anthropologist Cynthia Bull (1997), formerly known as Cynthia Novack,[2] interspersed with other relevant sources. In turn, this will lead to an exploration of how dance as a situated aesthetic embodied practice can be used as an exemplar, to highlight the notion that 'bodies have histories'. Here, I will use *modern dance* as a case study.

'The sensible and the intelligible'

[A] close study of the physical, sensuous experience of dancing provides us with knowledge as unmistakable as that provided by the more conventional study and analysis of cultural beliefs and concepts and of other aspects of emotional life. (Bull, 1997, p. 268)

Dancing, for Bull, unlike Cunningham for example, is not 'just dancing'. For the former, interpretations of the 'act of dancing' from the performers' or observers' points of view are not simply the product of personal preferences, but are constituted in and through our lived experiences in a variety of contexts and events, 'social and theatrical' (Bull, 1997, p. 267). The task of the dance analyst is to find 'ways to reveal and understand the webs of meaning created through the dance event' (ibid.). Dance writers, Bull notes, can make rather hurried cultural generalisations from the particular, without paying much attention to what is taking place in the event under consideration. Alternatively, there are those who produce a descriptive account of the immediate lived experience of the event without fleshing out the analysis. The first approach directs attention towards an 'extrinsic' analysis (Thomas, 1995). That is to say, dance provides an occasion for commenting on a range of other external factors: social, cultural or artistic. This approach, like the social constructionist approaches to the body discussed in the previous chapters, takes little account of the immediacy of the sensual qualities of the embodied practices under consideration, in this case dance. The second model focuses on the 'intrinsic' (ibid.) elements of the phenomenon and is often associated with phenomenological accounts of dance events, which 'can capture the sensual qualities of experience' (Bull, 1997, p. 270).[3] There is a tendency, here, to 'ignore how shared meanings shape the most "natural" of human actions and perceptions in dance and life' (ibid.).

The first method highlights the outer, appearing, social body, while the second involves the inner, experiential body. This either/or tendency in dance writing, which Bull highlights, resonates with the opposition between the concepts of *Körper* (the objective, instrumental, institutionalised body) and *Leib* (the subjective, lived, experiential body) discussed in Chapters 1 and 2 in the context of anti-foundationalist and foundationalist approaches to the study of the body. It will be recalled that Turner (1992, p. 41), following the ideas of philosophers such as Schilder (1950) and Merleau-Ponty (1962), argued that human embodiment is at once 'personal and impersonal, objective and subjective, social and natural'. Studies on the body need to take account of this simultaneity, as opposed to privileging one aspect at the expense of the other. Bull cautions dance writers in a similar manner. She stresses the interrelatedness of the 'sensible' and the 'intelligible':[4]

> The challenge in writing about dance from an anthropological perspective lies in simultaneously evoking the particular experiences and shimmering life which it refracts and reflects; the meanings and implications of dance,

indeed of all art, are embedded in the experiences of the art itself – learning, teaching, creating, performing and watching. (1997, p. 270)

Bull explores the relations between what we feel (the domain of the sensible) and what we know (the intelligible) by focusing on what Foster (1997) has called the 'meat and bones' of dance practices and the conceptual schema that informs them. The intent is to avoid the trap of the either/or positions indicated above.

Bull compares the role of the senses of sight, touch and hearing in classical ballet and contact improvisation through an examination of choreographic form, technique and audience perception. She argues that the former privileges sight over touch and hearing, while the latter emphasises touch. Bull treats the forms to some extent as ideal typical constructions. Being only too aware of the problems of overgeneralising dance forms which are ethnographically 'more complex and diverse', she cautions against viewing them in essentialist terms. The activity of dancing, as Bull (1997) notes, involves all of the senses to varying degrees. For the dancer, the kinaesthetic sense is perhaps the most important and immediate.[5] The dancer 'experiences the act of dancing within her own body and feels the physical sensations of dancing as basic and fundamental' (ibid., p. 286). This may also be the case for audiences depending how near or far away they are from being able to sense the physical, breathing, lived presence of the performer.

The celebration of the visual in ballet

Ballet is the most dominant and recognisable theatre dance form in the west. Its roots can be traced back to the European courts of the sixteenth and seventeenth centuries, where it was developed as a courtly spectacle to glorify and sanctify absolute monarchical power.

Ballet as we know it today can be dated from 1672, when Louis XIV of France created a dance academy designed to train artists for the newly emerging form of ballet-operas (Clarke and Crisp, 1973, pp. 28–30). Louis had been a very enthusiastic dancer from a young age. He took the central role in the lavish court ballets and became the living embodiment of his favourite dancing role of the Rising Sun in the ballet *Le Ballet de la Nuit*, which in part led to his title of 'Le Roi Soleil' (ibid.). Under monarchical rule, as Foucault has argued, the king's actual body was the political body: 'Its physical presence was necessary for the functioning of the monarchy' (1980, p. 55).

From the point at which Louis stopped appearing in ballets in 1670, theatrical professionalism increased. In establishing a dance academy,

Louis was effectively giving up his role as the 'absolute' performer of
noble dances to newly emerging professionals, who had hitherto played
character roles. It was around this period that the technique began to
be codified. The vocabulary and movement in ballet is written and
spoken in French to the present day. The first ballerinas took to the
stage in 1681. Gradually, female dancers became increasingly important, reaching their ascendancy over male dancers in the romantic era
in the nineteenth century. The teaching, training, theory, choreography
and direction remained under the control of men.

The dance academy that Louis created was superseded in 1713 by
the establishment of a professional school at the Paris Opéra, which
soon began to produce good dancers who were acclaimed throughout
Europe. In a short space of time, opera houses, theatres, ballet companies and schools were established under royal patronage in Italy,
Austria, Russia, England and Scandinavia.

The vocabulary of contemporary ballet, as Bull argues, is clearly
recognisable by the time of the romantic era in the first half of the
nineteenth century:

> In the romantic ballet, the former specific meanings of the movement had
> been clearly transformed into a more generalised signification of beauty
> and elegance, while the visual design of individual bodies in the stage
> assumed primary importance. Today, ballet ... represents ideals of exquis-
> itely controlled technical precision and emotional expressions combined
> within a classical (traditional) framework. (1997, p. 272)

The basis of classical ballet training is the five positions of the feet.
'All traditional schooled action', as the ballet theorist and aficionado
Lincoln Kirstein has noted, 'starts and stops with these positions which
have the subliminal logic in the carrying of the torso by legs and
feet and, initiating movement for every key hinge of the body' (1971,
p. 5). The legs and feet are turned out from the hip. The desired 180
degree 'turn-out', achieved only through a long period of training, provides support for an 'erect upper body', a wide base for turning and
jumping. It also offers the spectator a maximum view of the dancer's
body. ' "Turning out" ', according to Adrian Stokes (1934, p. 78), 'is
the essence of ballet.' The codified positions of the feet and the arms,
body shapes and steps can be combined to make choreographic forms.
Ballet for Stokes is nothing less than the 'embodiment of European
theatre' (ibid.). The 'geometry of classical ballet', its 'outwardness' and
the 'harmonious gradualness of its forms' symbolise the 'European
spirit' (p. 88).

Like Stokes, Kirstein (1983) maintains that ballet's technical requirements, which were developed over three centuries, are 'not arbitrary':

> These determine the greatest frontal legibility and launch of the upper body as silhouette framed in the proscenium. Ballet-repertory was calculated for opera-houses with orchestra pits, and balconies rendering the stage-floor a virtual backdrop for half the public. It is not the only form of theatrical dance; it is the most spectacular. (Kirstein, 1983, p. 240)

The mastery of the codified positions, shapes and 'steps' constitute the core of the ballet student's training in pursuit of the idealised body, based on the aesthetic ideals of classical beauty (Foster, 1997). Although the value of one method of professional training over another is the subject of much heated debate in the ballet world at particular periods in time, for example, the Cecchetti system over the Vaganova style, the core values of the tradition remain intact and are made manifest in the ballet class (Sayers, 1997). As Kirstein (1971, p. 5) has noted, 'at no stage in the instruction is there room for improvisation, experiment or doubt'. The first aim is 'correctness': the ballet dancer has to comply with the rigorous demands of the system to control and mould the body to its ideal image.

Professional dancers and the many thousands of ballet class students who did not make the grade will have spent about half of their class time at the barre. The following two passages describe the first section of the ballet class. They were written by different authors and published more than thirty years apart. They strike a similar note in their respective descriptions of the dancer's bodily image and comportment at the barre. The first passage by Lincoln Kirstein offers a more detailed description of the stance and the positions:

> The pupil grasps the bar. Before moving one must stand well. Pelvis is centred, neither tipped back or forward. Abdomen is drawn in, diaphragm raised. Shoulders drop naturally; head is straight, eyes front. Arms are carried downward, rounded from shoulders to fingertips. The desired 'turn-out', with heels together, the feet are spread to form an angle of 180 degrees, supporting the erect upper body, is only slowly gained. ...
>
> Each exercise is planned to prepare one part of the body for ultimate virtuoso requirements ... [The] exercises are repeated often, usually in four directions in units of eight – front, side, back and side. Starting with the five positions in succession, practice at the bar commences with half-bends (demi-pliés), slow continuous lowering and straightening of the knees, followed by deeper full bends (grands pliés), in which the heels leave the ground. Arms coordinate large sweeps with the deeply sinking and fully rising body. Port de bras, or carriage of the arms frames the body, as next

it dips forward and back. A large family of elementary 'beats' (battements tendus, simples, battements jetés, petits battements, frappés, soutenus) forms the subcultures for smaller movements of the feet. (Kirstein, 1971, p. 5)

The second account by performer/writer Susan Foster offers a more minimalist but, nonetheless, vivid impression of the typical ballet class:

Dancers begin a standard daily sequence with one arm stabilizing the body by holding the barre. They perform movements (announced in French) by the teacher, originating in and returning to, basic positions – first on one side and then, switching arms at the bar, on the other. The movements work the legs (always in a turned-out position) and, to a lesser extent, the arms to create variations and embellishments on circular or triangular designs. The torso provides a taut and usually erect center connecting the four appendages and the head ... Descriptions of movements and corrections are phrased so as to ask parts of the body to conform to abstract shapes; they place the pelvis or head in specific locations, and extend the limbs along imaginary lines of space. Additional criteria based on the precision of timing, clarity of shape, and lightness of quality all measure the student's performance. (Foster, 1997, p. 243)

Both commentators, the first more pro-ballet than the second, point to the emphasis on placement, line and the harmonious spatial designs created by the dancer's body in ballet in pursuit of the ideals of the form: geometry, extension and measured harmony (Stokes, 1934). The ballet class for Kirstein (1971) is a spectacle in itself, which prepares the dancer for the spectacle of the stage. Bull notes that although ballet students are trained to 'feel the flow of the movement', their training stresses 'sight as the primary process of artistic conception, perception and kinesthetic awareness' (1997, p. 272).

The power of the visual in ballet should not be underestimated. Ballet dancers are scrutinised and corrected by teachers or choreographers as they are put through their daily paces and they also scrutinise themselves by watching their performed movements in the ever-present mirror, rather like a knowing spectator. The preeminence of the visual in western culture, as demonstrated in the previous chapter, has been the subject of much criticism in social and cultural studies in recent years (see Jay, 1999). The principles of observation and causation were central to positivistic conceptions of sociology as a science, which were founded on the 'picture theory of truth'. Sight, after all, is implicated in the act of observing, as is the search for 'fact'. The dictionary definition of the verb to 'observe' includes: 'to keep in view: to watch: to subject to systematic watching: to regard attentively: to direct watchful and critical attention with a view to ascertaining a fact'.[6] As shown in the previous chapter, the method of participant-observation, from the participant-as-observer mode through to 'going native', has been central to the ethnographic study of 'other' cultures in anthropology. Postmodernist and postcolonial anthropologists, whose aim, in part, is to deconstruct the politics of the visual, have called the method into question in recent years. Feminists, too, as indicated in Chapter 2, have argued against the subjection of women to the power of the 'male gaze' or 'look'.[7] Sandra Bartky's construct of the 'panoptical male connoisseur' (cited in Wolff, 1995, p. 127) imbued in women's consciousnesses implies that women carry around with them an image of 'the male in the head' (Holland *et al.*, 1998). Bull's idea of the dancer holding an image of the ideal dancer/performance in their head is rather similar to this:

> As a dancer moves, she or he carries a mental picture of the perfect performance of each step, comparing the mirrored image with that ideal. (1997, p. 272)

The importance of sight in ballet extends to audience perceptions and the choreography. The audience is captured in the darkness of the auditorium, often at a long distance from the lighted proscenium stage upon which the action takes place and to which the spectators' attention is drawn. The sounds of the dancers' pointe shoes, their breathing, their physicality, may be obscured in the huge gulf between the performers on the stage and the spectators in the balconies. Moreover, the dancers are trained to minimise these effects. 'What always remains', for Bull, 'is the moving pictures, the extended lines which make the images visible from a distance' (1997, p. 274).

Ballet is almost always performed to music, and often to live music, and the choreography, as Bull notes, generally attempts to 'visualise' the sounds or the mood of the musical structure. 'Synchronised movement', Stokes (1934, p. 19) maintains, can 'give power to the music' and make the music 'an embodied thing'.[8] The musical sounds rise out of the orchestra pit situated in front of and below the baseline of the stage where the musicians are out of comfortable view of the audience. As a consequence, for Bull, the relation between music and the dance in ballet performance is not one of reciprocity; rather, the music is 'cultivated in relation to visual perception' (1997, p. 274). The sound of music or the sight of the musicians playing does not impede the primacy of the spectacle unfolding on the stage. This does not mean that that the music does not add to, counter or alter the ballet and the spectator's experience of the dance performance. As Stephanie Jordan demonstrates in her illuminating study of the 'musical-choreographic styles' of three ballet choreographers, George Balanchine, Antony Tudor and Frederick Ashton, 'when we go to the theatre ... music can be just as important to our experience as dance' (2000, p. ix).

Ballet choreography also places great importance on spatial design. The lines and bodies of dancers as they create shapes in space and the floor are an example of this. The dancers in the corps de ballet should give no sign of their individuality; rather, they should strive to move as one body in 'perfect unison' (Bull, 1997, p. 274). The whole, that is, the corps, is more than the sum of the individual parts. It should function like a 'collective organism' (Kirstein, 1971, p. v). One member moving out of step with the others, lifting an arm too high or too low, spoils the line of the corps and the visual movement patterns it creates. The uniformity of the corps stands in sharp contrast to the virtuosity, flair and individuality of expression expected of the soloist. The soloist, as Bull notes, plays 'at the edges of the strict boundaries to which the corps must adhere' (1997, p. 274).

Bull argues that whilst other senses such as touch and kinaesthesia play a role in ballet, they too are subjugated to the 'organising principle' of sight and the 'visual appearance of design in space' (ibid.). Touch, for example, is important in ballet, for both audience and the dancers, and is particularly visible in the duets with the male and female soloists (pas de deux). Touching involves technical competences and carries symbolic meanings. The spectators come to understand the meanings of the physical interactions between the dancers as either 'social encounters' or just 'dancing'. The former usually involves 'arm gestures and conventional embraces', while the latter entails the male dancer's 'physical manipulation of the ballerina (his hands on her back, waist, armpits, hips, pelvis and thighs)' (ibid.). This is an interesting divide. The social touching, for want of a better term, corresponds roughly to what would be deemed acceptable behaviour in public places between potential intimates (see Hall, 1969; Goffman, 1972, 1979) in the USA and Britain. The 'dance touching', on the other hand, involves a meeting of hands and parts of the body that are deemed risky in public places, even between those who are intimate, precisely because they are deemed to have sexual connotations. Although some twentieth-century ballets introduced more sexually explicit gestures into the conventions of social touching in ballet, Bull argues that audiences are able to decipher whether the touch is expressive, technical or a mixture of both by the 'dancers' execution of touch and the choreographic context' (Bull, 1997, p. 274). That is, the placement of touch is highly codified.

The kinaesthetic energy that ballet requires of the dancer, as indicated above in the section on the ballet class, is predicated upon the visual. It also highlights, as Bull and others (Daly, 1987; Foster, 1996a, 1997) have argued, issues around gendering and heterosexuality in dance. Both men and women ballet dancers require considerable strength and bodily control, which the training is meant to achieve. In general, although by no means always, men's movement in ballet should have the appearance of exerting energy and force, while women's movement should appear to be effortless and weightless. The fact that she will be dancing in pointe shoes contributes to this illusion of lightness, while the ideal female ballet body, slight and slender, gives support to the illusion of fragility. The gendered heterosexual partnering in ballet has been criticised by dance scholars and feminists alike (see Carter, 1999). Bull, however, here and elsewhere (Novack, 1993), avoids the trap of reductionism that has befallen others (see Thomas, 1996). The problems associated with gender representations in dance will be addressed in more detail in Chapter 6.

The primacy of sight in ballet, then, as Bull demonstrates, saturates the form on a number of interrelated levels: dance training, the performer, the performance, stage, music and the spectator. This is not to say that *all* ballet operates in this way or that the other senses do not predominate in certain instances. According to Laban movement analysts, although dance images are constantly changing within particular dances and across dance forms and styles, there are certain discernible characteristics or 'core values' that appear time and time again within the 'baseline of the movement style' of any dance form (Lepczyk, 1990).[9] Ness (1992), for example, as discussed in the previous chapter, identified a 'bouncy movement phrase' involving 'whole body weight shifts' as a significant movement symbol in the three variant forms of sinulog dancing in Cebu City. In academic ballet, by contrast, as movement analyst Billie Lepczyk (1990) demonstrates, the upward, vertical axis of the body is highlighted and given expressive value. The characteristic of verticality in ballet is given expression in the female dancer by the emphasis on 'pointe work and the concentration on airwork' (Lepczyk, 1990, p. 83). The focus on bodily extension and the turn-out of the legs complements the visual appearance of the upward striving of the form away from the floor. The key movement dynamics are 'lightness and directness', which, combined with verticality, contribute to a sense of stability and bodily centredness. There is an emphasis on peripheral body movement: 'the movement of the upper torso, arms and head accompanies the leg movement' while 'the pelvis appears quiet' (ibid.). In ballet, as Stokes (1934, p. 23) has commented, 'every-thing is, artificially ... put outwards: and in the interests of this effect, all movement is raised on to a level of airiness, grace and ease'.

Contact improvisation, as Bull's (1997) analysis shows, takes its point of departure from a different sense, that of touch. The floor in contact improvisation, unlike ballet, is not an enemy; it is 'an ally' (Banes, 1980, p. 67).

The sense of touch in contact improvisation

Contact improvisation is a form involving an exploration of the body's weight in relation to other bodies in the flow of movement in which 'Touch, weight and momentum' predominate over the visual aesthetics (Bull, 1997, p. 277). It is generally performed as a duet but, unlike the pas de deux in ballet, which is predominately a woman and a man, the partners in contact improvisation can be either. There is a shared sense of the reciprocity of movement and bodies in contact improvisation, which is exemplified in the mutual taking and giving of weight between partners and the falling and rolling of contacting entwined bodies. The dancer's focus is inner-directed, in contrast to ballet where, as we have seen, the dancer's intention and attention are projected outwards. While ballet is mostly always performed to music, contact improvisa-tion is usually performed in silence. The performer/audience separation in more traditional theatrical dance forms is countered in contact improvisation, as is the rigid distinction between teacher and student.

Contact improvisation developed in the USA in the early 1970s as a result of a group of dancers experimenting with 'catching each other and falling together':

> The form developed into a practice of moving while constantly touching, leaning on, lifting, balancing on, or supporting another person. The result-ing duet intertwines two bodies in a fluid metamorphosis of falls and suspensions, propelled by the dancers' weight. (Bull, 1997, p. 277)

Contact improvisation has been described as both 'an artistic and social movement' (Foster, 1997, p. 150). Unlike other contemporary dance techniques, it does not derive its name from an individual dancer, as in the Cunningham or Graham technique. Nor does it belong to a particular company. Steve Paxton was the initiator and guiding light of the contact improvisation movement (see Novack, 1990, pp. 63–103). The early development of the technique came about through a collaborative process involving Paxton, Nancy Stark Smith, Lisa Nelson, Curt Siddall and others.[10] It gathered momentum and developed through the dispersal of teachers, students and groups across the country and travelled to Canada and Europe. In a manner similar to social dance events, practitioners of contact improvisation (teachers, students, lay and professional) would come together for informal 'jam' sessions, where they would dance and socialise with others. Contact improvisation, like other body-centred techniques that gained currency in the 1970s, for example, the Alexander technique, became a 'way of life' for many practitioners. The body was perceived to have its 'own intelligence' (Foster, 1997) or 'truth' (Novack, 1990), which had been damaged by culture and civilisation and which could be born again, as it were, by listening internally to the body through the exploration of weight and touch.

By means of a newsletter, and through the establishment of a dedicated magazine in 1976, *Contact Quarterly*, key figures in the movement like Paxton and Smith were able to voice informally the aims, objectives and the teaching framework of the form (Novack, 1990, p. 81), without fixing it to a specific company brand. It became, at least in its early stages, ' an alternative structure for organizing dance in America' (ibid., p. 82).

Contact improvisation, also known as 'art sport', draws on other movement practices: social dance, sport and martial arts such as aikido. Paxton, for example, experimented with the techniques of falling, rolling and partnering that he had learnt while studying aikido. From its earliest beginnings, contact improvisation dances were not intended to be formal staged performances. Rather, the dancers provided 'informal demonstrations' or showings of their experiments, and people were invited to come to see and experience what they did, as the title of the first tour of the West Coast in 1973 suggests – 'You Come. We'll show you what we do'. The informal character of the dance events, the fluidity between performers and non-performers and teachers and students, is evident in the following description of the early performances:

> The performances were like a demonstration. It was very rough and you could drop in and out and it was okay … Duets would last ten or fifteen minutes, sometimes even twenty. The solo work in between was more episodic, usually very weight-oriented, jumping and falling, and falling and rolling … When everyone had a chance to dance with as many people as possible, it would be over. As a person in the audience and as a learning performer, you really got to see how the different levels would occur, starting from the more tentative contact, perhaps to a real physical contact, bumping up against each other, to some very soft communicative duet … there was a sense of danger in it, always. (Lisa Nelson, cited in Novack, 1990, p. 71)

By the 1980s, the stylistic characteristics of contact improvisation indicated above 'had become more facile, fluid, controlled and outwardly focused', according to Novack (1990, p. 12). The informal style of performance also gave way, to a large extent, to a more clearly defined 'presentational style'. Contact improvisation companies did not stay together very long. Novack suggests that this was because of the fluid character of the form itself and the non-hierarchical ideals that it embodied, which were difficult to sustain in practice.[11] Although dancers carried on teaching and practising contact improvisation in the late 1980s, and occasionally performing, scores of others incorporated the technique into other dance styles, without necessarily taking on the cultural values that it espoused. In this way, the technique of contact improvisation had a profound effect on the development of the independent dance movement in North America and Europe.

Touch, as Bull (1997) notes, is not only central to the technique of contact improvisation, it is also symbolic, just as sight is to ballet:

> Awareness of touching a partner and following 'the point of contact' provides the impetus for movement, which adheres to no preset pattern and relies on a general vocabulary of falling and rolling varying from one individual to another ... Touch joins the two dancers, tuning them to each other's weight and momentum as they move. (p. 276)

Students, according to Bull, are often initiated into the form by inviting them to bracket out their sense of vision. As they lie on the floor with eyes closed, they are requested to focus on their bodily sensations. They may be asked to 'make simple movements over a long period of time' and to feel and 'give into' the sensations of the 'changing patterns of their own bodies on the floor' (ibid.) Contact improvisation, in effect, stresses the 'how' of movement rather than the 'what' of movement. That is, the technique does not have a set vocabulary like ballet or the Graham technique, rather, 'students explore through improvisation the movement territory established by the stylistic and technical rules of the form' (Foster, 1997, p. 250). In class, for example, students will practise certain falls and rolls and techniques for transferring the weight of the body to different body parts and explore the taking or giving of weight through touch with a partner. They may also be taught how to jump into the arms of a partner and to catch a partner who is 'falling from a great height' (ibid.).

Developing a deep sense of trust in one's own body's sensations and sharp reflexes is crucial to dance safety in contact improvisation where the body can be propelled at great speed. As one dancer/writer has commented, 'One had best be able to trust one's reflexes when 150 pounds of weight are suddenly thrust upon one's shoulders' (Steinman, 1986, p. 98). For Paxton, the import of fast reflexes goes deeper than this. It reveals something about the skill of a dancer, his or her bodily sense or 'bodily intelligence' through touch, trust, and communication:

> The mark of the dancer used to improvisation is his quickness of response. This quickness is faster than habitual movement/thought and is based on acceptance of imminent forces, letting the body respond to the reality it senses and trusting it to deal with the situation intuitively. Trust is an organic form of communication. (Paxton, cited in Steinman, 1986, p. 98)

The student/teacher relation in contact improvisation is again different from that in ballet. In the former, the teacher acts as an adviser or 'guide', not as a master or tutor as in the ballet class. In most classes, even with beginners, students will have some time to experiment 'within the structure of staying in contact' (Bull, 1997, p. 276). The teacher may also join in the class or dance with the students to assist them with the tasks they are involved in at that point in time. Attention is directed towards the student's internal experience of the body in motion and stillness in the context of the class at that point in time, not on the external presentation of the body *per se*. The concern is to feel what is happening in the body, not to survey it from the outside or the mirror.

Contact improvisation performances usually take place in smaller and more informal spaces than traditional dance forms such as ballet. This means that the performers' bodies, their smell, their breathing, and sounds as they fall, catch and move together with weighted momentum are all vividly present for both the performers and the spectators. In this way, the performance can become a kinaesthetic experience for the spectators as well as the dancers. The kinaesthetic experience can impact upon the audiences' responses and their sense of their own bodies in the context of the performance, which, in turn, can result in a 'shared experience' of dancers and performers. Nelson's comments on typical audience responses she witnessed in the early days of the movement demonstrate this clearly:

> I always remember the same response, basically. The space would get warmer and warmer throughout the performance, and when it was all over there would be a lot of dancing in the audience. People would be jumping all over one another. They would stick around afterwards and really want to start rolling around and want to jump on you. The feeling was of a real shared experience among performers and audience, a tremendous feeling

of physical accessibility between performers and audience. (Nelson, cited in Novack, 1990, p. 72)

Unlike ballet, as Bull (1997) points out, there is no requisite ideal body for practising and performing contact improvisation. For example, dancers with disabilities, perhaps using wheelchairs as bodily extensions, can and do practice contact improvisation. In addition to being a willing participant, which is a necessary qualification for all dance forms, contact improvisation calls for a willingness 'to give up control over one's movement' to the touch of another (Bull, 1997, p. 277) and 'go with the flow' (Foster, 1997, p. 250):

> For the dancer, the body's edges seem to change and to meld with one's partner: Likewise, the sense of weight shifts in response to the partner's movement and the movement itself seems generated by and through the points of contact. (Bull, 1997, p. 277)

In contact improvisation, then, the dancer becomes 'immersed in the body' (Foster, 1997, p. 249). But it is not an individualised, essentialist bodily immersion. Rather, the impetus comes through the power of touch, which facilitates the coalescence of the movement of two bodies so that the surfaces and boundaries of the individual bodies seem to disappear in the flux. The kinesphere of the one dancer is inextricably entwined with that of the other, literally and symbolically.

This is rather like the notion of a 'with', which Goffman (1972) described in regard to the 'interaction rituals' that sanction the 'territories of the self' in the activity of walking in public spaces. Goffman, as indicated in Chapter 2, argues that individuals have an invisible psychological and social 'bubble' that surrounds them. The bubble is not fixed; it expands and contracts, depending on the context. The body, then, is not necessarily the stable, fixed, bounded entity we commonsensically assume it to be. A wheelchair, for instance, can become an extension of the body of its owner, as can a car, in which case the personal space surrounding 'the body' expands to accommodate the extended body. There are occasions when one person's bubble joins together with that of another so that they appear to themselves and to others as if they were one. When two people are walking together and communicating with each other, they become a 'with', in Goffman's words. The focus of attention is mostly directed towards each other, not outwards to the surrounding environment. They may or may not be physically touching each other, but will be closer together and walking more or less in time than they would be if they were strangers. If a person wishes to overtake the pair or pass them when coming from the opposite direction, the convention is to go round the 'with'. If that is not possible and the 'with' bubble is traversed so that it is effectively broken in two, then some 'excuse me' is likely to be offered by the bubble breaker. One member of the 'with' may sense that someone wishes to pass them and may step to one side, opening up the bubble, to let the person pass through, or may guide the self and the other member away from the source of intrusion, thus maintaining the unity of the 'with'.

In the social dance context of contact improvisation, the focus is centred on the 'connection of one's self and one's partner' (Bull, 1997, p. 277) to the exclusion of everything else. In performance, the dancers also need to be aware that there *is* an audience. This can lead the dancers to adjust their inner-directedness (their 'withness') outwards, towards a reflection of the appearance of the performance (from another's point of view), by attending to spatial design, timing and sequential movement patterns. Hence, although touch may be the primary signifier in contact improvisation, other senses also come into play in performance.

In contact improvisation the conventions of 'where' and 'how' to touch are very different from those in ballet. The distinctions between social touching and dance touching in ballet discussed earlier do not signify in contact improvisation, at least in the theory of the form. In the latter, any part of the body can be touched and no particular body parts are assigned specific meanings. The idea that body parts hold no meaning and that they can therefore be touched with impunity is a difficult one in cultures where there is a high degree of formality in bodily matters (Douglas, 1975b). As the case study of the body rituals of the Nacirema in Chapter 1 revealed, in predominantly white Anglo-Saxon Protestant cultures such as those of North America and Britain, despite appearances, the body is treated as a dangerous instrument and is shrouded in rituals and sanctions.

Contact improvisation invites participants to bracket out the everyday meanings of touching, which is easier said than done, or seen to be done. Indeed, Paxton warned against using sexual or psychological encounters as a focus for movement as opposed to touch and weight, because he believed it had implications for the dancers' safety and would stifle the development of the form (Novack, 1990, p. 168). Contact improvisation, as one teacher commented, is 'intimate but it is public' (Ellen Elias, cited in Novack, 1990, p. 168). It aims to reposition the body in a way that cuts across the binary divide between the private and the public. The values inscribed in the form are sanctioned and reinforced through practice in the presence of others in the class-room, social dance or performance space. The contact improvisation dance context, then, is viewed as a key factor in legitimating the form as a body-centred practice and neutralising the codes associated with touching in everyday life and in other theatrical dance forms, such as ballet.

As suggested earlier, the partnering in contact improvisation is also very different from the pas de deux in ballet. The gender distinctions between the appearance of strength of the male dancer and the light-ness and fragility of the ballerina in ballet are countered in contact improvisation. A small man can take the weight of a large woman or vice versa, which widens the range of kinaesthetic experiences of danc-ing and partnering for the dancers and spectators. Moreover, partner-ing itself is not conceptualised as a gendered activity; women routinely partner women and men partner men. In this way, as Bull points out, contact improvisation denies the compulsory heterosexuality that pre-dominates in ballet and other dance forms, as 'many different kinds of gender configurations and patterns may be implied or interpreted' (1997, p. 278).

Bodily sensing in ballet and contact improvisation

Contact improvisation and ballet seem to begin from opposite ends of the experiential body spectrum and yet, as Bull argues, they share certain things in common. They are both products of the western cul-tural and artistic tradition, although the former took its impetus from alternative social movements within that tradition. The practitioners of both forms in the USA and in Britain are mostly drawn from the white middle-class population, as is their viewing public, although ballet boasts many more participants and viewers. Ballet, in effect, is a global brand (with stylistic differences) with ballet schools and companies in, for example, South East Asia, North America, South America and Europe. Both forms emphasise the body, but they do so from different ends of the continuum.

The ballet body emphasises line, placement and visual spatial design. The ballet dancer's inner expression is given visibility through the 'looking-glass self', and the prescribed vocabulary and codes of the form. The body in western culture, as noted in Chapters 1 and 2, has been objectified through a range of discursive practices. The ballet body provides a striking example of this process of objectification through its celebration of the ideals of visualism and the pursuit of the mastery of the body over nature. It is an athletic, highly tuned instrument through which the dancer's inner expression is given an outward form. The virtuoso performance offers the audience a glimpse of the extraordinary possibilities of the moving body as it makes its trace forms in time and space, through, on the one hand, the male dancer's vigorous, energising sense of force and, on the other, the female dancer's defiance of weight and gravity.[12] The individuality of the principal performers, set against the backdrop of the sameness of the corps de ballet, not only provides a range of contrasting visual designs in the air and on the floor, it also gives visual expression to the system of social hierarchy, codes and manners on which ballet was founded. Several contemporary ballet choreographers, such as William Forsythe, whose work builds on the neo-classical tradition of Balanchine, have vigorously challenged this hierarchy of performance, while recognising their indebtedness to the form of ballet. Having said this, a brief glance at the repertoires of the major national ballet companies shows that the hegemonic draw of 'classic' ballets like *Swan Lake* and *The Nutcracker*, which stem from the nineteenth century, remains intact. Even the iconoclastic versions of these ballets by contemporary modern dance choreographers, like Matthew Bourne's highly successful male *Swan Lake* (1995)[13] and Mark Morris's gender-troubling *The Hard Nut* (1991) (see Morris, 1996b), pay tribute to the staying power of the form.

Contact improvisation begins from the opposite end of the scale from ballet. Its roots are in the counter-cultures of the 1960s and in the emergent critiques of the star images, hierarchies and codified techniques of western theatre dance (ballet and modern dance), epitomised in Yvonne Rainer's much-quoted blast at modern dance written in 1965:

> NO to spectacle no to virtuosity no to transformations and magic and make-believe no to glamour and transcendency of the star image no to the heroic no to the ant-heroic no to trash imagery. (Cited in Banes, 1980, p. 43)

The contact body directs attention inwards to the body of the self through touch and weight. The body is ideally the subject and the object of attention in contact, in contrast to ballet where the bodily focus is objectified and fashioned through its visual appearance and projections in space and time. While ballet conspires with the visualism of western culture, contact improvisation colludes with the 'truth of the body' ideology encapsulated in a range of alternative body reeducation techniques, such as the Alexander technique, which gained some ground in the 1970s. In line with its egalitarian principles, the form emphasises reciprocal relations between contact partners, who take and

give weight, whilst accommodating individual differences in movement. The democratic ideals have not always been sustained in practice,
particularly in the professional performance context (Novack, 1990).
While ballet stresses the powers and possibilities of the body through
control, contact improvisation invites the performer to 'let go' and see
what new movement possibilities emerge when the body is set free from
the strictures of ballet codification, although the former also has techniques for falling and so on.

The dancer in both forms, reflecting the spirit of 'possessive individualism' (Macpherson, 1964) inscribed within western thought, is an individual. The manner of experiencing individuation, however, is somewhat
different, as Bull points out. In contact improvisation, the dancer is
guided by the experience of physical sensation, 'responding to another
with bodily intuition and sharing this experience with an audience'
(1997, p. 284). In ballet 'the dancer feels herself to be a special being',
whose honed physical competence and emotional powers of expression
are made manifest, under the direction of a choreographer, by 'pre-set
choreography and music in presentation to an audience' (ibid.).

The preceding discussion aimed to compare and contrast certain
underlying qualities of the dance forms in question, as opposed to
drawing out significant differences within each form. This approach is
useful, precisely because it leads us to pay close attention to the ways
in which the body is constructed, instructed and experienced through
the movement vocabulary, technique and ideals encapsulated in these
forms. It also enables us to locate the forms within the socio-cultural
conditions of their emergence and development. Having said this, there
is a danger that the forms themselves become ossified and the
multifarious aspects of the dancing body, once more, end up as a single
entity – the body. The generalist approach, then, needs to be tempered
by attention to specific case studies.

Technical shifts and aesthetic transformations

Dance forms, of course, do change over time and dancers' bodies,
in their idealised and realised form, are also subject to change over
time. For example, although ballet as a form may display certain core
movement values, there are differences in the positions of the arms
(*ports de bras*) and the shoulder movements (*épaulement*) in the Russian,
French and Italian schools of ballet technique and training. These
colour the movement and thereby contribute to subtle differences of
meaning (see Lepczyk, 1987).

Developments in dance techniques and/or training can contribute to shifts in the aesthetics of given genres and alterations in the physical appearance of the dancing body, and vice versa.[14] Consider, for example, the soft shoulder line and subtle flexibility of the upper body that marked the Ashton dancer of the 1950s and early 1960s, or the speed, flexibility and hyper leg extensions which have become the marker of the female Balanchine dancer. Melissa Hayden, a former principal dancer in Balanchine's company, seems to confirm the transformational qualities of the female body under the tutelage of the *master* in stating that, 'You make yourself a Balanchine ballerina by dancing his ballets ... Your legs change, your body changes, you become a *filly*' (cited in Jowitt, 1988, p. 265). Hayden's words not only provide a clear example of the objectification of the (female) body in much of western theatre dance, they also suggest that the individual body is an unfinished entity, even the trained, fully formed dancing body, which can be transformed physically and aesthetically through training and practice.

In addition to the possibility of change within the history of an individual body, a brief glance at ballet history books, as Sayers has observed, reveals that the image of the ideal dancing body has been subject to change and revision across time:

> compare ... those ethereal sylphs hovering about the earth in romantic lithographs with photographs of buxom Victorian ballet dancers peering flirtatiously over their fans; or compare the demure, downcast gaze of later British heroines – the queenly Markova and Fonteyn, with the splayed body of Sylvie Guillem setting out the extended compass points of today's increasingly svelte balletic body in space. (Sayers, 1997, p. 132)

Modern dance has a shorter history than ballet. It emerged almost simultaneously although somewhat differently in Germany and the USA in the second decade of the twentieth century. American modern dancers like Martha Graham took from and challenged the work of the preceding generation of 'modern' or 'interpretive' dancers/choreographers such as Isadora Duncan and Ruth St Denis. Duncan was notoriously anti-formalist and blasted at ballet's artifice and hierarchical structure in her dancing and writing. Graham's technique, based on the principles of 'contraction and release', was forged out of the demands of her early choreography. The action of contraction is a concentration of the body's energy, which, initiated by squeezing out the breath, begins sharply in the pelvis and goes through the whole body. The force of the contraction can pull the body off balance and carry it from one plane to another. With the intake of breath, the action of release begins in the base of the spine and continues through the back, restoring the body to a 'normal state' (see Terry, 1978, pp. 53–61). The Graham technique, like ballet, became codified and since the 1950s has been taught as an alternative to ballet in dance schools and universities in many different countries.

The dancers in Graham's early company, such as Bonnie Bird, did not look like the long-limbed sylphs of contemporary ballet; nor did they resemble the slender dancers of Graham's later, postwar companies. Rather, these early dancers looked as if they were built to pound into and rebound off the floor (Bonnie Bird interview, 1984). In contrast to ballet, early modern dance choreography used the floor and gravity, although not in the inner-directed, playful sense that came to characterise contact improvisation half a century later. Modern dance was forged out of the individual dancers'/choreographers' bodies of ideas and physical aptitudes. Until recently, modern dancers tended to be trained in the work of a particular choreographer's style or technique. Ballet, which involves a very long period of training, does not easily translate onto the bodies of modern dancers, whose training can begin at a later age. The individual styles and techniques of modern dance choreographers do not necessarily look right on ballet dancers, whose bodies are so deeply marked by their training. Ballet dancers performing works created for modern dancers may be likened to classically trained singers such as José Carreras or Kiri Te Kanawa singing songs from musicals like *West Side Story*; the end result does not feel quite right. But specific modern dance techniques, as Foster (1997) argues, can also mark the bodies of dancers so thoroughly that they might not be able to adapt to another modern dance style. Having said this, the advent in recent years of what Foster calls the 'hired body' in contemporary dance means that dancers are increasingly required to have a 'flexible' body that can adapt to the demands of different choreographic styles. The idea of the flexible body is that performers might shift seamlessly from dancing in the performance style of perhaps a Christopher Bruce composition to that required for a Merce Cunningham work and on to a Glen Tetley piece, in the same programme. But shifts in training and/or the techniques of specific dance forms over the years can also alter or modify the look and the experience of dancing bodies, so that modern dancers in the here and now may find it difficult (or impossible) to get particular movements into their bodies that were important and/or routine in the bodily techniques of an earlier period.

The final section of this chapter centres on a case study of a reconstruction of a 'classic' early modern dance work, *Water Study*, which was choreographed by Doris Humphrey in 1928. Humphrey, like Graham, was a leading figure in the development of American modern dance. The discussion draws on my observations of two groups of third-year university dance students who were learning the dance in 1997. Semistructured group interviews were conducted with the students after class. A much longer interview was conducted with the students' lecturer, Lesley Main, who directs and performs works by Humphrey, in order to clarify and flesh out my initial observations and discussions with the students.[15] Quotations from the transcripts of the interviews are cited in the discussion. Attention was also directed towards ascertaining how the students perceived and learnt this dance, which was created in the early stages of Humphrey's choreographic development, when her technique was not fully formed. The basis of the technique, however, is already much in evidence in *Water Study*.

Humphrey, like Graham, recognised the dramatic effect of gravity in choreography. She developed a technique based on 'fall and recovery', which she construed as 'the arc between two deaths', the 'static death of the horizontal plane' and the 'dynamic death' of the vertical plane (Cohen, 1972, p. 119). Falling away from and returning to a state of equilibrium constitutes the continuous flux in the human body: 'giving in to and rebound from gravity' (Humphrey, 1959, p. 106). Life and dance, for Humphrey, occurs in the drama of motion between the horizontal and the vertical axes. The triumph of recovery from the fall occurs at the moment of suspension when 'the person asserts his freedom from the powers of nature' (Cohen, 1972, p. 119). The point of drawing on this case study is to further reflect on the discussion of histories of bodies in Chapters 1 and 2. In so doing, the problems of authenticity and reproducibility in dance emerge, which will be taken up and explored more fully in the next chapter.

Water Study – then and now

In her illuminating movement analysis of a reconstructed version of *Water Study* in 1976,[16] Siegel describes the dance as follows:

> *Water Study* is a collection of images of water. In silence, fourteen dancers create these images both collectively and individually, using movement that does not *describe* the movement of water but corresponds to its energies and configurations. (1979, p. 29)

In *The Art of Making Dances* (1959), Humphrey comments that dancing in silence was popular in the 1920s and 1930s because the new generation of modern dance choreographers was attempting to demonstrate that dance was an independent art and not a mere visual frill of music. Humphrey suggests that dancing in silence does not empty the theatrical space as one might expect. On the contrary, it facilitates an increased 'concentration and attention to movement' (1959, p. 142), which was a key concern of the modern dancers. Although there is no external musical accompaniment in *Water Study*, the dancers[17] use the inhalation, suspension and exhalation of their breath as the rhythmic source to create the phrasing of the movement, which in this instance was determined by the choreographer. Humphrey believed that the use of breath rhythm in dance did not have to be restricted to the rise and fall of the breath in the chest; it could be transposed to different areas of the body:

> The idea of breath rhythm – the inhalation, the suspension and exhalation – can be transferred to other parts of the body. One can 'breathe' with the knees, or the arms or the whole body. (1959, p. 107)

The rhythm and the pulse of the movement in each individual dancer in *Water Study* ideally accords with, although not necessarily corresponds to, that of the group, to create 'the ebb and flow of energy' (Siegel, 1979, p. 29) of the water, through expanding or shrinking the body from the centre, or by travelling across the space at speed to a different location.[18] The dancers are not identified as individuals; rather the impetus for movement is 'motivated towards an effect outside of themselves' (Kagan, 1978, p. 82). The whole in this dance is more than the sum of the individual parts. In order to achieve a unity of expression, the performers are required to listen with their bodies, to be sensitive to their own and to each other's movement, which is forged by the use of breath rhythm.

Humphrey told the dance critic Margaret Lloyd (1974, p. 87) that her starting point for *Water Study*, was 'human feeling...with body movement and its momentum in relation to the psyche and to gravity, and as it developed the movements took on the form and the tempo of moving water'. Lloyd indicates that, even at this early phase of her career, Humphrey's 'desire to get to the living source' of human movement led her to direct attention towards 'natural rhythms', like breath rhythm and 'natural movement'. That is, she wanted to find out what a body does when the layers of performance styles are stripped away. Thus, she was attempting to get to the nuts and bolts of human movement and to use these as the basis upon which to create movement designs. In a programme note for *Water Study*, Humphrey stated that the elimination of the measured beat of musical rhythm in favour of breath rhythm in the dance enables the rhythm to flow in natural phrases as opposed to what she calls 'cerebral measures':

> There is no count to hold the dancers together in the very slow opening rhythm, only the feel of the wave lengths that curve the backs of the groups. (Cohen, 1972, p. 85)

What interested me in the sessions I observed and in the discussions with the students was how they managed or did not manage in a number of cases to get the feel of the Humphrey movement style into their bodies. Of particular interest in regard to this dance were the various successive movements that start in the centre of the body and ripple all the way through the torso to the head and the arms in one direction and through the pelvis and the thighs in the other direction, sometimes with the spine curving the body inwards, and at others with the back arching the body outwards, and hurtling the dancers across the floor.[19]

Two groups of dancers were learning the dance in the same session and each group, in turn, watched the other rehearse what they had learnt. The students had had previous exposure to aspects of the Humphrey technique in the first two years of their programme. Initially, none of them appeared to be able to get the successive movement into their bodies. The successions, as Main pointed out in the interview cited above, are extremely difficult to do and although they look very easy, they require considerable strength, particularly in the thighs, which the majority of the students did not have at that point in their training. The dance begins with the dancers on their knees curled up in a tight ball. One by one, they unfold from the centre of the body to create the image of a small ripple across the floor. 'Continuity' as Elizabeth Kagan's movement analysis reveals, is a central component throughout this dance:

> The dancers' primary concentration ... is on maintaining a sense of continuity. Even the held shapes at the beginning of the piece must be performed with a free, or at least a neutral flow in the upper body, and although the arms become somewhat bound, they must never stop. (1978, p. 84)

The dancers' movement at the beginning of the dance in particular looked stilted and comic at the same time; it seemed as if they did not quite know how to control the flow of the movement through the body and into the arms. At times, the movement flow through the arms seemed to be halted too abruptly and then go into a slight recovery, giving a kind of bouncy appearance, instead of giving the impression of not stopping even in stillness.

At other points in the rehearsal, the successive flow, given impetus with an intake of breath, seemed to stream out of the dancers' fingertips into the space beyond, when it should have been hovering on the tips of the fingers so that with the expulsion of breath, their bodies would surge of necessity to a different point in the dance space.

The students' bodies generally appeared much softer and fleshier than I usually associate with modern or contemporary dancing bodies, particularly around the area of the abdomen. Moreover, it was evident that a number of them did not possess the flexibility in the spine that is so necessary for this dance. This improved measurably when a number of the dancers managed to listen to their breath rhythm.

At first, the students found the dance very difficult. Although it does not look particularly strenuous because of the emphasis on flow, it requires considerable strength and control 'to support, prepare for and accent the expression' (Kagan, 1978, p. 84). The dance is particularly hard on the knees and thighs, especially at the beginning. When the title of the dance was put up on the notice board prior to rehearsals it was accompanied by the words 'Remember to bring your knee-caps'. The students thought that the early modern dancers might have paid less attention to safety issues at that time, whereas the students are very conscious of dance safety. They also indicated that they found the dance extremely strenuous in the first few weeks of class. One dancer summed up the feeling of the group when she said that initially she felt as if she had 'a brick in each thigh'. As the students became more familiar with the technique through practice, they were able to 'relax' and 'release' into it. Thus, the students used terms that are common in contact improvisation and release techniques to think themselves into the demands of this dance:

> We started it [*Water Study*] in January ... we thought, you know, 'This is going to be really, really painful on our thighs and things' ... As we went along, it wasn't new anymore ... and more normal I suppose. We could start bringing the techniques we learned ... the words Lesley was using ... 'release into it', 'breathe into it' ... made sense, but the movement was initially painful. (Middlesex University dance students, group interview, 1997)

The differences in dance training over time also affected the way the students ran in this piece, which, in turn, led to a jarring of the on-going movement flow of the dance. In interview, the students' lecturer pointed out that while Humphrey's dancers ran in a 'naturalistic' way, that is, in parallel, contemporary modern dancers 'are formally conditioned to be turned out' and to 'think of placement'. But in Humphrey's time:

[The dancers] did not even think about it, they just did it, so there was an inherent naturalness in the way they moved anyway, and they were not concerned with ... turning their leg out at fourteen [years old] ... The sort of quality of movement was very different because of how they moved then. (Lesley Main interview, 1997)

The point is taken here that Main was discussing differences in training between early modern dancers and contemporary modern dancers. The construct of 'naturalistic' running might be questioned, given that running as a technique of the body involves training, while at the same time recognising the fact that the human species is bipedal. If we compared Humphrey's dancers running on stage with people running outside in the street, for example, would they look the same, or is dance movement always transformational in terms of its context?

Towards the end of the first session, one particular student, who was beginning to stand out in terms of her ability to get the rhythmic movement flow into her body and her commitment to the work, commented with visible pleasure to another member of her group, 'I can feel it now when I get it wrong'. This is a rather interesting comment. The student was implying that she does not feel the movement when it is right, her body now knows that in its bones; it has almost become part of her 'natural attitude' (Schutz, 1967). Rather, she suggested that her awareness is raised when she moves in an inappropriate way: that is, when she is out of style. This brings the taken-for-granted bodily knowledge of the Humphrey style, that is, the rules or codes, into bodily consciousness, which, in turn, can be drawn on reflexively for the purposes of corrective action. It could be suggested that this dancer had acquired, to borrow Bourdieu's (1993) terms, the bodily 'habitus' or 'hexis' of the movement style which this dance requires to be recognisable (in a practical bodily sense), for both dancer and the informed viewer, as a successful reworking of a dance from this choreographic position in the modern dance 'field'.

As indicated in Chapter 2, Bourdieu conceptualises the body as an unfinished entity, which, as a bearer of symbolic value, develops alongside other social forces and is crucial to the maintenance and reproduction of inequalities in society. In the process of its formation, the body becomes deeply inscribed by class, race and gender distinctions. The social construction of the body is bound up with individual history, which means that there is a relationship between the represented body and the embodied subject.

The bodily habitus, in Bourdieu's framework, is viewed as productive as well as reproductive. Bourdieu (1990a, p. 9) uses the term 'agents' rather than 'subjects' or 'actors' to indicate that individuals are neither passive nor do they act according to free will. The habitus is generative but it is acquired through experience and therefore will vary according to its formation in time and space. Individuals acquire a 'practical sense' or a 'feel for the game' (ibid.), which facilitates a whole variety of different 'moves' to be made. So habitus is sometimes called a 'feel for the game', which translates into a 'practical sense' that predisposes individuals to act and respond in given social contexts (ibid.). The habitus, in Bourdieu's formulation, is not conscious in the sense of bringing something into being by sheer will. However, it may be awakened in the bodily consciousness under certain conditions, supplying the potential for generating strategies for constructive action and/or change, which is not quite the same as free will. What Bourdieu is pointing to is that individual bodies have histories, but that these histories are not entirely of their own construction. Although this complex construct is being used, here, in a somewhat liberal manner in relation to the artistic field of dance, I think it provides potential for a discussion of the transmission and embodiment of dance techniques and styles, in a way that other more discursive or representational models such as that of Foucault do not (see Csordas, 1994b). Other writers such as Ann Daly (1995), Jane Desmond (1998) and Gay Morris (2001) have applied aspects of Bourdieu's theory of practice (1977) to the analysis of modern dance. Loïc Wacquant (1995) has developed the notion of bodily capital in the context of his ethnographic study of professional boxers. The centrality of the body for boxers, as Wacquant notes, is closely allied to the body-centredness which dancers experience on a daily basis.

Over the following session of the reconstruction process, a number of the members of the group, of which the student who knew when she had 'got it wrong' was part, also managed to get some of the required movement qualities into their bodies. As a consequence, their version of the dance was transformed, as was their experience of it. It was clear from the discussions I had with them that the dance had become more meaningful to them as performers. It was also evident that this had affected their group experience, as it had affected my experience of their performance of this work.

When this group was asked how they now knew they had incorporated the required movement into their bodies, they indicated that they did not really know how they knew, or perhaps could not bring it into verbal language. They implied that it was a kind of bodily sensibility, similar to the notion of 'bodily intelligence' articulated by Foster (1997) and Mabel Ellsweth Todd's (1972 [1937]) idea of the 'thinking body'. As the following four separate responses to the query show:

S1   That's an interesting one!
S2   It doesn't matter, because if you feel it, you don't have to think. If you feel it, you are doing it for the movement rather than thinking.
S3   You're not going through a checklist.
S4   No, that's right, it's not like 'I should do that a bit more' ... You just get there. (Middlesex University dance students group interview, 1997)

When pressed further about how the movement just got there, the students invoked the notion of bodily memory:

S1   It is a memory thing as well ... the memory in a sense is in your body.
S2   ... muscle memory. (Ibid.)

A unified use of dynamic breath rhythm in *Water Study* promotes a sense of the group being more than the individual members who comprise it. The students in this group declared themselves enriched by their experience of oneness with the group, which they found they could achieve by listening to the breath rhythm and the movement that is initiated through it. As one of the group suggested:

Actually ... I think that the way we do it, the way we feel it, the way we remember it all at once is [when] we start thinking about the breath and that means that we've got it ... Once we just think about the breath, and not having to think about the change [of position] ... we can feel the movement. At least we can *feel* the movement. We may not look right, but at least we can feel it. (Ibid.)

Note how the tone, here, invokes the group 'we' and not the individual as in most of the interview talk apart from the very first quotation. This group of students indicated that they thought the observed differences between the two groups were a result of the other group having recently lost two of their dancers. Because each dancer is required to be 'ultra-sensitive to everybody else', the drop in numbers would have made the group 'feel really unbalanced' (ibid.). A sense of group harmony and balance, from this group's perspective, is central to this dance.

While contact improvisation and ballet prioritise the sense of sight and touch respectively, *Water Study*, I would suggest, privileges a sense of listening and feeling from the inside out. The breath rhythm connects the movement of the individual bodies of the dancers with that of the group through flow, weight, rising and sinking, and moving out from the body's centre and returning to it.

This chapter set out to focus on specific dance forms and practices in an attempt to counter the lack of attention given to the moving body, its possibilities and limitations, in social and cultural studies. Through a close examination of the prioritising of the senses of sight in ballet and touch in contact improvisation from the performers' and spectators' perspectives, the dualisms in western culture were highlighted and explored. The chapter also opened up the notion that 'bodies have histories' through an examination of a reconstruction of an early work from the modern dance tradition. Certain differences between the training of contemporary modern dancers and earlier modern dancers were raised in order to show how these could restrict the abilities of the former to create a believable or workable version of the dance in the image of the latter. But it also pointed to ways in which unfamiliar movement can become familiar, resulting in the dancers experiencing and being enriched by a strong sense of knowing in and through the body of the self in relation to others.

These observations also suggest questions around 'reproduction' and 'authenticity' in dance. What are the problems of passing down modern or contemporary dance forms, which do not have a standardised vocabulary like ballet, from generation to generation, and in what sense, if any, can we speak of this passing down? Moreover, dance is an ephemeral medium. Indeed, we might ask if dances can or *should* be resurrected or reconstructed on other bodies in an authentic manner. And what do we mean by authenticity in this context? After all, when Balanchine's moves break with the conventions of ballet, he is not doing so from outside the system, as were the early modern dancers. Rather his iconoclastic moves invoke and sustain the tradition of ballet. As Deborah Jowitt (1988, p. 254) has noted:

> [In] ... Balanchine's ballets to contemporary music ... classical tradition may seem to be subverted, but a turned in leg is understood in terms of the turnout that follows, a flexed foot in relation to a pointed one; a swing out of a centred posture imprints its in-balance counterpart in our brains.

These themes of reconstruction and authenticity in dance will be explored in the following chapter.

Chapter 5

Reconstructing the Dance: In Search of Authenticity?

> Dance exists at a perpetual vanishing point. At the moment of its creation it is gone ... [it is] an event that disappears in the very act of materializing.
>
> (Siegel, 1968, p. 1)

Introduction

The history of western theatre dance can be seen, in many respects, as a history of 'lost' dances. As the above quote from Marcia Siegel suggests, dance, unlike other arts, does not leave a record of its existence in the form of a tangible object, like a painting, a script or a musical score. Rather, as it comes into being in performance, so it is gone. In recent years, with advances in film and video technology and dance notation, there has been a growing interest in resurrecting some of these lost dances from the early period of modern dance and modern ballet. The aim of this was to 'fill in the blanks' of the (hi)story of dance and provide some continuity to the tradition (Kriegsman, 1993; Morris, 1993). This quest for a 'retrievable past' (Copeland, 1993b) has also given rise to a variety of questions that centre around the complex relationship between 'authenticity' and 'interpretation' in the context of the politics of reconstruction (Marion, 1990; *The Drama Review*, 1984; Berg, 1993; Jordan, 2000). With this in view, this chapter will explore a range of theoretical and practical issues surrounding the concepts, processes and products of dance reconstruction. The exploration of the problematic issues that the desire to generate a 'usable'[1] or 'retrievable' past raises begins, in a sense, where the last chapter left off. In the final section of the previous chapter, which was based on observations and interviews with two groups of students learning to perform Humphrey's *Water Study* (1928), I referred to an open-ended qualitative interview with the dance lecturer, Lesley Main (interview, 1997). Main is also the Director of the Doris Humphrey Foundation, which was established in 1995, to mark Humphrey's centenary. Main's approach to bringing Humphrey's work to contemporary audiences, which she set out in an article in 1995 and elaborated on in the interview, provides the starting point for the discussion on dance reconstruction.[2]

The real thing?

In 1995, Main's group performed three early Humphrey solos (*Quasi Waltz* (1928), *The Call/Breath* (1929/30), and *Two Ecstatic Themes* (1931)), which were 're-created' by Ernestine Stodelle, who was a member of the Humphrey–Weidman company between 1929 and 1935 when the dances were created. The group also performed Humphrey's *Passacaglia* (1938) and this version was 'directed' by Main.[3]

In an essay entitled 'Preserved and Illuminated', Main (1995, pp. 14–15) discusses the aims of the Doris Humphrey Foundation and also the programme of Humphrey's dances cited above, which were performed at different venues during 1995.[4] In this paper and in the interview referred to above, Main speaks with conviction of what she sees as the need to perform work 'as it was' in some instances and 'as it is' in others. In so doing, she provides us with a good starting point for beginning to tease out various representations of reconstruction and the problems they give rise to. Although Main pointedly casts discussions of 'authenticity' and 'interpretation' to one side in her essay (and to be fair, this is not the point of the piece), her words and talk, as I shall demonstrate, constantly invoke these ghosts that seem to haunt the historicist dance and musical world. Main (1995, p. 14) suggests that some dances are 'of their time', while others can 'transcend their time of origin'. In other words, some work should not be tampered with because it has what we might term locally situated historical significance, while other work has a greater 'universal' time reach in that it can have relevance for a contemporary audience. The first type, then, according to Main (ibid.), can provide a 'living illustration' of modern dance *as it was*. According to a number of scholars, this recovery is sorely needed if dance is to move out of the shadows of the arts and into the light (see discussions in, for example, Topaz, 1988; Adams, 1992; Copeland, 1993b). The second type can provide more of a lived 'interpretation' of a choreographer's breadth of vision and movement ideas, or what Main referred to in the interview in 1997 as the 'spirit' of the choreographer that spans time and space and can speak to contemporary audiences in terms of their *now*.

Here we have two different views of reconstruction, the one 'authentic' to the original work, the other 'interpretative' of the spirit of the work. The idea of a 'dance work' as a thing in itself, as Siegel (1968) suggests in the first quotation, also presents us with a number of problems which will be addressed throughout the chapter (see Rubidge, 1996). Main (1995, p. 15) is not suggesting that one type should take precedence over the other. Rather, she maintains that both are required in order to aim for an 'accurate representation of Humphrey's legacy'. It is worth noting that there is an assumption that there can be such a thing as a correct or true representation of Humphrey's work, and therefore presumably of the work of other choreographers. The evaluative discourses concerning notions of good and bad representations are worth further consideration because they enable us to uncover the grounds that underpin them and offer us images of the character of the work (dance), and the perceived relationship between the maker of the work (choreographer) and the performer (dancer).

Reconstruction in context

The 1980s and early 1990s witnessed an increased interest in reconstructing choreographic work from earlier periods of modern dance, with a view to taking dance out of the 'vanishing point' where Siegel (1968) suggests it resides, by giving textual visibility to at least some aspect of its 'modern' past. Some writers suggested that the increasing passion for reconstructing past dances reflected a 'sign of impoverishment' and could be seen as 'a declaration of the bankruptcy of the present' (Schmidt, 1988, p. 32). 'The "Me" generation' of the 1960s and 1970s, as Roger Copeland (1994, p. 18) put it, had increasingly given way to the ' "Re" generation'. This shift was accompanied by the emergence of debates on the positive and negative aspects of reconstructing dance *per se*. Questions were also raised regarding the adequacy of the term 'reconstruction' to describe the activity or the dance performances that resulted from the process.[5] Some detractors felt that the term was restrictive because it conjured up an image of replicating the original, which, it was argued, was impossible to achieve because dance is a performed art constituted through the embodied practices of the performers on each and every occasion of its performance. As such, it cannot be fixed or located in any one performance. Depending on the theoretical stance adopted, it was deemed to be more appropriate to speak in terms of 're-creating' (Cohen, 1993), 'reviving', 're-staging' (see Forster, 1990), 're-envisioning' or even 'constructing' dance

(Franko, 1989). The advocates of reconstruction, on the other hand, were concerned to point to the disadvantages of not having a usable dance past to draw on for present-day performers and audiences, and for future generations. Comparisons were drawn with the other arts, which, unlike dance, do at least leave traces of their existence behind them in the tangible form of objects, canvases, scripts or scores. Moreover, some considered that 'dance has been written out of history, pushed to the margins of aesthetic and philosophical discourse' (Elton, 1992, p. 22), as a consequence of its lack of a retrievable past.

As indicated in Chapter 3, there is a lively but less well-known folk dance research tradition emanating from the folklorist, ethnochoreological tradition, which, to a greater or lesser degree, has its research base in eastern and central European countries. The concern within this tradition is to document and provide an accurate record of 'lived', but vanishing, folk dance traditions. In Hungary, for example, which boasts a folk dance research tradition spanning seventy years, the concern was and is to 'collect documents of "authentic folk dance" and music into an extensive archive and distribute knowledge systematically in the form of academic monographs, compendia, type-catalogues and motif-indexes' (Felföldi, 1999, p. 55). This folk dance tradition has a more sustained and empirically grounded 'social scientific' research base within eastern and central Europe than is evidenced in western theatre dance research. Although methods of collecting data have been traditionally more important than generating theory within this framework, theoretical issues such as those indicated above with regard to the preservation of modern dance have begun to emerge here too. László Felföldi (1999, pp. 55–6) has commented that the drive towards nationalising cultures and the search for 'pure' local dance forms by educators, artists and politicians in Hungary has effectively rendered the folk dances archaic. This has resulted in a 'specifically shaped, indeed distorted picture of the traditional cultures of eastern and central Europe' (ibid.), which, in turn, has impacted upon the dance traditions themselves. Felföldi notes that central and eastern European researchers have had to take into account complex considerations of authenticity and preservation on the one hand and the ossification of tradition on the other, when conducting their folk dance research. I am not going to draw on this tradition of research in any detail in this chapter. Nevertheless, it is instructive to note that certain of the key concerns that animate the debates on the reconstruction of early modern dance works are also visible in the ethnochoreological tradition of central and eastern Europe.

The debates surrounding reconstruction in dance studies began to raise questions about authenticity and interpretation, reproducibility and the 'aura' of the work of art, tradition and the relation between past and the present, and the symbolic capital of dance as an art form. Similar questions were also being raised elsewhere in social and cultural studies in the late 1980s and early 1990s. For example, there was a renewed interest in the work of Walter Benjamin in cultural studies, particularly in connection with his analysis of modernity and his insights into the fate of high art in the era of mechanical reproduction (see McRobbie, 1992). In the field of musicology, questions regarding musical authenticity and reproducibility, particularly in connection with what appeared to have become the orthodoxy of 'historical music', gave rise to a great deal of controversy in the 1980s.

These debates were of a theoretical and practical nature and this chapter will seek to draw these out more fully by examining the underlying concerns and by making reference to a range of materials. I shall focus primarily on western theatre dance and particularly modern dance, as this was largely the point of convergence for the debates in dance studies in the 1980s and 1990s. I shall use some of the debates on historical music performance as a background to the discussion. There is a close relationship between dance and music in the western theatrical dance tradition and several scholars have shown that the examination of musical/choreographic aspects of a work can provide significant and subtle insights for dance reconstruction (Cook, 1990; Hutchinson Guest, 1991; Jordan, 1993). Further, as indicated above, the 'authenticity' debate in musicology resonates strongly with emergent debates on the politics and practice of dance preservation. I shall also draw on Benjamin's ideas in his essay on 'The Work of Art in the Age of Mechanical Reproduction' or 'technical reproducibility' which, according to Hal Foster (1997, p. 218) 'is the more accurate term',[6] towards the end of the chapter.

Varieties of musical authenticity

The relationship between authenticity and creative interpretation, as indicated above, has been fiercely debated in the field of musicology since the 1980s. As Shelley Berg (1993, p. 109) has pointed out, these debates surrounding the performance practices of historical or early music have 'a particular resonance for dance' today, when those involved in dance theory and/or practice are increasingly having to confront questions of the authenticity of dance performance. I would also suggest that these questions have been pursued more rigorously in musicology than in dance studies, perhaps because musicology has a more sustained tradition within academe.

In the 1970s and 1980s, early music achieved great popularity with performers and the listening public through the revival of lost or forgotten music played on 'original' instruments, and with more familiar music played in a radically different manner to the conventional 'romantic' style of the nineteenth century. Nicholas Kenyon (1988, p. 6) notes that such was the sway of the historical performance movement that the words 'performed on original instruments' came to all but stand as a marker for ensuring that a performance was 'authentic'. Initially, criticisms of historical music performances were directed towards the performing competence and artistry of the musicians and to the historical faithfulness of the performance. To begin with, the question of the viability of the construct of historical faithfulness in itself was not an issue because authenticity was assumed or was taken for granted. The question of the limits of authenticity did not emerge until the 1980s.

The proponents of faithful historical music performance sought to locate authenticity in terms of the original intentions of the composer and the original audience's hearing of it, which implied that there was a 'single, true, certain authenticity' to be found (Tomlinson, 1988, p. 115). Hence, the historical performance movement adopted a positivistic approach to music performance. Richard Taruskin (1995), the musicologist and performer, railed against what he saw as the 'intentional fallacy' of the historical musical performance credo. The term 'intentional fallacy' first came to prominence in the late 1940s and early 1950s in the field of literary criticism. In an article with that title, W.K. Wimsatt and Monroe C. Beardsley (1946) attacked the dominant positivist approach within literary criticism for reducing the search for meaning in a literary work to a causal explanation of authorial intention, thus ignoring the potential for meaning in the work itself. Like Wimsatt and Beardsley, Taruskin (1995, p. 98) argues against the notion of 'consulting the oracle', maintaining that the composer's intentions are not accessible to us in the present day. He maintains that the need to justify a particular performance on the basis of its closeness to the composer's original intentions 'bespeaks a failure of nerve, not to say infantile dependency'. He also argues that the concern with generating a historically authentic performance is a modernist invention and not a historical restoration. It should be noted that Taruskin does not reject the notion of authenticity *per se* (although he does not like using the term). Rather, he shifts the site of its belonging away from the composer and places it firmly in the hands of the performer. He maintains that authenticity is to be found in the 'performer's imaginative conviction' (Tomlinson, 1988, p. 117).

Gary Tomlinson (1988), the music historian, suggests that by invoking the outmoded 'intentional fallacy' theory, Taruskin gives rise to a highly restricted version of music research, which is solely locatable in terms of the performer in performance. Tomlinson wishes to replace the term 'authenticity' with 'authentic meanings', on the grounds that we cannot possibly know with any degree of objective certainty the composer's true intentions in creating the work, or what the audience felt when it heard it for the first time. Rather, authentic meaning refers to

> the meanings that we, in the course of interpretative historical acts of various sorts, come to believe its creators and audience invested in it. (1988, p. 115)

Tomlinson advocates a 'post-positivist approach to the discovery of historical intent', which is founded on the 'nature of meaning' and a 'metaphor for the transaction by which the historian conceives of the past' (1988, p. 118). Meaning, for Tomlinson, is contextual and therefore the more we delve into the context, the wider the potential for meaning. Borrowing Geertz's (1975) hermeneutic model of culturalist interpretation, Tomlinson perceives of the practice of history as 'a conversation' between the historian and the agents in the past that he or she is studying.[7] As Tomlinson notes, whilst the notion of 'conversation' in anthropology is real (real people are in conversation), in history it is more metaphorical. Meaning, for Tomlinson, does not only reside in the work, as, for example, a structuralist approach would suggest; rather, meaning is fluid and not fixed in any one site. Tomlinson argues that meaning arises from the relationship of the work to 'things outside it' (1988, p. 122) in the wider socio-historical context. As such, he maintains that meaning cannot be grasped fully through performance, as Taruskin (1995) argues. Rather, Tomlinson advocates the notion of 'multiple meanings' in that 'depth of understanding increases with the complexity and richness of the context in which we find it' (1988, p. 134). This suggests that the authentic meanings of a work, which facilitate musical knowledge, are not necessarily found in the musical score itself, nor in the performance of the score, but in things which lie outside of the work, 'from an ideological context external to all its elements' (p. 135). The authentic meanings of a work, for Tomlinson, are not located in the music itself (the relation between the performance and the score) but in the discursive practices from which they emerge (pp. 135–6). Indeed, Tomlinson goes further than this and suggests that authentic meanings may be better revealed 'on the page', as it were, as opposed to by the performance or the score:

> There are deep and rewarding kinds of musical knowledge that involve neither the score nor its performance. The most profound and authentic meanings of music will not be found in the musical works themselves but behind them, in the varieties of discourse that give rise to them. The deepest interpretation of such meanings will spring from minds caught up in the mysterious and fundamentally human act of pondering the past. (p. 136)

Despite their differences, both Tomlinson and Taruskin (1995) argue against the orthodoxy of the historical performance movement, which insists that authenticity is to be found in the composer's intentions and the original audience's hearing of it, through the use of original instruments. By their different interpretative strategies, Tomlinson and Taruskin seek to open up the authenticity problematic by shifting the focus away from the creator's intentionality and towards historicity for the former and the act of performance for the latter.

Peter Kivy (1995), in his philosophical analysis of the construct of authenticity in musical performance, argues against a singular notion of authenticity. Instead he speaks of 'authenticities', which range from faithfulness to the composer's intentions, performance practice and original sound in the composer's lifetime to the performer's own self and his or her original way of playing. The first three meanings of authenticity pertain to original intentions, practice and sound, and these, according to Kivy, correspond to the orthodoxy of 'historical authenticity in musical performance' (1995, p. 5). For Taruskin (1995), the performer is not simply a vehicle through which the composer speaks but is an artist in his or her own right whose authentic understanding of the music is available through performance. Thus, Taruskin perceives a gap between the music and the score. Although Kivy (1995) rejects Taruskin's disregard for the composer's intentions, he agrees that there is a fundamental gap between the text (the score) and the object (the performance), which relates to his fourth sense of authenticity. Kivy's fourth sense of authenticity corresponds to Taruskin's idea that authenticity can only be found in the act of performance. Kivy argues:

> the gap between 'text' and 'performance' is not only a necessary evil but at the same time a *desired, intended* and logically *required* ontological fact. It is in that gap that the work of art is produced that we call the 'performance', and that I have likened to an 'arrangement' of the work. It is that gap that personal authenticity can either be or not be. (1995, p. 272)

Within the framework of historically authentic music, the gap between the text and act is of a different order from that indicated above. Kivy argues that within historically authentic music the construct of 'performance' given above, which implies a notion of the performer as collaborator, is reduced to that of 'production'. In the final analysis, because it brackets out the interpretative act of performing, the 'quest for the historically authentic performance is a quest for closure' (ibid.).

The preceding discussion offered four variations of the meaning of authenticity. First, from the perspective of the historical music performance movement, authenticity is achieved by replicating the composer's intentions and the original sounds. Second, from Taruskin's viewpoint, authenticity resides in the performer's imaginative act. Third, from Tomlinson's post-positive perspective, authentic meanings are located in the multiple, contextual meanings and discourses that lie outside of the work. Fourth, according to Kivy (1993, 1995), authenticities may be sought in a variety of factors. These varieties of authenticities provide a basis for pursuing our discussion of reconstruction in modern dance. With these viewpoints in mind, we can now return to Main's (1995) notion of dance *as it was* and dance *as it is*, which was touched on earlier in the chapter.

Dance *as it was*

The idea of reconstructing a dance *as it was*, that is, not tampering with it, retaining its original condition, resonates strongly with the quest for authenticity with regard to historical music. In her discussion of the three dance solos by Humphrey cited earlier, Main (1995) suggests that the dances were performed as they would have been at the time of their making. Ernestine Stodelle did not update the costumes or the movement to suit contemporary audiences, we are told, but, rather, reconstructed them in accordance with the way in which they were originally conceived and performed. If we transpose the criteria set out by the historical music movement onto dance, these dances could be said to conform to that restricted sense of authenticity. These solos, according to Main, constituted a 'living illustration' (1995, p. 14), of Humphrey's choreography in the late 1920s and early 1930s. Although there is a close relationship between music and dance, the music/dance analogy does not fit completely (Ryman, 1992). It may be that the differences between the two forms are sufficient to render the idea of performing a dance *as it was* an impossible pursuit from the outset.

In western music, performers and conductors can have access to the composer's score, which they can read, learn and interpret, because there is a 'universally' accepted way of writing western music which is part and parcel of musical education. The same cannot be said of western dance, despite the fact that there have been numerous attempts to devise a form of movement notation for over five centuries (Hutchinson, 1977). Music and dance, as the choreographer Merce Cunningham (1985) has pointed out, share time in common, but dance exists in both time and space. A viable dance notation, unlike its musical counterpart, has the problem of incorporating the third dimension (space) into its scoring frame. Significant advances in the development of dance notation have been made in the past century. As a result, notated scores have come to be used increasingly 'as the basis for enabling dancers to perform works with which they have had no personal contact' (Van Zile, 1985–6, p. 41), although these scores are not without problems (see Hutchinson Guest, 1984). As Judy Van Zile (1985–6) has pointed out, choreographers, unlike composers, seldom create their own dance score, and dancers, unlike musicians, are not generally 'literate' in movement notation. Therefore, choreographers generally need to rely on a notation expert if they wish to have the work scored. This raises the consideration of whether the score is an accurate translation of the choreographer's intentions or a reflection of the notator's interpretations of the choreographer's intentions, a second-hand construct in social research terms (Geertz, 1989). Does it mean that the score is less accurate because someone other than the choreographer has notated it, as opposed to the usual method of passing down dances from dancer to dancer?

As a consequence of the lack of dance literacy, the majority of dancers, unlike their counterparts in music, cannot take their parts home to learn and come in prepared to work with the director or the choreographer with a view to generating a performance. Accordingly, as Van Zile notes, dancers have to be 'taught' their parts by the 'choreographer, a rehearsal coach, another dancer, or a "translator" – most frequently referred to by Labanotation practitioners as "reconstructor" – who, in effect, personally translates every instruction provided in a notated score' (1985–6, p. 41).[8] When a dance is scored by someone other than the choreographer and mounted on the dancers by a notator/reconstructor who reads from the score, there is a sense in which the notator/reconstructor is placed in a privileged relation to the choreographer and the dancer. The dance, in effect, becomes fixed in the score which itself is constructed through a process of interpretation. As in the debates surrounding the limits of authenticity in musicology, dance scholarship in the 1980s seemed to be caught up in questioning how much interpretation of the dance work was possible or appropriate in notation and reconstruction. Some considered the score sacred (Hutchinson Guest, 1991) – that it contained the 'essence' of the work (see Topaz in Copeland, 1994). From this position, the dance work, in effect, is the score. This fixing of dance in the score seems to run counter to the evanescent character of dance in performance (see Siegel, 1968; Croce, 1977; Sheets-Johnstone, 1979). It also presupposes that the system of notation, which in the cases cited above is Labanotation, is complete enough to record all the complexities of the form and content.

A similar scenario may be said to exist in regard to the filming of dance. As film and video technologies become more readily available and comparatively cheap, so more dances are being recorded for training purposes and/or for televising. The 'documentary' film, that attempts to show the whole dance on the stage through a single camera, as Siegel (1993, p. 23) has pointed out, 'is invaluable to students and researchers hunting elusive lost dances', but it seldom equates to public broadcasting standards. Moreover, the idea of documentary film as a 'living record' in itself has increasingly been called into question and is viewed as a construction:

> In the past few years, there has been a growing acknowledgement that films and pictures needn't be merely expedient reflections of dance; they can in fact do their own dance. (Ibid.)

The way in which the dance is shot, of course, positions the gaze of the audience in a more fixed manner than a live performance. In live performance, audience members have more freedom to decide what they wish to focus on and to redirect their gaze, to edit and cut at will. Although a number of choreographers such as Merce Cunningham and Twyla Tharp have taken up the challenge of creating dance works for the camera, choreography is still mostly created to be performed live and to be entered into the repertory of a dance company (Brooks, 1993, p. 25). As the foregone discussion has demonstrated, the task of maintaining a 'living' choreographic record is so enormous that the majority of dance works of the past have been lost. Moreover, the early modern dancers and the majority of contemporary choreographers, for the most part, have been much more concerned with developing new works than in reworking old ones.

As dance becomes more readily available through video and television, so the experience of dance for a large number of viewers comes to reside in the recorded image rather than the live performance. Let me give an example here. As part of my research on the relationship between modern dance and the other arts in America in the inter-World War years, I made a detailed study of a section from *Appalachian Spring* (1944) which was choreographed by Martha Graham. The analysis of *Appalachian Spring* (see Thomas, 1995, pp. 149–63) was largely based on a close examination of a film made in 1976 and, for comparative purposes, an earlier film made in 1958. When the Martha Graham Company performed in London in 1999 they revived a number of Graham's earlier works, including *Appalachian Spring*. During the performance of the dance, as it was unfolding before my eyes, I found myself comparing and contrasting the dance with the 1976 film of the dance and not a previous live performance I had seen many years before. In this instance the film had become fixed, it suddenly took on the status of the original, *it was* the dance, and at the same time, the performance took on the character of the copy, the quality of which was measured against the film. This is a kind of reversal of the 'aura' of the work of art within the era of technological reproducibility of which Benjamin (1973) wrote; I shall return to this later in the chapter.

The idea that the dance reconstructor takes the choreographer's intended dance off the page and puts it on the stage operates on the positivist premise of the picture theory of truth, which, as Tomlinson (1988) has argued in regard to music, has long been questioned and found lacking. This view does lurk around in the shadows and emerges on a fairly regular basis in music and in dance. For example, the view that dancers can be 'taught' their parts, as Van Zile (1985–6) indicates, implies that they are passive recipients, the instruments through which the choreographic artist or 'oracle' speaks, as opposed to being interpretative artists, as Taruskin's (1995) equivalent stance in music proposes. The notion of the separation of the performer and the artist, as Amy Koritz's (1995) fascinating study of dance and literature in early twentieth-century England demonstrates, was not entirely innocent. It was set in motion at that time through a series of shifts in aesthetic ideology which were given impetus by the emergent canons of symbolism and modernism and which were also tied in with shifts in gender and class ideologies. Koritz notes that as the stigma attached to women performers diminished around the turn of the century, space was opened for the entry of middle-class women onto the stage.[9] This freedom to perform without being thoroughly stigmatised was accompanied by the gradual devaluing of the performer as artist. Ultimately, the performer came to be viewed as a vehicle through which the creator's/author's/choreographer's genius could be transmitted to the audience. The separation of the performer from the artist was in line with tendencies to incorporate aesthetic theories and values from the non-performing arts, which denied the authority of the performer, into the theatre and which in turn enabled the theatre to gain more 'artistic' status. In the case of dance, following the impetus given in other arts, that genius came increasingly to reside in the 'increased status of a male-dominated hierarchy of creators or "authors" of the ballet production' (Koritz, 1995, p. 3).[10]

The separation of the artist from the performer assisted the ascendancy of Sergei Diaghilev's Russian ballet to the position of an elite art form, with increasing precedence being given to choreographers/dancers like Vaslav Nijinsky and Léonide Massine. At the same time, it restricted the careers of early modern dancers such as Isadora Duncan, Maud Allan and Ruth St Denis on the English stage. In American modern dance, the separation between choreographer and dancer was not quite as striking in the initial stages of its development, perhaps, in part, because performers like Martha Graham and particularly Doris Humphrey were valued as choreographers (creators) as well as dancers. As it became more established, however, the status of the choreographer increased at the expense of the dancer as artist, so that dancers came to be identified with the work of particular choreographers. Dancers of today have to be much more flexible (see Berg, 1993; Main, 1995; Foster, 1997). As indicated in the previous chapter, professional dancers are required to work with many more choreographic styles than in the past. Nevertheless, apart from a handful of star performers in the transnational world of ballet,[11] the work tends to be treated as the property right of the choreographer. Despite the fact that the symbolic capital came to reside in the choreographer's work, in practice, that is, in production and performance, it may be argued that the choreographer and the dancer(s) were and are co-creators. As Ann Dils has argued:

> The process of choreography, of working with dancers, is as important to the dance as its formal elements, those attributes such as spatial structure and relationship to a musical score. (1993, p. 223)

Dils's perspective offers a more flexible and perhaps realistic view of reconstruction and the choreographic process than the more restricted sense discussed above.

Dance *as it is*/dance *as it was*

In her discussion of two different approaches to reconstructing two choreographic works by Doris Humphrey which were performed in 1989 and 1990, Dils makes the point that Humphrey's dances are not hers alone and that dancers, both past and present, are co-authors of the work.[12] Recognition of this, according to Dils, 'can provide greater clarity, and a critical sense of play and experimentation in reconstruction' (1993, p. 223). Ray Cook, a professional Labanotator and reconstructor, prefers to use the term 'dance director' to describe his role in the process of bringing into performance past or lost dances, in an attempt to shift the focus away from the 'truth as copy' version of reconstruction. Dils describes Cook's reconstruction process of Humphrey's *Dawn in New York*,[13] which was created in 1956, as 'a compelling scavenger hunt, an act of scholarship and an artistic venture' (1993, p. 224). This process is similar to that employed by Millicent Hodson and Kenneth Archer in their recovery of Nijinsky's lost dance, *Le Sacre du Printemps* (1913) for the Joffrey Ballet in 1987 (see Archer and Hodson, 1994). However, although Dils suggests that Cook seeks to achieve 'a balanced interpretation of the work' (1993, p. 224), it should be noted that Archer and Hodson (1994, p. 103) maintain that their aim is to 'reconstruct the original ballet, as it was performed on the opening night'.[14]

For his reconstruction of *Dawn in New York*, Cook used a variety of resources including an unfinished Labanotation score, photographs, reviews of the work at the time of performance, interviews with dancers who were cast in the work and Humphrey's writings. Cook had to find a way of filling in the movement that was missing in the score and completing the final five minutes of the work (Cook, 1990). As he 'fleshed out the dance' (Dils, 1993, p. 224), the dancers were encouraged to 'contribute movement phrases based on imagery and the previously established movement' (ibid.), providing another example of how dancers contribute to a work. In certain respects, this co-authoring is reminiscent of the way in which Ferdinand de Saussure's *Course in General Linguistics* was 'put together from the lecture notes of students, who thought that the master's teaching should not be lost' (Culler, 1976, pp. xvi–xvii), and the manner in which George Herbert Mead's students compiled his ideas in *Mind, Self and Society* (1934).

Dils considers that 'Cook created a thought provoking reconstruction and a successful performance' because he took into account 'performative as well as structural elements' (1993, p. 225). Thus, he was not operating on the basis of a 'choreographic archaeology' (Rosenstein, cited in Dils, 1993, p. 225) but was seeking to bring together these fragmented elements of a past dance, to bring the dance to life in the present. There is a strong sense in which this corresponds to Main's notion of dance *as it is*, as indicated earlier in the chapter. Cook is as much a collaborator in the work as the past and present dancers. However, it should be noted that he did not attempt to fit the movement style to the bodies of the contemporary dancers he was working with. Rather, two former dancers who had been members of the Juilliard casts came in to coach the dancers in the Humphrey movement style of the 1950s with which contemporary dancers are unfamiliar. As discussed in the previous chapter, dancing bodies and techniques change over time and what would be considered routine, everyday movement techniques for dancers from a former era may be utterly foreign to present-day dancers. Dils makes the point that initially the dancers were 'uncomfortable' as they were encouraged to work in 'the non-contemporary style of exaggeration in modern dance' (1993, p. 224). So the dancers had to de-familiarise their bodies from their taken-for-granted body techniques to realise and 'make familiar' the unfamiliar movement qualities of older modern dance, that is, to incorporate them into their bodily habitus. Dils comments that once they had assimilated the exaggerated movement qualities into their bodies, a 'clarity of movement' resulted that enabled her to 'see things in *Dawn in New York* that might not have been apparent with a more contemporary performance approach' (ibid.). What is interesting, here, is that it indicates a process of not simply dance *as it is*, but also an attempt to realise dance *as it was*. So there is still a sense of recovering the past work even as there is a vivid presentness in performance.

It is clear from Main's article (1995) and her interview (1997) that she considers that even those past dances which transcend their time and can be categorised in terms of dance *as it is* also require a very strong dose of authenticity in terms of dance *as it was* when they are brought back into performance. Like Cook, Main also calls herself a dance director. This she perceives to be different from the efforts of Ernestine Stodelle, her teacher and mentor, to bring back the three early Humphrey solos cited at the beginning of the chapter, which are better seen as recreations:

> Ernestine [Stodelle] calls what she does 're-creating'. But that involved bringing the pieces [the solos] back ... from nothing, from old film archives and notes and things. (Main, interview, 1997)

Cook's recovery of *Dawn in New York*, from Main's perspective, would also seem to fall into the recreation category. As indicated above, Humphrey worked with her dancers in a collaborative manner and as a result her dances can be viewed in terms of what Rosalind Krauss has defined as 'compound artworks' (cited in Dils, 1993, p. 223). It will be recalled that Stodelle was performing with the Humphrey–Wiedman group at the time the solos were made. She had, then, direct 'experiential' bodily knowledge of the dances themselves, the ways in which Humphrey worked, and as a dancer in the company, she would have been integral to that collaborative enterprise. For Main, this further authenticates Stodelle's reconstruction of these Humphrey solos as dance *as it was*. Dance directors like Main, who do not have first-hand knowledge of working with the original choreographer, have more resources at their disposal because of the foundational work that 'original' dancers such as Stodelle have done on Humphrey's work. Interestingly, as indicated above, Stodelle was Main's teacher and in the past she has also staged Humphrey dances, such as *Water Study* (1928), with Stodelle. This, in turn, suggests that Main also has a line of access to Humphrey's work via her teacher and mentor and Main implied as much in the 1997 interview.

In the interview, Main insisted that directors must be 'knowledgeable in the style'. Style cannot be fully revealed through the score because 'the score can't record style'. This access to what Taruskin (1995) refers to as 'the oracle' (the composer or choreographer) extends to Main preferring the scores of Humphrey's dances that were constructed by former company members like Stodelle, Eleanor King and Lucy Venable. Main considers that the score can only be a starting point, because the system (Labanotation) cannot record the complexities of a dance for a performance. Nevertheless, she still insists that some scores have a 'greater feel of the movement style', because the notators had also been performers in the company. In other words, they have a greater sense of authenticity. But the real clues to getting to the 'heart of a piece', according to Main (interview, 1997), are to be found, first, by following what Humphrey herself said about it in her notes and in her writing; second, through consultation with the dancers such as Stodelle and King who performed in the piece; and third, by attending to what they have written about it. This could imply that choreographers remain consistent over time in their approach to a work and that the original dancers' recollection of the work is also consistent over many years in terms of their movement memories and dance context. It further raises questions about which performance of a work, if any, may be said to constitute *the* work. When asked if the method of drawing on the memories of the first generation of Humphrey dancers had drawbacks in terms of fading or changing memories, Main responded:

> It does, and you have to take that into account. You're not going to get anything hard and fast from someone who's eighty-five because she danced these pieces sixty years ago, but you'll get what she feels about them, what's still in her. Even though it's changed over the years, you get *clues*; all you're going to get is clues. (Interview, 1997)

Whilst there is recognition that memories do fade, the words also indicate that the kernel of what 'really' was is retained within the former dancing self. This further implies that there is still an authenticity of the self at work. I would suggest that the notion of memories being put forward here refers to kinaesthetic memories which have been incorporated in the dancer's bodily habitus, although Main did not discuss what the dancer retains within herself in this way. In addition, individual bodies change over time and the older or former generation of dancers will not have the technical competence that they once had when they were performing those now lost or forgotten dances. Despite this, it is almost always taken for granted that the dancers' experiential knowledge of the dances, which is contained in their movement memories, is potentially recoverable. That is, even though they can no longer do it, the knowledge of how it was done is contained within them and can be brought out in, say, the context of the rehearsal studio. In this way they become invaluable, authenticated resources for assisting the reconstructor or dance director to piece together parts of the lost dance which is to be resurrected, and/or for assisting the dancers who are to perform the work to bring their past roles to life in an authentic manner (Cook, 1990).

As indicated earlier, Main (1995) considers that Humphrey's *Passacaglia* (1938)[15] is one of those dances that can potentially transcend their time and place of creation and performance and have relevance for a contemporary audience.[16] The dance provides an insight into 'the development of Humphrey's movement style of the 1930s, particularly her noted use of the ensemble' (Main, 1995, p. 14). Main suggests that the ideals of humanism and the emphasis on group cooperation, which Humphrey sought to convey in her work and which are evidenced in *Passacaglia*, transcend their time. Humphrey expressed these ideals in her published letter to John Martin, the critic for the *New York Times* in 1943, who had criticised her for putting on an all-Bach programme of dances that season.

> Now is the time for me to tell of the nobility that the human spirit is capable of, stress the grace that is in us, give the dancers a chance to move harmoniously with each other, say, in my small way, there is hope as long as corners remain where utility fails. (Humphrey in Cohen, 1972, p. 256)

The 'nobility of the human spirit' is also given voice through her technique of 'fall and recovery', the 'arc between two deaths', the 'dynamic fluctuation between resistance to and giving in to and rebound from gravity', which for Humphrey constituted the 'very core of all movement' (1959, p. 106):

> All life fluctuates between resistance to and the yielding to gravity... There are two still points in the physical life: the motionless body, in which thousands of adjustments for keeping it erect are invisible, and the horizontal, the last stillness. Life and dance exists between these two points and therefore form the arc between two deaths. (Ibid.)

Main considers that both the humanist sentiments expressed in Humphrey's words, and the 'endless possibilities' contained within 'fall and recovery' – 'the eternal optimism coupled with the danger and drama' – have relevance for today (1995, p. 14). Other writers, such as Selma Jeanne Cohen (1972) and John Mueller (1974), suggest that the sentiments Humphrey sought to realise through her work were already becoming out of date in the artistic climate of the 1950s. Despite this, Mueller considers that 'Passacaglia is fully capable of communicating to a modern audience – of being profoundly moving in fact' (1974, p. 25). Its power lies in the 'careful craftsmanship' (ibid.), its theatricality and its uncompromising movement style that resisted, according to Siegel, 'the time-honored forms of ballet' (1979, p. 91). Indeed, as Siegel points out, contemporary modern dancers often find the movement 'unnatural' because the 'balletic line is so ingrained and the sense of weight is so habitually avoided' (1979, p. 98). As discussed earlier, the dancers who were working on the reconstruction of *Dawn in New York* also initially found some of the movement uncomfortable for their modern bodies. While Siegel implies that the polemic that is contained in Passacaglia can often make today's dancers uncomfortable, Mueller (1974) considers that it can be appreciated as 'an abstract movement statement' without making explicit Humphrey's programme. This is because the drama is not located in terms of a narrative plot or referential movement, but, rather, through the kinetic possibilities unleashed in the idea of the 'arc between two deaths'.

Although Main suggested in the 1997 interview that when she starts directing a Humphrey work such as Passacaglia she wants it to be 'of

Humphrey' and not the 'imagination', she nevertheless will alter certain aspects of the dance if she considers them to be anachronistic to contemporary audiences. She is prepared to make 'legitimate' adjustments to the work because of the constraints of different performance spaces, and to update or change the costumes, if appropriate. When directing *Passacaglia*, Main allowed the female soloist to perform the ending of the solo section in a slightly different way than Main herself had performed it some years before on the basis of the Labanotation score. Although the solo was not very different, it was 'right' for the dancer and instead of continuously correcting her 'it made sense to leave it with her, because it just felt right' (interview, 1997). This approach resonates with that of Cook (1990) discussed above. The director and the dancers are to a certain extent co-authors of the work, but at the same time, the performance has to be rooted in the authentic character of the choreographer's work and movement style. Such an approach, then, locates itself in terms of dance *as it is* and, at the same time, dance *as it was*; that is, the coexistence of interpretivity and authenticity, which, at least, retains the gap between performer and text that Kivy (1995) argues is crucial to 'performance', as opposed to that of (re)production, which is constituted through closure.

Dance *as it is*

While recent interest in reconstructing lost or past dances has centred on early modern dance of the twentieth century, such as Isadora Duncan and modernist experimentalists such as Graham, Nijinsky and Humphrey, there has been a longer-term interest in the subject of baroque dance, or pre-classic dance forms. As Mark Franko (1993) has pointed out, it is hardly surprising that these particular periods have been chosen as important because each in its own way points to the beginnings of different kinds of dance genres. The dances of the Italian and French courts, for example, are generally viewed to have formed the basis for the development of classical ballet. Early twentieth-century modern dance artists, such as Isadora Duncan and Ruth St Denis are usually treated as the precursors to the development of modern dance and subsequently postmodern dance.

The old-fashioned approach to reconstruction sought to replicate the dances of past eras and stage them in a literal manner. In the 1980s, this approach gave way to more innovative practices in which the thematic content and structure of particular dances were given a theatrical edge, which afforded them a living presence as opposed to mere imitation. The Humphrey reconstructions discussed above and the imaginative reconstructions of Duncan's work by performers such as Annabelle Gamson (1993) exemplify this shift in perspective. Franko suggests that the era of baroque dance, which 'served as a springboard for modernist experimentation', can 'take on an added meaning' (1993, p. 134) now, when the canons of modernism itself have been called into question by postmodernism and deconstruction:

> it is through our newly gained distance from the historical avantgardes of the twentieth century that the baroque period crystallises in its historical significance. In periods of transition, it is important to look back to our origins: our historical perspective on modernism presupposes a more acute sense of the radicality of the baroque. (Ibid.)

Franko maintains that it is not sufficient simply to consider the implications of conventional reconstruction strategies as outlined above, we also need to consider reconstruction in relation to postmodern art, particularly the way in which the latter signals or makes reference to former periods. In so doing, we might enquire if the concern with recycling and the appeal of retro within postmodernism offer a radical critique of the modern, or if these are simply empty gestures that constitute a nostalgic return to the past.

Perhaps we can make sense of this more readily if we consider briefly the example of fashion. Fashion is one of those cultural systems that continually reappropriates dress codes and aspects of style from the past and reformulates them into the new mode. Thus, contemporary designers find innovation in the old specifically to generate a new mode of dress or fashion. In this way, we may say that nothing is simply recycled or reproduced as it once was, rather it is transformed into something new which might contain references to the old. The tendency in historicism, as Franko points out, is not to see the new in the old, but rather to see the old in the new, which affirms the notion of continuity in the cycle of tradition and revolution in art. Reconstruction's 'master conceit', according to Franko, 'is to evoke what no longer is, with the means that are present' (1993, p. 135). In an attempt to counter this historicist tendency, Franko argues for the notion of construction through deconstruction, as opposed to reconstruction or replication in dance:

> Construction sacrifices the reproduction of a work to the replication of its more powerful intended effects. (Ibid.)

Franko's method of constructive choreography in his own work, *Harmony of Spheres* (1987), which took its impetus from an early baroque ballet, was to construct through deconstruction and, as a result, to reinvent a work. For Franko, the constructionist approach is 'forward looking in its utopian vision of an unattainable form of theatre. It generates manifestos' (1993, p. 150). The project of reconstruction, however, he argues, is 'reactionary, seeking the truth in its own "still-life" reproduction. It generates performance museums' (pp. 150–1).

Franko's polemic against construction focuses on the issue of 'repeatability' rather than authenticity. He argues that the desire for repeatability is underpinned by a tradition of theatrical theory from Diderot to Edward Gordon Craig and that this has been an impetus for the reconstruction project. This positivist notion of repeatability needs to be replaced with a kind of dance theorising, which he associates with what Susan Foster (1986) has called 'writing dancing'. Let loose from the chains of repeatability, 'construction can practice cultural critique as a form of active theorising on dance history. It consists of inscribing the plurality of visions restoring, conceptualising and/or inventing the act' (Franko, 1993, p. 152).

Although Franko views the reconstruction project as retrogressive, other dance scholars have developed an innovative approach to reconstruction. Susan Manning (1993a), for example, uses the word to refer to her insightful yet rigorous 'on the page' reconstructions of the work of Mary Wigman (Manning, 1993b) and Martha Graham (Manning, 1996). Manning (1993b) makes a distinction between the notion of reconstruction and revival. The former mostly involves the notated score or film while the latter involves oral transmission from dancer to dancer. These two positions are not treated as binary opposites but, rather, as operating on a continuum. Although the term 'reconstruction' is usually associated with reconstructions for the stage, Manning considers that there are points of convergence between reconstructions for the stage and her own reconstructions 'on the page'.

Both dancer and scholar have access to the same kinds of 'evidence', oral, kinetic and archival sources. The dancer coalesces 'these sources of evidence in the studio' (Manning, 1993b, p. 16), striving towards a performance that works in kinaesthetic and theatrical terms. The scholar brings together the same sources 'in the study', with a view to generating 'a descriptive account that supports a theoretical argument and a historical inquiry' (ibid.). Although their ends are different, the dancer and the scholar, Manning argues, operate along a continuum in terms of 'shared assumptions about authenticity and identity of dance reconstruction' (ibid.) and not in opposition. At one end of the continuum is the concern to get as close to the original (however that is defined) as possible, whilst the other end of the continuum stresses the inevitability of interpretation in reconstruction. The procedure of the former, according to Manning, is exemplified in Hodson's and Archer's reconstruction of Nijinsky's *Le Sacre du Printemps* (1913) for the stage and in Siegel's vivid descriptions of dance 'on the page' in *The Shapes of Change* (1979). Manning's own reconstructions on the page have veered towards the interpretative end of the continuum and thus highlight her 'intervention in the process of reconstruction' (1993a, p. 16). Manning operates on the basis that the scholar should reveal the grounds of his or her reconstruction speech act, which means that the scholar should proceed with a strong sense of reflexivity. This textual approach to 'performance on the page' resonates with Tomlinson's (1988) post-positivist non-performance version of reconstruction in musicology. Whilst it is not as radical as the deconstructive approach to construction favoured by Franko (1993), Manning's approach prods the process of reconstruction one step further along the interpretative pathway than that taken by Cook (1990), Dils (1993) and Main (interview, 1997) discussed above.

'Performance museums' and lived traditions

The foregone discussion provides an overview of some of the key issues surrounding dance reconstruction and offers a range of approaches to retrieving lost dances. Although most reconstructors now recognise that there is at least some interpretation involved in the process, the concern for authenticity and making 'real' the work of the choreographer remains dominant. This approach is expressed clearly by Jill Beck (Topaz, 1988), who considers that the task of the 'dance director' is to maintain the essence of the piece. By this, she means that the vision of the choreographer should be brought to life, and that this process is dependent on intuiting the ideas of the choreographer. For the most part, the drive in the 1980s and 1990s to reconstruct dances of the early modernist era, as Sally Ann Kriegsman (1993, p. 15) has pointed out, centred on a concern for continuity and 'to fill in the blanks' of the story of dance. But this sense of continuity (or evolution) was alien to the modern dancers who sought to break with the very idea of tradition. Moreover, American modern dance, as John Martin (1965) indicated, did not constitute a system, but was founded on the creative interests and practices of particular individuals. Consequently, it may be argued that any reconstruction or restaging of modern dance works refers back to the creators, *not* the tradition. That is, it is the 'aura' of the individual creator that is invoked in modern dance reconstructions, as opposed to the idea of a tradition. Walter Benjamin, in his important and much-quoted essay on 'mechanical reproduction', or more accurately 'technical reproducibility' (Foster, 1997, p. 218), defines the concept of the aura as 'a unique phenomenon of difference, however close it may be' (Benjamin, 1973, p. 224). The aura, according to Benjamin, is distant, unapproachable, the very opposite of closeness; its unapproachability constitutes a 'major quality of the cult image. True to its nature, it remains "distant, however close it may be" ' (ibid., p. 245).

'The presence of the original', for Benjamin (1973, p. 222), 'is the prerequisite to the concept of authenticity'. Developments in technical reproducibility in writing and photography and film in particular in the late nineteenth and early twentieth century destabilised the sanctity and authority of the work of art. Technical reproduction, according to Benjamin, displaced the authority of the original because it was largely independent of it. That is, technical reproduction detached the reproduced object from its domain of authority. By making many objects from the one, technical reproduction substituted plurality for uniqueness. In bringing things closer, technical reproducibility encompassed a democratising spirit capable of shattering the sanctity of the aura. The work of art becomes, in contemporary life, a work that is capable of being reproduced. We can, for example, make any number of prints from a negative and it becomes pointless to ask which is the original, just as it becomes useless to ask whose dance is this (alone). In the case of fine art, the market value accorded to the original 'one-off', signed and authenticated 'art' work of a past, present or future 'master' has increased exponentially with developments in reproductive technologies.

The extended use of film or notated scores of modern dance could contain a democratising spirit, in so far as their usage offers the possibility of transmitting a sense of tradition for future generations, which is necessary for cultural reproduction (Williams, 1981). As James Pernod has indicated, the practice of dance reconstruction has become a 'cultivated addition to the curriculum in a large number of dance departments in the US today' (Pernod and Ginsberg, 1997, p. 4). The result is that 'knowledge of our dance heritage', in kinaesthetic, visual and cultural terms, 'informs and gives meaning and context to the dance works being created today' (ibid.). But, and this is a very important 'but', the strength of this democratising spirit is largely dependent upon the concept of reproduction that is being invoked.

The idea of producing an exact copy along the lines of technical or mechanical reproduction, as Raymond Williams (1981) has pointed out, can lead to the ossification of a *lived* tradition. In turn, it could lead to the reinforcement of what Lincoln Kirstein aptly termed the 'apostolic succession' in dance (cited in Garafola, 1993, p. 168), or as Franko (1995, p. ix) put it following Lyotard, the 'modern-dance master narrative'. In this case, rather than the aura being jeopardised by reproduction, it becomes sanctified. This construct of reproduction leaves little room for the emergence of different possible readings of choreographic voices of the past to be viewed from the standpoint of a history of the present (Foucault, 1986). Nor does it invite a critical approach to the creation and establishment of a dance canon, in light of who or what gets recorded or does not get recorded.

The idea of 'genetic reproduction' that Williams (1981) favours as a metaphor for the transmission of culture is more hopeful. It offers the possibility of conjoining tradition and innovation, of making anew.[17] This does not invoke the notion of 'performance museums', but, rather, the possibility of generating *lived* and *living* traditions. It is arguable that dance's difference and power lies in its non-reproducibility (Phelan, 1993), as a consequence of its existence at the 'vanishing point', to quote Siegel (1968, p. 1) once more. To a large extent Benjamin would agree with this. In an endnote, he states that from his perspective, the 'poorest provincial staging of Faust is superior to a Faust film in that, ideally, it competes with the first performance at Weimar' (1973, p. 245). The implication of this is that the first per-formance, for Benjamin, is the yardstick by which all subsequent per-formances are measured. Thus, the 'aura' of the work is left intact, while subsequent performances remain mere shadows of the original.

Throughout this chapter, it has been shown that there are a range of possibilities between authenticity at one end of the scale and interpre-tivity at the other for reconstructing, recreating, reinventing, directing or retrieving dances from former eras. It is important to note that the choices that are made in reconstructing 'an event that disappears in the very act of materializing' (Siegel, 1968, p. 1) are not only practical but are underpinned by theoretical frames. These frames reflect how the reconstructor positions him/herself on the scale of authenticity and interpretivity.

Dance often looks longingly at other art forms that leave sustainable evidence of their pasts. Feminist art historians have clearly demon-strated just how partial the tradition of art is and the ways in which women artists have been systematically written out of it (Parker and Pollock, 1981). Feminist art history's concern to recover lost, passed over or silenced women artists, according to Griselda Pollock, entails 'a double project':

The historical recovery of data about women producers of art coexists with and is only critically possible through a concomitant deconstruction of the discourses and practices of art history itself. (Pollock, 1988, p. 55)

Pollock's comments could equally apply to the recovery of lost or past dances. The dance reconstruction project must go hand in hand with the deconstruction of discourses and practices in dance history itself.

In the following chapter, I will consider the discourses on representations of gender and sexuality in recent approaches to dance history and dance anthropology, which have been influenced by feminist and poststructuralist perspectives.

Chapter 6

Dance and Difference: Performing/ Representing/Rewriting the Body

Introduction

Feminist scholarship, as indicated in Chapter 4, has had a major impact in dance studies since the late 1980s, as have recent debates on the body in social and cultural theory. The influence of feminist discourses is perhaps most evident in the study of western theatrical dance forms. This is hardly surprising, given that the body is generally the primary means of expression and representation in western dance and the majority of performers are women. Moreover, the majority of dance scholars are women. As indicated in previous chapters, this traffic has been largely one-way from feminism to dance studies (see Thomas, 1993a; Foster, 1997; Desmond, 1998). Relations between gender and dance have also surfaced in studies of social dance. The first half of this chapter centres on a discussion of gender, race, sexuality and dance in four ethnographic studies of social dance. This provides a more empirical focus and extends the examination of gender in the direction of race and sexuality. Attention is then directed towards a consideration of the ways in which representations of women and sexuality in dance have been analysed in recent studies in dance history. Finally, I consider the often unquestioned linking of dance with liberation or resistance and, by extension, the feminine, in certain dance studies approaches and contemporary cultural criticism.

Exoticism, eroticism and auto-eroticism

Anthropological studies of dance have long featured the dances or movement systems of males and those of females (see Hanna, 1987, for an extensive cross-cultural survey of these studies). Surprisingly, as Susan Reed (1998) has noted, the debates on gender which took place in anthropology in the 1970s and which were addressed in Chapter 3 seldom found their way into these ethnographic studies. In the late 1980s, in the wake of the turn to postmodern ethnography in anthropology, women ethnographers and anthropologists were debating the pros and cons of developing a feminist ethnography. The pursuit of a feminist dance anthropology or ethnography, however, was not exactly a top priority for the majority of dance anthropologists at that time. Even Hanna's (1987) ambitious cross-cultural study of *Dance, Sex and Gender*, despite the tantalising words 'identity', 'desire' and 'sexuality' contained in the subtitle, displayed little evidence of engagement with debates in the field on gender and sexuality at the time of writing, as a cursory glance at the extensive bibliography at the end of the book reveals. Having said this, over the past twenty years, anthropological studies have made significant contributions to the 'politics of dance, and the relations between culture, body, and movement' (Reed, 1998, p. 505) and, clearly, gender and sexuality are strongly implicated in these. In so doing, a number of ethnographers, although by no means all, have drawn on approaches which were key to debates and developments in anthropology and other areas of social and cultural research in the 1980s: semiotics, poststructuralism, postmodernism, postcolonialism and feminism. These 'isms', in turn, contributed to the 'crisis in representation' (Boyne and Rattansi, 1990) in the social sciences and the humanities, which, in large part, led to a loosening of traditional disciplinary boundaries.

In an overview of dance anthropology over the past two decades, Reed (1998, p. 519) acknowledges that dance anthropologists have raised issues regarding gender and sexuality in the course of their inquiry (see Spencer, 1985; Wild, 1987; Kealiinohomoku, 1989; Grau, 1993), which point to the non-essentialist, performative, discursive character of gender identities. However, she notes that very few dance anthropologists have 'explicitly drawn on feminist approaches'. As suggested above, this is in contrast to dance historians who have argued that feminism and dance studies share much in common (see Daly, 1991; Manning, 1993a; Cooper Albright, 1997; Carter, 1998, 1999). It is possible that dance ethnographers have been concerned to analyse the dance forms in question in the context of a wider range of social issues; for instance, the politics of racial identity and class, as well as gender and sexuality. Gender, then, becomes one important factor among, but not necessarily separable from, others (for example, Meduri, 1988, 1996; Cowan, 1990; Novack, 1990; Daniel, 1991, 1995; Browning, 1995; Savigliano, 1995). That is, whilst these writers are feminist in orientation, they also incorporate other social factors into their analysis of social dance. Reed (1998, p. 50), for instance, considers that recent historical and anthropological research, such as Meduri's (1988, 1996), on *bharatha natyam* and the dances of the female temple dancers of South India, the *devadasis*, offer important insights 'into the ways in which identities of indigenous dancers shifted as they became implicated in the changing discourses of colonialism, nationalism and Orientalism'. Indeed, I would suggest that such studies are richer precisely because they make such interconnections[1] and this is a further reason for including this kind of work in the next section, which focuses on three Latin American dance ethnographies and an ethnography of a Trinidadian dance. For example, Yvonne Daniel's (1991, 1995) studies of the Cuban national dance, the *rumba*, reveal how idealised representations of gender difference are articulated in the dance, by means of a close analysis of the different movement qualities that men and women are required to exhibit in performance. Rumba, she argues, is a site for the men to 'exhibit strength, courage and bravado, while the women's dance is generally softer, subtler, more cautious and graceful' (Reed, 1998, p. 517). The central thrust of Daniel's studies, however, is directed towards political ideology, race and identity in Cuba.

Rumba, traditionally, was associated with black or 'dark-skinned' working-class people in Cuba. Before the revolution in 1959, both ballet and modern dance in Cuba were highly acclaimed nationally and accordingly occupied a higher status position than Cuban folkloric dances. The rumba was selected as *the* national dance of Cuba by the revolutionary government over other more popular forms, such as the conga and the son. This was because it was seen to encapsulate the ideals of equality and the African aspects of Cuban cultural heritage which the socialist state was seeking to promote.

Rumba, as Daniel notes, is both a 'dance/music tradition' and a secular 'event or celebration'. The 'rumba complex' (dance/music) is not a single dance and should not be confused with the ballroom version of the rumba, which is entirely different from traditional rumba, although it utilises 'traditional folkloric musical structure' (Daniel, 1991, p. 1). Through a detailed ethnographic account of the variety of contexts (historical and contemporary) in which a range of types of rumba are performed, along with verbal and notated descriptions (musical and Labanotation) of the different types, Daniel elucidates how the phenomenon of rumba can be viewed 'as an indicator of social conditions' and 'of governmental efforts to change social attitudes' (1995, p. 13).

The revolutionary government's attempts to appropriate the rumba as the symbol of an egalitarian, non-racial society holding firm against the outside (capitalist) world, as Daniel argues, have not been entirely successful. Daniel (1991) points to contradictions surrounding skin colour and class on the 'world view' level of analysis and the social and choreographic levels. For example, while the promotion of the rumba as a symbol of national identity entailed an acknowledgement of the country's debt to its African heritage and to contemporary 'dark-skinned' Cubans, the fact remains that rumba is mostly performed by 'dark-skinned' Cubans, 'with relatively little direct participation from other segments of society' (p. 1). Thus, despite government efforts to reeducate the people, the rumba is 'still identified with a non-prestigious group, the former lower class, and many Cubans do not readily adopt its practices' (p. 4).

Daniel's analysis of rumba also points to contradictions between female liberation and the culture of machismo in Cuba. The female dancer initially appears to be the focus of attention in rumba, 'giving the impression that she is dominant, powerful, in control, or at the very least, the central attracting figure' (p. 5). Close analysis of the movement and the choreographic types of rumba, however, reveal a rather different picture. In reality, it is the male who predominates and sets the pace of the (dance) action, exhibiting movement traits that are associated with nineteenth- and early twentieth-century machismo figures, particularly the 'free blacks and mulattos', who dressed in highly decorative, flashy clothes, rather like rumba dress today. Thus, 'race' is once again brought into play and at the same time erased. The women dancers 'react and respond' to the men's movement in the chase/courtship and rarely take up the offensive. Just as some women are entering the traditional masculine provinces as executives and managers in Cuba's economic sector, so they are making some minimal headway in rumba. Nowadays, as Daniel observes, women sometimes perform a particular type of rumba called 'columbia', which traditionally was danced only by men competing against each other. This offers a small window of opportunity for women dancers to 'express equal status and exhibit new power through rumba' (1991, p. 5). However, this is by no means the norm and, just as in the economic sphere, a culture of machismo in rumba lingers on amidst desires for a 'new egalitarian culture':

> Rumba is a performed contradiction in terms of dance, expressing both respect and honor for the sexes through courting/chasing sections and simultaneously expressing inequality and oppression through limited movement participation by women. (Ibid.)

Poststructualist and/or postcolonial theories, perhaps, constitute the most obvious influences in some recent ethnographic studies of dance (Ness, 1992, 1997; Browning, 1995; Savigliano, 1995), although feminist scholarship also informs the work. Barbara Browning, for example, in the final chapter of her ethnography of the Brazilian *samba*, invokes Judith Butler's (1993) construct of 'gender as performance' for her analysis of race, sexuality, exoticism and transvestism read through the spectacle of the Bahian carnival. However, poststructuralist literary studies constitute the theoretical backbone of the ethnography. Browning, who trained in literary analysis and African Brazilian dance, contends that her 'understanding of the significance of writing has been informed by dance and vice versa' (1995, p. xxiii). As with the Cuban samba, the Brazilian national dance should not be confused with its 'sanitised' ballroom version.

Browning's study is mapped out in a way that is usually associated with certain 'literary principles'. For instance, she 'reads the samba... as a form that narrates a history of cultural contact between Africans, Europeans and indigenous Brazilians' (1995, p. xxiii).[2] This narration is not enacted 'mimetically', but, rather, is 'compressed into a single musical phrase'. Thus, Browning rejects the realist, reflection theory, or dance-mirrors-society approach. Samba, for Browning, is a history 'without closure', as is the capoeira, an Afro-Brazilian dance/game/ martial art 'which embodies the history of racial struggle' (p. xiv) in Brazil and which is the subject of Browning's third chapter. Capoeira is 'played in a circle with musical accompaniment' with 'two players who try to take each other down, or otherwise dominate each other, while demonstrating mastery of movement' (Lewis, 1995, p. 222). Blacks in Brazil became skilled in capoeira to defend their communities, comprised of escaped slaves, from attack. As one might well imagine, Portuguese colonial power prohibited the practice. But it was practised subversively within a protected circle, with choreographic elements and music added to disguise 'a fight as a dance' (Browning, 1995, p. 91). Prohibition of capoeira remained in place many years after slavery was abolished in Brazil. In the academies where the capoeira is taught, students are reminded that as they are practising, they are 'also embodying a historical racial struggle' (p. xv). In this view, our bodily histories are not only entwined with our individual biographies and social location, as perhaps Bourdieu's (1977) approach suggests. Our bodily stories have a much longer history, as Elias (1978) argues, and these histories are not necessarily of our own making. Contemporary bodies are deeply marked by histories of race, class and gender (see Gilman, 1992; hooks, 1992). The 'story' (and there are many competing ones) of the capoeira, as Browning (1995) shows, is difficult to fix in 'descriptive writing' because 'its strategy is one of constant motion – both literal and figurative. Just when we ascribe a straightforward meaning to it, we find it is turning itself upside-down with self-irony' (p. xiv).

Becoming involved with the dances of *candomblé*, the 'African religious ceremonies in Brazil', led Browning to reconsider the grounds of her writing and authorship. Like the capoeira, the candomblé dances were suppressed in Brazil by the white authorities for many years. Browning argues that they only became sanctioned when it became noticeable that increasing numbers of white middle-class Brazilians were participating in them and the tourist industry spotted an opportunity to cash in on the 'exotic appeal' of the forms. The dances of the candomblé are 'understood to be embodiments ... of the principles of beliefs that bind a community together', in contrast to western dance where 'authorial innovation' (1995, p. xii) is viewed as an expression of the individual creator/performer. 'The [candomblé] dances', as Browning shows, 'rewrite the significance (including the sexed and sexualized significance) of the bodies that actualize them' (p. xxiv). In order to write 'significantly' about candomblé dance choreographies, Browning sensed that she had to give up her 'authorial' (literary, western) voice and write in the service of the divine sources that bestowed meaning upon them.[3]

In Cuba, as Daniel's (1995) ethnography of rumba demonstrates, the socialist government has sought to abolish or erase racism and class divisions by means of statutes and reeducation, but they live on and are articulated in the rumba. Brazil is often heralded as a culture where observable inequalities are not founded on racial discrimination but on class differences. Browning argues that there has been in effect an 'erasure of race' from the political agenda, from the time of abolition of slavery in Brazil in 1888 when the historical records relating to slavery were destroyed, including the importation of slaves, to the present day. Racial democracy is inscribed in the Constitution. If racism does not exist, then how can one explain the fact that the majority of black Brazilians live in a state of economic destitution and that there are virtually no leading politicians of colour?[4] Whilst race might have been erased from the historical records, historical narratives and political legislation, it is present in the complex compressed polysemic movements of the body in samba, which Browning describes as 'the body articulate' and as 'resistance in motion'. Samba 'speaks with the feet' and the body:

> Samba is the dance of the body articulate ... The dance is a complex dialogue in which various parts of the body talk at the same time, and in seemingly different languages. The feet keep up the rapid patter, while the hops beat out a heavy staccato and the shoulders roll a slow drawl...

Samba narrates a story of racial contact, conflict and resistance, not just mimetically across the span of musical time, but also synchronically, in the depth of a single measure. (1995, p. 2)

The year of 1995 was a good one for dance ethnography. Not only were the national dances of Cuba and Brazil the subjects of study, so too was the national dance of Argentina, the *tango*. Marta Savigliano's complex study of the Argentinian *Tango and the Political Economy of Passion* (1995) is informed by and comments on the recent 'post' theories – postmodernism, poststructuralism and postfeminism. It also draws on postcolonial theory. Daniel's (1995) approach to studying the Cuban rumba, which incorporates the tools of movement analysis, embraces a more traditional style of ethnographic writing. Browning's study of Brazilian samba, with its wonderful, impressionistic vignettes, adopts a more literary approach to ethnography. Savigliano's (1995) approach to the Argentinian tango, as discussed below, may be defined as choreographic and experimental.

The history of tango, for Savigliano, is a complex 'history of exiles' (1995, p. xiv). Like Browning, Savigliano refuses to employ a linear narrative in telling the stories of tango. She maps the travels of tango from its origins with the exiled slaves in Rio de la Plata via the Spanish and Italian immigrant slums of Buenos Aires to the ballrooms and clubs of the elite cultural metropolises of Paris, London, New York and Tokyo, and then back again to Argentina in its newly de-authored and recodified forms. The narration moves between the then and now and back again in a non-linear, synchronic manner. There are many competing voices in Savigliano's text shouting out to be heard, just as there are different voices in the bodily articulations of the dance, and in tango lyrics and stories. The presentational format draws on a range of writing styles, personal, polemical and performative: introductions and reintroductions and different conclusions are offered; political debates and theories are set up and immediately deconstructed; descriptions of tango dance are set out like performance scripts, with stage directions and so on. Savigliano is clear that the study is not just about tango; rather tango *is* both the project and the methodological tool for this political analysis of the 'economy of passion' (pp. 16–17).

The notion of employing choreography as a tool for the analysis of the body across and between disciplines is also evidenced in two edited collections by Foster (1995, 1996b).[5] As noted in Chapter 3, constructs of gendered performance and performativity (Butler, 1990b) and choreographing difference (Derrida and McDonald, 1995), which have found their way into gender studies and cultural studies in recent years, seldom, if ever, attend to the enactment of performance or choreography (Wolff, 1995; Foster, 1998). The slippery, ephemeral character of the moving body, which resists easy translation into the written text, however, is central to this 'writing at the intersection of dance studies and cultural studies of the body' (Foster, 1996b, p. xiii). Here, choreography, defined in the *Chambers Dictionary* as 'the art of making dances' (Chambers, 1972, p. 231) is treated 'as a theorization of relationships between body and self, gender, desire, individuality, communality, and nationality' (Foster, 1996b, p. xiii). The concern is to reveal 'how the crafting of moving bodies into a dance reflects the theoretical stance towards identity and all its registers' (ibid.). Dance, then becomes a theoretical apparatus and a heuristic device for helping us to comprehend the fleetingness of the body and assisting 'in the task of transposing its movements into words and its choreography into theory' (quoted on the back cover of Foster, 1996b). Savigliano's text clearly lies within the province of these studies in 'choreographing history'.

Experimental, reflexive, performative writing in sociology and anthropology has been in evidence since the 1970s, as indicated in Chapter 3.[6] Norman Denzin (1997; Denzin and Lincoln, 1994), the champion of postpositivist qualitative research in sociology, cautiously applauds experimental, performative writing that runs counter to the tropes of realism employed in traditional or 'positivist' sociological or anthropological studies. The new ethnography, according to Denzin, echoing Victor Turner (1982) 'has crossed the liminal space that separates the scholarly text from its performance' (Denzin, 1997, p. 123). Denzin writes in admiration of 'new journalists' in the 1960s and 1970s like Tom Wolfe, whose texts blurred the boundaries between fact and fiction. Savigliano's performative strategy also blurs the distinction between fact and fiction.

Like Browning, Savigliano is a key protagonist in the study. Browning (from the USA) started out from the position of an outsider and largely 'went native', with all the contradictions that this entails. As Savigliano is Argentinian, she can speak from the position of an 'insider', as one of the colonised. Somewhat ironically, however, she discovered her passion for tango while studying in the USA, where she now resides, which also makes her an 'outsider'. Savigliano, as Grau (1997, p. 86) comments, 'is a Third World intellectual using the tango to decolonise herself'.

Like samba and rumba, tango enacts a story of desires, passions, tensions and contradictions. Tango, according to Savigliano, speaks of female resistance while at the same time, like rumba, 'it is implicated in the machismo and in the exploitation of women' (Foster, 1996b). Savigliano refuses to see a simple one-to-one relation between macho culture and women's exploitation. While the tango has been traditionally created, controlled and dominated by the figure of the male and the celebration of male bonding, Savigliano (1995, p. 69) argues that 'women have never been just "docile bodies" or "passive objects"'. Rather, in its songs, stories and choreographies, tango 'has recorded women's abilities to subvert and negotiate' (ibid.). Savigliano is a feminist who seeks to deconstruct feminist discourses. The tango, she argues, echoing Foucault, is about 'the struggle for power' (p. 70).

Decolonisation, in its many shapes and forms, lies at the heart of Savigliano's analysis, which draws sustenance from postcolonial theory. In her view, it does not simply take two to tango, but three: 'a male to master the dance and confess his sorrows; a female to seduce and resist seduction, and be seduced, and a gaze to watch these occurrences' (p. 74). The third party in the tango is principally 'the colonizing gaze'. It is this gaze, for Savigliano, following writers like Edward Said (1979), which has 'the power to exoticize':

> Exoticism and Autoexoticism are interrelated outcomes of the colonial encounter, an encounter that is asymmetric in terms of its power. (Savigliano, 1995, p. 75)

Tango, as Savigliano points out, 'was incorporated into the world economy of passion as one among many exotic dances' (1995, p. 82). At some point in their life cycle, tango, samba and rumba, all hybridised forms, were appropriated from their sources by the west (and in the case of tango, Japan) as exotic, erotic displays of sexual passion between men and women and transformed into popular ballroom dance forms. Once the raw edges had been smoothed out by the 'good taste' of (civilised) western culture, they were subsequently sold back to their country of source as 'authentic', where they were reabsorbed and reappropriated from 'the west' by 'the rest'.[7]

The construct of 'male gaze' in the context of film spectatorship (Mulvey, 1975, 1989) has had a significant impact on feminist approaches to western theatre dance and dance history (see Thomas, 1996; Manning, 1997; Banes, 1998; Carter, 1999, for summaries and critiques of this work). While Savigliano's analysis focuses on the colonising gaze, hardly any ethnographic studies of dance have addressed the problem of reception and spectatorship in dance (Reed, 1998). Daniel does pass comment on the ways in which gender can be read in rumba, as indeed does Browning in her analysis of samba. Neither of these ethnographers let the voices of participants speak for themselves (Grau, 1997). Daniel Miller's study of 'lower-income' women performing a dance called *wining*, which featured prominently in the 1988 Trinidadian carnival, however, does address spectatorship and reception in dance in a more systematic manner, although he falls somewhat short of providing a close analysis of the movement.

Wining, according to Miller (1991, p. 325), 'is a dance movement based on gyrations of the hips and waist and may be performed by individuals, or upon an other person, or in a line of dancers'. The dance can involve the contact of 'genitals to bottoms' between couples.

Wining is not exclusively associated with carnival and can be performed at fêtes and other social dance events. Although it is usually danced to the sounds of calypso or soco music, it can also be performed in response to other 'forms of excitement'. The 'contact of genitals to bottom' in the dance does not necessarily signify eroticism or sexual intention because, in Trinidad, as Miller notes, 'genital contact gives less cause for attention than oral contact' (1991, p. 326) such as kissing, at least among the lower-income groups.

It is in the run-up to the carnival period that wining becomes prominent, particularly at the fêtes where 'the men may gyrate against the bottoms of the women in front'. The couple 'may be enclosed within a line, or may gyrate front to front' (1991, p. 326). In this particular context, wining is generally seen in terms of relationships and what is considered acceptable wining becomes an issue for both men and women. Men, for example, may accuse their partners of exceeding acceptable limits when dancing with other men. During carnival, where a degree of licence is in order, the wining 'transforms from women and men wining on each other, to women wining alone or with each other' (ibid.). As they wine with each other the women parody the way in which the men 'respond to their assumed indiscretions' (ibid.) by, for instance, pretending to be angry and pulling off one woman from another and dragging her away.

Miller's study considers the responses of men and the press to the women performing wining with and upon other women during the 1988 carnival. The press in general treated the gyrating dancing women as 'vulgar and immoral', while Miller's male informants viewed their female wining as 'lesbianism gone rife' (p. 333). By contrast, the women performers viewed these interpretations as 'incomprehensible' given that as they became caught up in the dance, they had little concern as to with or on whom they wined.

Miller sets his interpretation of wining against the backdrop of complex cross-gender relations, sexuality and kinship networks of contemporary Trinidad. Cross-gender relations in Trinidad, as he shows, have been reduced to 'a few acts of exchange of which sexual relationships are predominant' (pp. 333–4). He argues that this all-female form of wining enacts a sexuality that has no need of men: 'it is not lesbianism but auto-sexuality' in which the women's object of dancing is centred on their selves. However, it would be a mistake to see wining as an expression of 'female solidarity', according to Miller. Because the wining is inner-directed and self-contained, it enables the women to be as little concerned with other women as they are with men. Rather, Miller considers that the dancing, by evoking a sexuality that is not dependent on men, momentarily inverts the 'normal' cross-gender relations that these women experience on a daily basis. Wining, in this instance, may be interpreted as a negation of 'sexuality as an act of exchange' (p. 334). It constitutes a moment of transcendence from the everyday, and as such may be understood as an act of 'Absolute Freedom'. The construct of absolute freedom, as Miller notes, was developed by the abstract enlightenment philosopher, G.W.F. Hegel. This freedom is achieved through the enactment of auto-sexuality in wining and the inversion of the normal codes of cross-gender relations. Miller indicates in passing that dance movements involving pelvic gyrations are also to be found in Latin America, particularly around the Bahia region of Brazil, which, it will be recalled, featured strongly in Browning's (1995) study of samba. Browning also considers samba's 'autoerotic potential to be extraordinarily liberating' (1995, p. 33).

Miller's interpretation of female wining resonates with Bakhtin's (1968) idea of the 'carnivalesque', which, interestingly, Alan Swingewood (1998, p. 127) describes as 'a utopianism of absolute equality and freedom', in which 'social hierarchies and social distance' are suspended. In Bakhtin's conception of carnival, the established rules of social order have been inverted, 'as carnivalised forms subvert and transgress the official symbolic order' (ibid.). Miller is careful, however, not to make sweeping generalisations regarding the inversion of normal social relations and codes of behaviour from this particular case study to the Trinidadian carnival *per se*. Nevertheless, he suggests that, for the majority of the participants, the 1988 carnival may be interpreted in this light.

The powers unleashed through the carnivalesque are incomplete, momentary and unstable, according to Bakhtin (1968). This instantiation of auto-sexuality through wining is also brief and unstable. It soon gives way to a return to 'normal sexual relations' at the end of the carnival, which is traditionally viewed by most people as a period 'when older relationships are ended and new ones are begun' (Miller, 1991, p. 334).

Browning's (1995) discussion of her participation in and observations of the Bahian carnival reveal that in addition to economic and racial occurrences of inversion, gender inversion, particularly for men, is also allowed during this brief period:

> On the first night of the Bahian carnival... the traditional game is transvestism, for both men and women. But men generally take a more enthusiastic part in the switch... men with lurid eye makeup, inflated breasts and wobbly high heels fill the square. A man's participation in this event is no indication of his year-round sexual behavior, although it is a moment that suggests that the machista stereotype of Brazilian straight men covers a more complex sexual identity. (p. 152)

Some of the participants, however, may be cross-dressers and carnival time is a moment when 'their sexuality and validity are acknowledged' (p. 152) and celebrated.

Bahia has a significant population of transvestites, the majority of whom, as Browning indicates, are black or mixed-race, poor and usually on hormonal medication. Their position in society, outside of carnival is contradictory. Browning notes that whilst they occupy a permanent 'carnivalised' position in Brazilian society, they are also routinely 'whistled at and hooted in a manner that seems ironic, aggressive, affectionate and genuinely sexual all at once' (p. 152) by straight men. In carnival week and the gay balls, however, the transvestites are celebrated and applauded by both men and women for 'their beautiful adolescent breasts' (ibid.). Cross-dressing or drag performances, however, do not always subvert the dominant codes of gender and sexual behaviour. As Butler (1993, p. 125) points out in her analysis of the film *Paris is Burning*, 'there is no necessary relation between drag and subversion'. Contrary to the way in which many readers have interpreted her discussion of drag performances in *Gender Trouble* (1990a) as a way of undercutting the symbolic order, Butler stresses 'that drag can be used in the service of both the denaturalization and reidealization of hyperbolic gender norms' (1993, p. 125). Other cultural critics (Garber, 1992; Wolff, 1995) have also argued against a simplistic assessment of drag or cross-dressing as transgressive and/or liberatory. By taking this view on board, Browning's comments about cross-dressing on the first night of carnival, cited above, could be interpreted in a less positive light than

she proposes. The spaces of production for the celebration of transvestism in the Bahian carnival also raise a question mark around the total
suspension of the established social ordering of gender and sexuality during the Bahian carnival. Browning notes that despite the fact that 'transvestism surrounds' the street festivities, the transvestites 'are not
integrated into the organised processional groups of carnival' (Browning,
1995, p. 152). Although she does not pursue this, Browning's observations, here, suggest that the everyday world is not completely turned
upside down in carnival: residual gender, sexual and racial norms still
may be traced through the spaces of performance and the bodies of the
performers. Samba, for Browning, drawing on Butler's discussion of
race, sexuality and gender in colonial and neo-colonial states,[8] 'is a racial
history lived through the modality of sexuality' and 'gender *is* constructed in specifically Afro-Brazilian terms' (1995, p. 159).

The four studies discussed above, from their various ethnographic
perspectives, address issues of gender and sexuality in dance in relation
to a broader range of concerns, particularly race and class in the context of colonialism and the neo-colonial nation state. Although they
draw on feminist approaches at some point in their discussions, or at
least the first three do, they perhaps have a much looser affiliation than
is evidenced elsewhere in recent studies in dance. Since the late 1980s,
there has been a proliferation of studies in dance history which address
gender representations and sexuality as they are articulated in and
through the body in western theatre dance in particular. Much of this
work bears witness to the influence of cultural studies, critical theory,
particularly poststructuralist and postmodernist and recent socio-
historical approaches to the body on a rapidly developing field of dance
studies.[9] And it is to this that I now turn. Rather than provide a
detailed discussion of this work, I will offer a brief overview of the key
issues. I will then focus on a particular case study (Daly, 1995), which,
in turn, will lead me to point to other studies and developments in
the field.

Representations of women in western theatrical dance

As indicated at the beginning of this chapter, the development of a
feminist dance anthropology or ethnography was not high on the
agenda of dance anthropologists in the late 1980s. But it was around
this time that the impact of feminist scholarship began to be felt in the
work of several dance historians and performers (see, for example,
Foster, 1986; Alderson, 1987; Daly, 1987, 1987/88; Goldberg 1987/88;

Boyce *et al.*, 1988; Dempster, 1988). In 1991, Ann Daly outlined the potential benefits to dance analysis and feminist scholarship if they joined in 'partnership'. Dance and feminism, she notes, 'are highly compatible'. The 'body' is central to both:

> The inquiries that feminist analysis makes into the ways that the body is shaped and comes to have meaning are directly and immediately applicable to the study of dance, which is, after all, a kind of living laboratory of the study of the body – its training, its stories, its way of being and being seen in the world. As a traditionally female-populated (but not necessarily female dominated) field that perpetuates some of our culture's most potent symbols of femininity, western theatrical dance provides feminist analysis with its potentially richest material. (1991, p. 2)

Daly, here, notes the import of the theory of the 'male gaze' to the study of gender representations in dance, although she recognises that it has 'become tiresome to feminists and non-feminists alike' (ibid.). Laura Mulvey's influential Freudian semiotic analysis of spectatorship and gender representation in Hollywood films, first published in 1975, proposed that women in film are represented from the standpoint of the male spectator. The female is the object of the 'male gaze' and the viewer (male or female) is entreated to see her through the male look. The woman in film is objectified and rendered passive by the active power of the male gaze. The structure of looking in film, according to Mulvey (1975), duplicates the unequal power relations between men and women in society. Mulvey argued that feminist film should 'disrupt' the pleasure of the gaze.

The male gaze theory was useful to feminist analysis because it offered a model for 'understanding the association and objectification of women through their bodies and their lack of cultural power within the discourses of patriarchy, which had been implicit in earlier second wave feminist analysis' (Thomas, 1996, p. 73). However, it had a number of limitations. For instance, it was criticised for proposing an ahistorical, universal structure of male, heterosexual looking, for presuming that men, unlike women, are not objectified through the gaze and for not taking account of difference, except along the lines of the Freudian male/female binary divide. Mulvey subsequently took some of these criticisms on board in a later paper (1989), but as Gamman and Makinen (1994) point out, because the revised model remained locked into psychoanalytic theory, it still cannot account for change across time. Thus, it is unable to address current postmodern practices such as parody or camp. Neither can it consider how women (heterosexual, lesbian, bisexual), as opposed to men, get pleasure from looking.

Researchers in cultural studies, postmodern anthropology (see Clifford and Marcus, 1986) and film studies (for example, Kaplan, 1983; de Lauretis, 1984, 1987; Doane, 1987) began to question and develop the gaze theory in other directions from the beginning of the 1980s. Dance researchers, coming to this material somewhat later, seemed to embrace the male gaze without much question, at least in the late 1980s and early 1990s (see Thomas, 1996, pp. 73–84), although they did not necessarily adopt a psychoanalytic model. Feminist critics in dance were interested in the ways that women are represented generally in theatre dance, on the one hand, and, on the other, how they might possibly transcend or subvert the dominant modes of representation. A central focus of attention and scorn in feminist dance scholarship, as Alexandra Carter (1999) has argued, was directed initially towards classical ballet, with its emphasis on bodily display and its gender-differentiating pas de deux form, as suggested in Chapter 4. The neo-classical choreographer Balanchine also came under feminist fire. Daly (1987) noted that while feminist critics had paid the ballerina scant attention, the Balanchine ballerina 'was strictly off-limits' (p. 8), as the legacy of this 'master' choreographer who stated that he sought to glorify woman through his art had reached mythic proportions during his lifetime and continued unabated after his death in 1983. Daly set out in effect to deconstruct the image of the Balanchine woman, which she characterised as an icon of American femininity. This artificial (patriarchal), idealised construction of femininity as represented in ballet, Daly argued, is 'naturalised' and in turn becomes the yardstick by which real women are judged in everyday life. Daly's 1987 much-cited paper clearly struck a chord with a number of performers and scholars who were voicing concerns about the negative effects of the demands of the profession and the regimes of training on dancers' health. It will be recalled from the discussion of feminism in Chapter 2 that 'fat' became a feminist issue in the 1970s and 1980s when alarm bells were sounded in regard to the sudden rise in reported cases of anorexia nervosa and subsequently bulimia in young women and young girls. The stories of two ballerinas who had performed in Balanchine's company, New York City Ballet, Toni Bentley (1982) and Gelsey Kirkland (1987), to a certain extent, added fuel to the fire in feminist dance criticism by revealing the closed world of ballet and the extraordinary lengths that some dancers go to to remain at their ideal dancing weight (see Novack, 1993). A few years earlier, the publication of *Competing with the Sylph* (1979) by L.M. Vincent had highlighted the relentless pursuit of thinness among classical ballet dancers of all ages. Vincent, a medical practitioner who worked primarily with dancers' injuries, also criticised the demands made on dancers by the ballet schools and companies to maintain a fat-free, almost prepubescent, ideal ballet body, and audiences for wanting to see sylph-like ballerinas perform before their eyes.

Susan Manning, in an insightful review of the application of spectatorship theory in dance criticism, notes that 'feminist critics who have applied gaze theory to ballet have reached strikingly similar conclusions' (1997, p. 151). The ballerina, like the woman in the Hollywood film, is conceptualised as a sight to be seen by the male spectator: 'as a spectacle, she [the ballerina] is the object and the bearer of male desire' (Daly, 1987/88, p. 57). As discussed in Chapter 4, the ballerina in the pas de deux has often been treated as a passive object, whose function was to be manipulated, dependent and supported by the male dancer. Furthermore, as indicated above, the training system has been criticised for moulding and crafting the bodies of women from a very young age to the requirements of the idealised ballet body of today: lean, flexible, long-limbed, good turn-out and appropriately arched feet (see Dempster, 1988; Wolff, 1990; Novack, 1993; Foster, 1996a).

However, even the staunchest critics of ballet revealed in their writings an ambivalent relation to the form (Dempster, 1988; Adair, 1992; Novack, 1993). Whilst arguing that ballet perpetuated stereotypical notions of women as fragile and in need of support by men, Novack (1993), for example, also remarked on the considerable physical demands, technical skills and strength that were required of the female ballet dancer. Although some feminist critics changed their minds or modified their position on the gaze over the course of the 1990s (Daly, 1992, 1995; Cooper Albright, 1997), the overwhelming tendency has been to see 'ballet as a vehicle for patriarchal repression' (Taylor, 1999, p. 177).

Despite the limitations of applying a monolithic gaze theory, male or otherwise, from the medium of film to gender representations in performance dance (see Banes, 1998), the shift towards a semiotic (referential) reading of dance by feminist dance critics was instructive for several reasons. By insisting that the body in dance is articulated in and through a range of discursive practices, it called into question the predominant notion of the 'natural' body, which, as we have seen, has underpinned and sustained theories of sexual difference. The focus on spectatorship indicated that the ways in which we look at dance are profoundly partial and social at the same time: they are inscribed in and through a chain of signifying practices and cultural codes through which we make sense of the world and 'through which our bodies, our subjectivities, are implicated' (Thomas, 1996, p. 83). As such, it offered a challenge to the abstract theories of beauty and perfection, which bracketed out the social and which had dominated the formalist tradition of dance aesthetics. In effect, what was at stake was the relationship between content and form. This content versus form debate has been more or less resolved, at least as far as feminist dance criticism is concerned, through recent moves by feminists to augment the one-sided focus on representation of women in dance with a consideration of the kinaesthetic aspects of dance performance, as discussed in Chapter 4. However, a very similar battle was fought out in the pages of the *San Francisco Chronicle* over the month of December 2000,[10] which, once again, cast a shadow over the discourses of classical ballet, which never quite seems to go away.

It began on 8 December when Jon Carroll wrote a column entitled 'Just Like a Ballerina' (http://www.sfgate.com/cgi-in/article.cg?file=/chronicle/archive/2000/12/08/DD15762.DTL). Caroll reported that Krissy Keefer, 'a dance professional', was suing the San Francisco Ballet School, which is a 'talent incubator' for the well-respected San Francisco Ballet, for not accepting her eight-year-old daughter as a student because 'she did not have the right body type'. The school declares on its website that it is seeking girls with 'a straight and supple spine, legs turned out from the hip joint, joint flexibility, slender legs and torso' (ibid.). Carroll raised the question as to whether the ballet school, which is supported in some measure by public funds, 'should be allowed to set its own standards' when the city recently 'passed an ordinance banning discrimination against people based on height or weight'. Carroll presented this as a 'public/private' clash over art. On the one side, he wrote, there are 'the acolytes of an aesthetic perfected by George Balanchine', which was formulated on the 'ideal of an ethereal woman'. On the other side there are the taxpayers of San Francisco, who might want to ask some questions of people who are paid to shout at children for being 'too fat' (ibid.). He also noted that modern dance choreographers, like Mark Morris, have demonstrated that 'dance need not be based on the Balanchine model': fat dancers, short dancers and so on can 'also interpret music with their bodies'. Carroll thought it would be interesting to see 'how the two sides lined up' and invited readers to think hard about the issues.

From this point on, there ensued a battle between the supporters or detractors of the ballet school's position and the mother's decision to sue, which soon spilled over into television, other newspapers and journals. The following day, Octavio Roca, a dance critic on the *Chronicle*, responded in support of the school. He pointed out that the San Francisco Ballet School is one of the 'two or three finest' pre-professional schools in the USA and that its published requirements are no different from the prestigious schools in the USA or in Europe (http://www.sfgate.com/cgi-in/article.cg?file=/chronicle/archive/2000/12/09/DD141289.DTL). Unlike modern dance, Roca stated, classical ballet 'calls for superhuman technical training and aptitude ... A ballet dancer's body is the instrument of ballet, as necessary to her as sight is to a painter' (ibid.). Another *Chronicle* dance critic, Allan Ulrich, waded in soon after to offer further support to the school. Once again drawing comparisons between ballet and modern dance, he stated that the former, unlike the latter, 'depends on the uniformity of body type, on rules and protocol'. The art of ballet, after all, he wrote, is 'predicated on physical architecture' (http://www.sfgate.com/cgi-in/article.cg?file=/chronicle/archive/2000/12/13/DD133935.DTL). There is no room here, then, for difference.

The critics' viewpoint was supported by a number of people but was also roundly criticised by others, lay people and professional dancers alike. The critics' detractors invoked a range of issues from cultural elitism to the increase of anorexia nervosa and bulimia among young women and girls, to which ballet, it was argued, through its emphasis on the perfect female body, was contributing (http://www.sfgate.com/cgi-in/article.cg?file=/chronicle/archive/2000/12/13/ED73230.DTL). One commentator noted with interest that questioning the 'strange cult of anorexo-mysticism' in ballet and the appropriateness of 'Balanchine's starved aesthetic' was enough to bring out elitist comments from ballet supporters and for the questioner to be labelled as an 'art bolshevik' (http://www.sfgate.com/cgi-in/article.cg?file=/chronicle/archive/2000/12/19/DD12635.DTL). A former professional ballet dancer who trained at the San Francisco Ballet School argued that 'sexism has always haunted classical ballet' and that the 'controversy over body type ignores male dancers' (http://www.sfgate.com/cgi-in/article.cg?file=/chronicle/archive/2000/12/29/ED166641.DTL). At the same time, she pointed out that although Balanchine is supposed to have 'imposed some unreal physical "ideal" on modern ballet', Suzanne Farrell, his most favoured ballerina, 'had wide hips, ample thighs and a foot that had been broken and healed in an odd way' (ibid.). Other dance critics have also noted that Farrell, who became the model for the Balanchine dancer, did not have the 'body type' that subsequently came to be associated with the idealised Balanchine ballerina. Kirkland (1987) offers a rather different view of Farrell's bodily attributes, from the wings of New York City Ballet. She recalls that when she was a young dancer in the company, all the dancers were jealous of Farrell and attempted to copy her appearance and style. They, too, wanted to be Balanchine's muse: 'Her long neck and legs, her exotic line and delicate features, made her Balanchine's perfect instrument' (p. 54).

In several of the articles, letters and comments in the *Chronicle* on this public/private arts clash, there is a perceived difference between the standardised, idealised ballet body and the variable modern dance body. As indicated earlier, feminist dance criticism has been concerned not only to analyse dominant representations of women's bodies in dance but also to consider how women performers could transcend or transgress their 'to-be-looked-at-ness' (Mulvey, 1975) status. That is, how could they resist 'being co-opted by the conventions and expectations of the male gaze' (Daly, 1991, p. 3) and, in effect, look back? While feminist dance writers have generally viewed ballet as bad, they have tended to treat postmodern or new dance as good (Foster, 1986; Wolff, 1990; Adair, 1992; Dempster, 1988). Foster (1986) proposed a distinction between 'reactionary' and 'resistant' postmodern dance;[11] that is, between those dances that appear initially to challenge the dominant systems of representation but in fact operate within them and those dances that reflexively disrupt the dominant canons of representation and offer alternative strategies. Despite this, most feminist criticism, Foster included (see Auslander, 1988), strongly suggests that dances of resistance are more likely to occur in postmodern or new dance forms than in other performance dance genres. In effect, this gives rise to a dance hierarchy with postmodern or new dance at the top and ballet at the bottom (see Thomas, 1996, pp. 82–3). However, as Jordan and Thomas (1994) have argued, feminist critics have tended to adopt an all too unitary, ahistorical view of ballet. They also fail to draw distinctions between the world of professional ballet training and the amateur, once-a-week ballet class (see Sayers, 1997; Taylor, 1999). Banes (1998) also criticises the 'ballet is bad' stance of much feminist research. Like Manning (1997), she rejects the notion that all women are either victims or heroines. Close analysis of choreography, combined with historical, political and cultural contextualisation, generates a more complex picture of 'dancing women' than that proposed by some feminist writers. Indeed, close analysis, Banes argues, is necessary in order to avoid 'essentialist characteristics of genre representations and conventions' (Banes, 1998, p. 4), and gender representations too, we might add.

Dance and body politics

If feminist writers have placed ballet in general on the negative side of the representations of women continuum and postmodern or new dance on the opposite, positive pole, modern dance, it has been suggested (Manning, 1997), occupies a more ambiguous position. Elizabeth Dempster (1988), for example, recognises that modern dancers, such as Isadora Duncan, started out by stripping the female body away from the colonising discourses of classical ballet into which it was framed, in order to reveal the 'natural' body and release the potential for expressing human emotion and feeling through new modes of 'writing' the female body in dance.

The body, for Dempster, like Bourdieu, is an unfinished, 'meticulously constructed artefact' (1988, p. 37). 'Social and political values are not simply placed or grafted onto a neutral body–object like so many old or new clothes' (ibid.). Rather, 'ideologies are systematically deposited and constructed on an anatomical plane' (ibid.) of the dancer's body. Although the rhetoric of the 'natural' female body, which is central to Duncan's philosophy, is anathema to much contemporary feminism, as it essentialises sexual difference, Dempster points out that it does not diminish the impact of Duncan's rhetoric or dancing on those who saw her perform. She also notes that although the 'natural' body was employed by other modern dancers later on, like Graham and Humphrey, they nevertheless produced very distinctive and diverse ' "unnatural" – female languages and texts' (p. 51). However, with the establishment of modern dance into a set of codified techniques, there was an erasure of the specificity of the natural body, which initially held the promise of a 'viable mode of self-presentation for the women who wrote and spoke it into being' (ibid.). Consequently the body in modern dance also became subject to colonisation. Thus, the female body in modern dance, ultimately, 'is as prescriptive as the system it originally sought to challenge' (ibid.). However, Dempster argues that postmodern dance, rather like a 'successor science' (Harding, 1987), rewrites the significance of the body by interrogating the language of dance itself (1988, p. 51). For Dempster, the bodily 'writing' of postmodern dance is partial, contingent and temporal, which means that by extension the feminine body is 'unstable, fleeting, flickering, transient – a subject of multiple representations' (p. 49).

In 'Reinstating Corporeality: Feminism and Body Politics', Janet Wolff (1990) considers the prospect of a feminist corporeality through a critical review of recent literatures on the body; for example, Douglas, Elias, Foucault, Kristeva, Irigaray, Grosz. She incorporates a discussion of the relations between 'gender, dance and body politics' as a brief case study to develop her argument. Wolff (1990) adopts a similar position to other feminist critics of ballet. The roles designed for women in classical ballet, she argues, 'collude in a discourse which constructs, in a medium which employs the body for its expression, a strangely disembodied female' (p. 136). Like Dempster, Wolff considers that modern dance 'has usually been viewed as an important breakthrough for women', particularly because it combined 'a conception of the natural body, and a commitment to women's stories and lives' (pp. 137–8). Thus, for many critics and performers alike, modern dance's 'aesthetic transgressions' were also political transgressions. Like Dempster, Wolff perceives the essentialism embedded in the natural body rhetoric of modern dance as problematic for a feminist corporeality, precisely because it erases the role of culture from the discussion. Dance, she argues, 'can only be subversive when it questions and exposes the construction of the body in culture' (p. 137) and these features are to be found, or potentially at least, in postmodern dance. Postmodern dance, as in the work of Yvonne Rainer, DV8 or Michael Clark, for Wolff, offers a window of opportunity for the emergence of a body politics that is not predicated on an ahistorical, essentialist image of the female body. However, neither Dempster nor Wolff offers a close analysis of particular dances to support or advance their argument and instead they rely on 'abbreviated, idealised descriptions of postmodern dance' (Manning, 1997, p. 158). In the end, as Manning claims, their arguments can be reduced to the blanket proposal that 'early modern dance produced a corrupt feminism, postmodern dance an authentic feminism' (ibid.).

Wolff rejects theories of the body that are wholly essentialist or wholly constructionist. As we have seen in Chapters 1 and 2, body theorists, such as Turner (1992) and Lyon and Barbalet (1994), have also rejected this type of either/or model and contemporary feminists have engaged in heated debates over the problem of essentialism and sexual difference (see Gatens, 1996, pp. 76–91). Wolff favours an approach that constitutes the female body 'as discursively and socially constructed, and as currently experienced by women' (1990, p. 134). Such a framework may provide 'the basis of a political and cultural critique', inasmuch as 'it eschews naïve essentialism and incorporates the self-reflexivity of a recognition of the body as an effect of practices, ideologies and discourses' (pp. 134–5). One way round this and other either/or positions in the study of dance history, as dance scholars such as Daly (1995), Bull (1997), Manning (1997) and Cooper Albright (1997) suggest, is to incorporate the kinaesthetic aspects of dance into the socio-cultural analysis. In this penultimate section, I focus on Daly's (1995) study of Isadora Duncan. Here, Daly offers an implicit rebuttal to Dempster and Wolff's essentialist readings of Duncan's conception of the female dancing body (or bodies as it turns out) and by extension perhaps, essentialist readings of modern dance, too. The study also offers a critique of the monolithic male spectatorship theory to which Daly formally attached great importance, although this critique was already evident in an earlier paper (see Daly, 1992).

Dancing bodies/subjects-in-process

Daly's study of Duncan (1878–1927), *Done into Dance* (1995), which is subtitled *Isadora Duncan in America*, sets out to rescue Duncan's serious artistic endeavours from the continual tide of sensationalist writings, biographies, plays and films which have focused attention on the dancer's unconventional and highly publicised personal and emotional life, and have all but ignored her innovative dance practice.[12] This reconstruction of Duncan's 'vanished practice' (p. x), however, is only achievable through 'an act of imagination' (p. 18). Duncan did not allow anyone to film her dancing. She preferred to be remembered as a legendary figure of mythic proportions. Although there are numerous other kinds of literary and photographic records, primary and secondary, which have their own problems, there are no recorded works available to enable a reassessment of her 'actual' bodily practice. This, as we have noted in the previous chapter, is more often the case than not in dance history, for several reasons, including its ephemeral character.

Daly aims to 'articulate the meanings of Duncan's dancing for her American audiences and the ways in which these meanings were produced' (p. xi). Despite the fact that Duncan worked abroad in Europe and Russia most of the time and indeed achieved greater acclaim there than in America, her ideas and practice, as outlined below, were deeply rooted in America. Moreover, she had a profound influence on the historical development of American modern dance: 'She [Duncan] set the agenda for modern dance in America, defining its terms and literally setting its practice in motion' (p. x). The study, then, has a decidedly 'local' focus. Koritz's (1995) study of early modern dancers such as Duncan and particularly Maud Allan on the English stage in the late nineteenth and early twentieth centuries, which was discussed briefly in the preceding chapter, also has a local focus.

Daly's analysis interweaves text with context on three interrelated levels that are not mutually exclusive: the descriptive and analytical; the interpretative; and the critical. The first level attempts to uncover Duncan's rhetoric and practice, and her audience's responses. The second interpretive level considers what Duncan's practices meant for her American audiences during her own lifetime. Here, Daly examines 'Duncan's body as a practice through which a variety of cultural issues such as self, race, Woman, art, democracy and America were negotiated' (p. xii). The third, critical level sets out the ideological implications of Duncan's practice. Daly draws on a range of contemporary social and cultural theory throughout the study, but her starting point for viewing Duncan's dancing body as a feminist practice is Julia Kristeva's (1984) feminist psychoanalytic semiotics, which, Daly proposes, opens up a theoretical space for 'culturally marginal' voices to be heard as 'culturally productive' (p. xii).[13]

In *Revolution and Poetic Language* (1984), Kristeva sets out 'a theory of the processes which constitute language' which 'are centred on the speaking subject' (Moi, 1986a, p. 12). In considering the 'signifying process', Kristeva not only addresses the vexing problem of *how* language comes to signify or mean, but also 'what it is that *resists* intelligibility and signification' (Moi, 1986b, p. 90). Kristeva draws on the construction of the subject and the concept of the symbolic order in the psychoanalytic theory of Jacques Lacan (see Mitchell and Rose, 1982). However, she questions the all-encompassing power of the symbolic order in Lacan's formulation and sets out a framework of the subject which is at once more fluid and multiple.

Kristeva proposes that the 'signifying process' is a result of the interaction of two orders or 'modalities'; the 'symbolic' and the 'semiotic' (Kristeva, 1984, p. 24). The symbolic order is constituted through the rules of language (the law of the father in Lacanian terms, the entry to which is marked by the child's entry into language). The semiotic, by contrast, is rooted in the prelinguistic phase (in the pre-Oedipal, maternal body, the 'imaginary' in Lacanian theory) and is comprised of bodily drives and 'pulsions', whose endless possibilities are gathered up in the semiotic 'chora'. Kristeva borrows the concept of the chora from Plato (meaning receptacle or space, unstable, changing, unfixed, becoming (see 1984, p. 239, note 12)) and reworks it 'to denote an essentially mobile and extremely provisional articulation constituted by movements and their ephemeral states' (p. 25). The chora is not yet in language, 'it is analogous to vocal or kinetic rhythms' (p. 26), but it is a precondition for the entry into the symbolic order. With the entry into the symbolic order, the semiotic is repressed, but it is not erased permanently. It resides in the unconscious and may be released into the dominant symbolic order at a later date. Thus, Kristeva's construct of the subject is not necessarily fixed or locked for all time into the symbolic order, but, rather, is constituted as a 'subject-in-process',

If the symbolic order is associated with 'the law of the father' (phallocentrism), then the semiotic is associated with the feminine (maternal body). The feminine (in a deconstructionist sense, not in a biological sense[14]) is located in the semiotic chora and is pushed to the margins of the logocentric, phallocentric symbolic order. It is from this space of endless possibilities, which cannot be contained by the rational structure of language, that there is the potential to disrupt, challenge, break out of or destabilise the dominant symbolic order. It is important to note that, for Kristeva, once the symbolic break has been instituted, the semiotic, which is a precondition for entry into the symbolic, 'functions within signifying practices as the result of a transgression of the symbolic' (p. 68). That is, the semiotic does not lie outside of language, rather, 'it exists in practice only within the symbolic' (ibid.). The original pre-symbolic semiotic chora, then, Kristeva stresses, is a *theoretical supposition*. Kristeva proposes that it is in the writing of the modernist literary avant-garde such as that of Joyce or Mallarmé that the repressed feminine finds a voice, where the bodily 'pulsations' and the unconscious break through the rational barriers inscribed in the phallocentric order.

What Daly finds useful in Kristeva's work is the notion of the subject-in-process, which means that the female is never fixed or stable, either in essence or in representation and is always relational to the dominant order. When compared to the ossified female subject in male spectatorship theory, which featured prominently in Daly's own earlier analyses of representations of women in dance, it offers a realm of possibilities of difference. The non-essentialist model of the feminine that Kristeva proposes, for Daly, makes possible new ways of reading how American audiences interpreted Duncan's 'female' dancing body. Kristeva's emphasis on the pre-symbolic body, which is analogous to 'vocal and kinetic rhythms', is clearly attractive to dance scholars keen to include the kinaesthetic elements of dance into their analysis.

Daly builds her imaginative reconstruction of Duncan's 'vanishing practice' through the identification and contextualisation of Duncan's five different but interrelated bodily practices: 'the dancing body, the natural body, the expressive body, the female body, and the body politic' (Daly, 1995, p. 19). These bodies are not discrete or linear and there is a continual overlap between them, with one or other becoming more dominant at particular points in Duncan's life, although the dancing body seems to operate as the connecting cog between the different bodies. It is in this way that the shifting, multiple possibilities of the processes of subjectivity which Kristeva's theory proposes come into being in Daly's analysis of Duncan's practice.

Duncan's dancing body, as Daly shows, emerged out of existing practices and discourses that the dancer had witnessed and experienced in America in the late nineteenth and early twentieth centuries. Her 'new dance' was forged out of three movement traditions, social dance, physical culture and ballet. Theatrical dance and dancers in late nineteenth-century America were viewed as being beyond the bounds of respectable social discourse. This was also the case on the English stage at that time where, as Koritz (1995) argues, dancing was equated with erotic female displays, which were viewed as morally dubious. In order for theatrical dance to be seen as a respectable pursuit for women to engage in, it had to be given a moral edge. Duncan's dancing body, as Daly demonstrates, was captured under the heading of a 'moral practice'. The grounds for this transformation of the dancer and the dance to the category of the divine creature were already inscribed, in part, in American culture in social dance. The hugely popular nineteenth-century dance manuals, with their emphasis on manners and grace, provide ample evidence of this (see Kendall, 1979). Moreover, the physical culture movement of the 1890s, particularly American Delsartism, stressed the emotional and spiritual aspects of harmonic exercise as well as the physical benefits (see Ruyter, 1979). Ballet, on the other hand, constituted the old (decayed) dancing order that Duncan sought to overthrow with her 'new' spiritually inspired and inspiring 'art' with a capital A. In an essay written in 1902 or 1903, Duncan blasted at ballet for its unnatural use of the body and particularly for its 'deformation of the beautiful woman's body':

> The school of ballet today, vainly striving against the natural laws of gravi-
> tation or the natural will of the individual, and working in discord in its
> form and movement with the form and movement of nature, produces
> sterile movement, which gives no birth to future movements, but dies as it
> is made. (Duncan, 1983, p. 263)

In order to convince her audiences that her new dance was significant, Duncan had to articulate a verbal discourse to run alongside her non-verbal practice. Unlike other dancers of her day, even high-status foreign ballet dancers and contemporary 'art' dancers like Ruth St Denis and Maud Allan (see Kendall, 1979; Shelton, 1981; Koritz, 1995), Duncan refused to dance on the vaudeville stage and instead performed in the 'legitimate theatre', concert halls and opera houses. She contrasted her 'natural' flowing movement style with the constricting bodily style and artificiality of ballet.

In Duncan's dancing, spectators found something new. She danced solo on the stage for the whole evening, which was almost unheard of at the time. She boldly pronounced her dancing as 'art' as opposed to entertainment, aligning it with the art of ancient Greece. She refused the typical construction of the female dancer as a titillating sight for the audience's pleasure. Rather, as Daly states, Duncan's dancing 'seemed to her spectators a vision of freedom, her tunic as alive as her body, the garment's light silk catching the force of her curving, swaying, onrushing movement' (1995, p. 64). She refused to be co-opted by the gaze.

Daly's analysis of the 'natural body' shows how Duncan offered her audience an illusion of natural movement. Illusion is the appropriate word, here, as Duncan carefully crafted and moulded her 'natural' dancing body by hard work over many years, paying mindful attention to the body in motion and stillness. However, there were inherent contradictions in Duncan's discursive bodily practice which Daly draws out. Duncan claimed her dancing sprang from natural impulses. Duncan's natural body was not rooted in primitivism. While Ruth St Denis and Maud Allan invoked the Orient as their source of inspiration, Duncan formulated her construct of the natural body through the idea of classical (natural) beauty, to give legitimacy to her artistic practice. Duncan's natural body was 'the artistic transformation of "Nature" into "Culture" ' (Daly, 1995, p. 112). In Duncan's dancing and verbal discourse, the natural body turns out to be the civilised body. Invoking Bourdieu's (1984) construct of distinction and cultural taste, Daly argues that Duncan's trope of the natural body encapsulated a racial and class hierarchy: 'it was artless artifice' (1995, p. 112). Daly's 'constructionist' account of Duncan's claim that her movement form emerged out of natural impulses of the (female) body counters Wolff (1990) and Dempster's (1988) perceptions of Duncan's practice and rhetoric as essentialist.

After she died, critics charged Duncan with bringing the cult of self-expression into American theatrical dance. The idea of 'the expressive body – that which makes externally visible its internal depths' (Daly, 1995, p. 19), which Duncan espoused, had come into play earlier through American Delsartism. However, Daly argues that, whilst Delsartean expression was a means for improving the self and for upward mobility, it was also an instrument for 'controlling the force of the female body, physically and socially' (ibid.). Duncan's theory of expression did not centre on self-expression. To begin with, 'it was dynamic, not static' (p. 136). Duncan believed that movement could not only reveal emotions but can also induce them. Moreover, 'what is expressed by the dancer (whether it be an emotion, a mood, a thought, an allegory) is not imposed by a single ego; it was acquired by merging the soul with the universe' (ibid.). 'By reconstructing the body as an expression of the soul, Duncan thus transformed her dancing into a means of prayer and effectively consecrated an art form' (p. 137).

Duncan's greatest claim to fame, perhaps, lies in her emancipating pronouncements on the female body, in dance and life. However, as Daly shows, Duncan's feminism is both more and less than it is usually portrayed. On the one hand, her public image was a traditional one of motherhood without sexuality, but she also advocated voluntary motherhood, which brings sexuality back into the frame. Duncan sought to demystify the female body through a celebration of it in life and art. In American culture, the 'female dancer per se was constructed as a highly paid, empty headed blonde soubrette of ill repute' (p. 157). Thus, she set out to dismantle the notion of the female dancing body as a prerequisite for the extravaganzas and spectacles that had dominated the American stage in the late nineteenth century. Daly argues that 'Duncan took advantage of the female body as a marginalised site of expression to make it a symbol of cultural subversion' (p. 20).

Once dance had become a legitimate art by the 1920s, Duncan erased the reference to classical Greece from her rhetoric. She became more concerned with paying close attention to content, particularly social criticism, rather than form. Her dancing body was also an explicit body politic. Like other aspects of her life and work, as Daly demonstrates, Duncan's body politics were founded on a series of contradictions. On the one hand, she espoused a Whitmanesque libertarian view of the American body, for all people, regardless of class, race or creed. On the other hand, the body she cultivated was one which was marked by class distinction, social status and racial superiority, and which she equated increasingly with 'America'. She hated ragtime or 'jazz dancing', which she identified with primitivism and excess, and a denial of 'culture and civilisation'. Daly argues that by 'defining her artistic practice in opposition to "primitive" modern [jazz-inspired] dance, Duncan was effectively constructing a genre of American dance as whiteness' (p. 219),[15] which, as indicated in Chapter 2, had serious consequences for the careers of African American concert dancers (see Perpener, 2001). Other feminist-inspired dance critics have also extended the analysis of gender representations to a consideration of the interrelationship between gender, class and race in modern dance (Koritz, 1995; Manning, 1996; Burt, 1998).

Daly's study of Duncan reveals the complexity of the shifting and contradictory qualities of Duncan's bodily practice in the context of America. In Daly's analysis, Duncan's dancing body was not simply a product of its social and cultural location, or a body on display, it was a product of a process, of becoming a self (a subject-in-process). Daly (1995) does not make generalising claims about modern dance, except perhaps to hint at the way in which it continued to sustain its constitution as 'whiteness'. Nevertheless, her analysis is more in sympathy with those who argue for the resistive possibilities of modern dance (for example, Copeland, 1993a) than those who, like Wolff (1990) and Dempster (1988) conclude that the transgressive potential of modern dance was colonised by the very forces it sought to counter in the first instance.

One of the implications to be drawn from all the case studies discussed in this chapter is that dance, to a greater or lesser degree, has the potential to disrupt or transgress the dominant social order. The association of theatre dance with the feminine in both positive and negative ways has also been noted. Although feminist and cultural critics, for the most part, have ignored dance as a topic of inquiry, some have used the word 'dance' as a metaphor for liberation. In the final section of the chapter, I draw on Wolff's (1995) assessment of the hidden assumptions that underpin such a move and the unintended consequences for critical cultural analysis.

Dance as a metaphor for 'writing the body'

In this more recent paper, Wolff (1995) questions an assumed connection between dance and liberation which is present in contemporary cultural criticism and feminist criticism and thus, by implication, her own assumptions regarding the resistive potential of some postmodern dance, as discussed above. Wolff considers that there is an all too easy slippage between the idea of dance, liberation and women in feminist and cultural criticism which misunderstands the 'nature' of dance. Wolff argues that this trope is founded on an unquestioned and erroneous assumption of dance 'as intuitive, non-verbal, natural and that it risks abandoning critical analysis for a vague and ill-conceived "politics of the body"' (Wolff, 1995, p. 70). She notes that feminist criticism generally invokes the idea of 'theory-as-dance' as 'a commitment to liberal pluralism' (p. 78). However, 'for Derrida and those who have taken up his notion of "incalculable choreographies"', the meaning is rather different in 'that it seems to inhere the very mobility of dance' (p. 79). Derrida 'dreams' of the possibility of a 'multiplicity of sexually marked voices' (Derrida and McDonald, 1995, p. 154) which go beyond binary gender oppositions. The dismantling of the gender and sexuality binaries, as noted before, has featured prominently in recent work in gay, lesbian, queer and performance studies (for example, Butler, 1990a, b, 1993; Garber, 1992; Case *et al.*, 1995; Grosz and Probyn, 1995; Desmond, 2001). Rather than address Derrida's 'dream of the innumerable' (Derrida and McDonald, 1995, p. 154), Wolff is concerned to ask why he employs the concepts of dance and choreographies 'to do the work of radical destabilization' (1995, p. 79). The answer, for Wolff, lies in the unfounded assumptions indicated above: first, that dance as a non-verbal mode of communication is either prelinguistic or lies outside of language's signifying process[16] and thus threatens 'phallogocentrism'; second, as the body is the instrument of dance, 'it provides access to what is repressed in culture' (ibid.). It has authenticity:

> Because, unlike walking or swimming, dance is perceived as creative, it is seen to articulate the authentic expressions of the body. From these assumptions the conclusions are drawn that dance is or may be liberating and, a fortiori, that metaphors of dance operate automatically as critical theory. (pp. 79–80)

Although there may be difficulties in translating dance into words, it does not necessarily follow that dance lies outside of language and is therefore 'ineffable'. Translation from one (verbal) language to another can also be very problematic but it would be strange to suggest that a language exists outside of or beyond its signifying processes. Moreover, as demonstrated in Chapter 4, both the realms of the intelligible and the sensible are implicated in theatrical dance forms, although certain genres may privilege some aspects over others.

Feminist criticism, as Wolff notes, has drawn on the work of French feminists such as Hélène Cixous (1981), who is largely responsible for the concept of an *écriture féminine* (Moi, 1985), and Luce Irigaray (1985) to develop a body politics. A few dance historians have drawn on the ideas of these particular French feminists (for example, Copeland, 1993a; Sanchez-Colberg, 1993; Kozel, 1997; Briginshaw,

2001), but not in such a sustained manner as, for example, Daly has done with the other major French feminist theorist, Kristeva.

Irigaray and Cixous, like Kristeva, are concerned to retheorise sexual difference (or deconstruct it) to explain and to find a pathway through the dominance of the patriarchal symbolic order. They draw critically on psychoanalytic concepts and deconstruction to understand the structures of femininity and masculinity within patriarchy in conjunction with the social forms that these structures engender. Both Irigaray (1985) and Cixous emphasise the heterogeneity of the feminine, but in rather different ways. For Cixous (1981), borrowing Derrida's terminology, male sexuality and male language are phallocentric and logocentric. The structure of meaning within this frame is ordered around and fixed in terms of binary opposites, woman/man, nature/culture, heart/head and so on, which are founded on the principal binary opposition of male and female. Feminine sexuality and feminine language are repressed by patriarchy, but they constitute a source of danger to phallocentrism. The phallocentric, logocentric social order, however, is not immutable. Feminine writing, according to Cixous, can challenge it. The patriarchal order can be transformed by freeing the repressed feminine located in the body to assert different meanings and values. It is through the reassertion of the feminine libido, a feminine 'writing of the body', that the possibility of change resides:

> By writing herself, woman will return to the body which has been more than confiscated from her, which has been turned into an uncanny stranger on display … Censor the body and you censor breath and speech at the same time … Write yourself. Your body must be heard. (1981, p. 250)

As Wolff (1995, p. 81) notes, 'a feminism that emphasizes the primacy of the body in writing is bound to identify the potential of the dancing body'. However, she argues, ideas of 'ineffable' areas of transcendence or liberation are not empirically testable. Wolff argues that there can be 'no pre-social experience of the body' (ibid.). Indeed, Kristeva (1984), as indicated earlier, is sensitive to this dilemma by her presentation of the semiotic chora as a '*theoretical supposition*'. The conjoining of the notion of a pre-discursive dancing body and liberation is problematic from another viewpoint. Theatre dance, and I would also want to argue the case for social dance, as Wolff suggests, 'is thoroughly mediated by cultural languages and practices' (ibid.), as the discussion of dance training and dance genres in this present chapter and Chapter 4 has demonstrated. Even Brenda Farnell (1994), who argues strongly that dance researchers (from whatever discipline) should use the (non-verbal) tools of movement analysis such as Labanotation to record movement, emphasises the necessity of talking with dance informants to ensure that the notator's script reflects 'native' understandings of movement. Like Foster (1998), Wolff proposes that choreography, which points to a heterogeneity of non-linear movement possibilities, within the framework of an artful (signifying, discursive) practice, might be a more appropriate metaphor for cultural criticism than an uncritical construct of dance as pre-discursive or extra-linguistic. However, as will be shown in the next chapter, the idea that individuals can experience a brief flash of freedom from everyday life through dancing continues to underpin cultural studies' interpretations of the role of dancing in youth cultures. In the past, this idea was often expressed in terms of the 'freedom of Saturday night' (see Ward, 1993).

Chapter 7

Dancing the Night Away:
Rave/Club Culture

Introduction

The focus of this chapter centres on contemporary popular social dance culture in Britain, which is often referred to as rave or club culture. At certain points in the chapter more traditional dance hall forms, which include modern ballroom and modern sequence, are brought into the discussion. Club culture is commonly associated with youth culture while ballroom dancing is linked with members of the older generation, who frequented dance halls prior to the rise of solo dancing and the advent of the discothèque in the 1960s. Indeed, the term 'club cultures', as Sarah Thornton points out, 'is a colloquial expression given to youth cultures for whom dance clubs and their eighties off-shoots, raves, are the symbolic axis and working social hub' (1995, p. 3). British club cultures 'have their roots in a blend of international musical and cultural influences that stretch back, at least in easily recognisable form, to 1945' (Malbon, 1999, p. 16). Of particular importance were the gay and black disco scenes that emerged from New York in the 1970s. People refer to club cultures or clubbing as rave, dance culture, social dance cultures, dance music culture or nightclubbing, depending on their age, experience and preferences (ibid.). Clubbing has continued to grow, fragment and diversify into a whole variety of genres and sub-genres. It has become 'a major cultural industry' (ibid.) in Britain in recent years, with revenue levels reaching 'over £2 billion per annum' and growing. According to surveys conducted in the latter half of the 1990s,[1] 42 per cent of the UK population (of all ages) attended clubs or discothèques (large and small) on at least one occasion in the year. In 1990, this figure was 34 per cent. In 1996, 43 per cent of 15–24-year-olds attended a club at least once a month. Eighty-five per cent of clubbers were under 30 years of age and the vast majority of participants in these dance events were between the ages of 20 and 24

(Malbon, 1999, p. 8). As people get older, according to the survey findings cited above, the less they frequent clubs or discothèques. Dancing, then, is an activity that generally is identified with the younger age ranges in the UK. Indeed, the history of social dancing from the late 1950s has chiefly been associated with specific youth subcultures and their identification with popular musical forms. In recent years there has been something of a resurgence of interest in modern ballroom (waltz, foxtrot, quickstep and tango) and Latin American styles (such as the salsa) which involve partnering, as well as the solo forms which entail set moves and dancing in unison, like line dancing (Thomas and Miller, 1997) and group dance forms involving open partnering, such as set dancing (O'Connor, 1997). These do not necessarily involve those who are long past the age of clubbing. For example, some Student Union ballroom dancing societies in English universities have reported a significant increase in membership and participation.[2] A detailed survey of competition ballroom, which draws on statistical data, indicates that the three styles included in competitive dancing (modern, Latin American and sequence) attract and are practised by 'people of every age, from childhood to well beyond retirement age' (Penny, 1999, p. 58). The spotlight of the chapter centres on a discussion of rave or club cultures in the context of youth cultures in Britain and cultural theory. At several points in the chapter, I draw on material from a recent study of people over sixty years of age in London and Essex who attend ballroom and/or modern sequence dancing events, *Dancing into the Third Age*.[3]

Like Jane Cowan (1990, p. 4), I begin from the premise that dancing comes under the umbrella of the special or out-of-the-ordinary 'areas of social life, such as ritual, play or the arts'. The dance event, following Cowan (ibid.), is conceptualised as 'a "bounded" sphere of interaction' in which ... individuals publicly present themselves in and through their celebratory practices – eating, drinking, singing and talking as well as dancing – and are evaluated by others'. The primary focus of the event can vary according to the context. In some situations, listening to the music and dancing is the centre of the event while the other social activities cited above are peripheral (Ronström, 1989).[4] Thus, in rave and club culture, as we shall see, music, dancing and drugs appear central to the event. In ballroom and modern sequence dancing, on the other hand, dancing and social interaction can be of equal importance to the older participants. Owe Ronström (1989) has argued that only when dance is the central perceptual focus of the event in question can it be properly characterised as a 'dance event'. By incorporating Cowan's broader definition, it is possible to describe the latter example as a dance event, although the focus on dancing may be given less weight by some participants in ballroom or modern sequence than perhaps in rave or club culture. Getting ready for the event as well as 'chilling out' at the end of the evening, as some commentators of rave and club culture have noted (Malbon, 1999; Pini, 2001), can be as important as the event itself. Older ballroom and modern sequence dancers have also indicated the importance of dressing up to go dancing.[5] These considerations beg the question as to where and when the dance event actually begins and ends. A similar problem arises in theatrical dance, particularly in contemporary dance, as indicated in Chapter 4 in the examination of contact improvisation. The idea of the 'bounded sphere' of interaction is useful, nonetheless, as it frames or marks the point of entry from the ordinary to the extraordinary. The concept of the dance or performance event grew out of the work of dance anthropologists (Kealiinohomoku, 1979; Royce, 1980) and other performance theorists (Bateson, 1972; Goffman, 1974; Stone, 1982). Rather than restricting the focus to particular dances or dancing, that is, the dance forms, the dance event takes into account the social situation in which the dancing is practised and performed. In this way, the form is considered to be separate from the context. Before embarking on the examination of club culture, I will set the scene by comparing and contrasting the following two 'dancing stories':

> In the Town Hall at Oxford, the people had a marvellous time. It was just great throbbing humanity ... great heat ... great noise. At the end of the dance-floor, by the band, there was a section for jivers, so of course the extroverts used to love to go and perform and we used to stand and watch them, because they were so splendid, you know; the men swinging the ladies between their legs and up again, swirling around ... What appealed to me was seeing twenty-odd musicians all together on a stage, all in uniform, and they all played the latest hits ... Waltzes, foxtrots, quicksteps, they played all sorts. When the dance-floor was full it was like Old Trafford on a full day, it was absolutely jam-packed.
>
> We used to go as a group of girls together and sit around and wait to be asked to dance, and the boys would come up and try to be very suave. These young men would sort of look at you and lift an eyebrow and expect you to jump up and dance with them. Or they'd say 'You dancing?' You'd say 'You asking?' ... 'Yes, I'm asking' ... 'OK, I'm dancing.' (A woman respondent's tale of her experience of dancing in dance halls in the early 1950s, in Everett, 1986, p. 15)

> The music dominated the dance floor. Everyone was dancing – on the balcony, on the little stages that projected out onto the dance floor like catwalks (look at me, 'cos I'm looking at you!), in the bar, behind the bar,

on the bar. I really enjoyed dancing. I felt myself slipping in and out of submission to the music. No sooner had I forgotten what I was doing, and my dancing had become almost automatic, than I was suddenly aware of myself again, conscious of my moving feet, looking at what my arms were doing. I looked at people dancing and noticed how overtly they were look-ing at everyone else. I don't mean glancing either. I mean really looking at someone, although that was completely normal. I could feel myself being scanned, but wasn't affronted or anything by this. We all seemed to want the music to take us over; to become us in some way. Okay, we each stamped our individuality on it in our own way – a neat little step here, an arm movement there – but the clubbers were essentially doing the same thing as each other and in the same place and at the same time ... Sweat becomes something to be proud of rather than a social stigma.

... There came a point when I was just taken aback by what I was witnessing, of what I was partly constitutive, of what we were and had become. Some form of extraordinary empathy was at work in that crowd, particularly when at the kind of extended climax of the evening the music and lighting effects combined so powerfully with the moving crowd on the dance floor. Clubbers were losing it all over the place. (A male researcher's tale of his experience of clubbing at 2 a.m. on the main dance floor of the Tunnel Club in London in the summer of 1997, in Malbon, 1999, p. xii)

The 1950s dance hall experience and the 1990s club experience compared

These two eye-witness accounts of memories and experiences of going dancing have much in common, despite the fact that the dancing events under discussion are set almost fifty years apart: the first refers to an era when Britain was recovering from the aftermath of the World War II in the early 1950s, and the second takes place at the *fin de siècle*. There are also some striking differences, which will emerge out of a brief discussion of the common elements in the stories.

To begin with, these stories of dancing pleasures in popular culture are centred on the urban experience of the crowd: 'Old Trafford on a full day', 'the moving crowd', 'jam-packed'. Both narrators speak of the importance of the music to their experiences of the dance events in question: 'twenty-odd musicians on a stage ... played the latest hits', 'music dominated the dance floor'. The mixing and sampling of recorded music by the DJ, mapped onto the baseline tempo of the beats per minute (bpm) in the 1990s replaces the presence of the live band in the 1950s story. In contemporary dance music cultures, the DJ is a musician, a producer of music too, not just someone who plays record-ings of other people's performances (see Thornton, 1995, pp. 62–3).

In the end-of-the-century story, the musical sounds permeate every corner of the space and the bodies of the dancers through large PA systems, whereas the sound emanates from the musicians playing on the stage out to the dancers on the floor in the earlier account.

In the contemporary clubbing event, dancing takes place everywhere and everyone is dancing, 'in the bar, behind the bar, on the bar'. Although everyone is dancing in an individualised manner, 'a neat little step here, an arm movement there', they are all doing the same kind of thing at the same time and in the same space. In the early 1950s story, the dance floor is partitioned into two separate dance-style zones. There is a small section in front of the stage designated for the more contemporary *jive* dancing. The remainder of the dance floor is for the more established and less physically exuberant dances such as the waltz, foxtrot and quickstep, which, nevertheless, require a sustained, contained energy and sufficient space so that couples can move around the dance floor. In this period, dance events, 'like the fashions and the songs' (Everett, 1986, p. 14), were not primarily organised around youth and therefore different kinds of dancing took place on the dance floor over the evening to cater for the various age ranges. These dances, including jive, involved dancing with a partner. All of this was in the process of dramatically changing.

There were two distinctive features in 1950s social dancing. The first was the continuing interest and development in Latin American dance forms, such as the rumba, samba and tango, which, as noted in the previous chapter, were forged out of various African European cultural practices. The second was the advent of *rock and roll* (rock 'n' roll). The latter dealt a serious blow to formal dancing. The roots of rock 'n' roll are to be found in the *jitterbug* and the *lindy hop*, the products of 1930s *swing*, which came out of the jazz era and were mostly danced by young people (see Back, 1997). African American music has had a powerful and sustained influence in the development of popular music and social dance in the twentieth century, although this influence has often been read in racist terms (see Frith, 1996, pp. 127–31, for example, on the 'burlesquing' of black culture by white performers of rock 'n' roll). Although the jitterbug and the lindy hop were still 'couple' dances, the dancers did not progress around the room as in previous dances such as the waltz or the foxtrot; instead the dancing was contained within an unmarked-out space. Some dance halls banned jitterbugging and jiving altogether in order to accommodate older dancers, while others sectioned off a portion of the dance floor specifically for the 'excesses' of the jivers.

In the 1950s example, because the dance floor is divided into two separate zones, traditional closed-couple modern ballroom dancing and the contemporary, youthful jive dancing, with its more open partnering format, could be performed at the same time and to the same music. Whilst the division between dance musical styles was organised on the horizontal level in the 1950s, in the contemporary club scene it is more likely to be ordered on the vertical plane with different floors, or separate rooms, designated to specific dance musical styles. The contemporary clubber is formally free to wander between the various ambient spaces, although there may be distinctions at work underneath the surface so that some spaces are less inclusive than others.

Both stories invoke a spirit of community or sociality, of a coming together of individuals with the group through music, the physicality of dancing and the sense of the crowd: 'great throbbing humanity ... great heat', 'we all seemed to want the music to take us over'. Moving together in time and place, as William McNeill's (1995) study shows, is a powerful force in the affective bonding of the individual with the group, which, he argues, is evidenced in different historical periods and in many different societies. This resonates with Victor Turner's concept of 'communitas'. Communitas, for Turner, involves rituals 'in which co-operative and egalitarian behaviour is characteristic, and in which the social distinctions of rank, office and status are temporarily in abeyance, or regarded as irrelevant' (1974, p. 238). The structure of social relations in the contemporary clubbing account of this coming togetherness appears more fluid and transient than the earlier one and more equal. A number of cultural analysts (Redhead, 1990c, 1993c; McRobbie, 1993; Rietveld, 1993; Jordan, 1995; Bennett, 2000) have suggested that participants in rave 'celebrations' lose a sense of their (everyday) subjective identity while dancing and 'merge with the crowd' into a kind of 'collective body' (Jordan, 1995). The idea of an emergent raving connectivity or sociality and 'losing it' on the dance floor will be explored later in the chapter.

Both accounts refer to 'looking' at others dancing although, again, the structure of looking in each case appears to be different. In the 1950s story, the woman narrator speaks of her pleasure in standing back and looking at the jivers' outgoing, virtuoso dancing performances. Malbon, on the other hand, articulates a more active, egalitarian mode of looking. As the individual dancers become less focused on their dancing self and become aware of others dancing, they can be seen to look at 'everyone else', while they themselves are being looked at by someone else in a focused and attentive manner that would be deemed inappropriate behaviour between strangers in the 'ordinary' world of public spaces outside of the club. Neither exhibitionism ('look at me') nor the colonising gaze ('I have you in my eye') is the issue here. Rather, it is as if there is an associative desire to 'become' the music at that particular moment in time, for however long it may last, creating a momentary 'us': 'a body without organs' (Deleuze and Guattari, 1982).

The gender hierarchy which is so apparent in the 1950s story of dance etiquette, characterised by the 'You dancing?' 'You asking?' dialogue, which was subsequently satirised in the opening voice-overs of the 1970s television series *The Liver Birds*, is absent in the clubbing account. The rise to prominence of solo or beat dancing in Europe, which took off with the *twist* in the early 1960s, signalled the demise of the traditional dance halls and the rise of club culture. The dance bands, which had long dominated the dance hall era, were displaced by the DJ who played the records for the clubbers to dance to in the 'new-fangled discothèques' that were springing up in major cities like London, Paris and New York (Brewster and Broughton, 1999, p. 64). Dancing in the 1960s revealed a gulf between the younger and the older generations. The older generation danced ballroom and Latin, jive and the twist, whereas the younger generation (the 16s–25s) focused on solo beat dances as an expression of their difference and individuality.

The idea of individuation in dancing has often been associated with the cult of self-expression, increasingly so since the 1950s, with the establishment of a powerful hedonistic youth culture. But it can also be interpreted in a more positive light as, for example, an expression of a sense of belonging to and identification with a particular group and as a reflection or celebration of sexual equality. From this point on, individuals did not have to dance with a member of the opposite sex; they could dance with friends. Tradition no longer compelled young women to stand around the edges of the dance hall and wait to be asked to dance, as was evidenced in the 1950s story. They could get up and dance on their own or with friends. Young men, too, could dance together in a group of other men. Moreover, since the advent of rave culture, it seems that young women do not have to go in a crowd to dance 'round their handbags', they can and do go clubbing by themselves (Pini, 2001). As will be discussed later in the chapter, women often cite the absence of the 'cattle-market' in rave culture as a significant element in their preference for rave over the more traditional nightclubs and discothèques (McRobbie, 1993; Pini, 1997b).

This chapter focuses on contemporary club cultures, particularly rave culture in the context of youth cultures in relation to the cultural theories and observations that researchers have drawn on to explain the emergence and rapid proliferation of this phenomenon. The discourses on contemporary clubbing generally generate a picture of a fragmented, unfixed, postmodern world in which new, fluid modes of 'sociality' and 'figurations' (gender, sexual, racial) are at least a possibility, if not an actuality. The question of authenticity, which was central to the discourses on dance reconstruction discussed in Chapter 5, emerges here, too, but in a different way (what counts as authentic 'cool' club culture and mainstream clubbing and on whose authority?). This section will also include a brief discussion of the influential subcultural theories of 'resistance' and 'style' that emerged from the Birmingham Centre of Contemporary Cultural Studies (CCCS) and the resultant hierarchical distinction between 'authentic' subcultures and popular, consumer-oriented youth cultures. Where relevant, I also refer to early twentieth-century social dance practices and the role of the dance hall as a leisure pursuit in the city. As indicated above, at certain points in the chapter I exemplify an argument or a statement by drawing on observations from the *Dancing into the Third Age* research project, which set out to assess the meanings that social dance has for people over the age of sixty who participate regularly in dance events in London and Essex. The participants in this study, like the woman in the first story, frequented the dance halls in the late 1940s and early 1950s and witnessed and participated in the shift from ballroom to jive and the end of the dance hall era as they knew it.

From acid house to rave culture

Towards the end of the summer of 1988, the tabloid newspapers in the UK reported the emergence of a new form of leisure pursuit for young people, which they characterized as *acid house* and which would soon mutate into rave. Acid house was a 'kind of music played in clubs and warehouse-parties' that seemed to stir the young people who danced to it into 'a state of raving frenzy' (Rietveld, 1993, p. 45). Acid house was much in evidence in Manchester in 1986/87 (Redhead, 1990, Rietveld, 1993). The specific origins of acid house, like those of rumba, samba and tango, as discussed in the previous chapter, are difficult to pinpoint precisely. Thus, there is some debate surrounding which groups of people first brought house music to Britain, in which cities it made its first appearances and at which point in time it developed a life of its own as rave and left its roots behind (Redhead, 1990, p. 2). Hillegond Rietveld defines the rave event as follows:

The rave is a dance party, where the music has its origins in Acid House from Chicago, techno from Detroit and garage from New York, which themselves have evolved from the dance musical-styles that were played in (black) mainly gay clubs, especially the Warehouse in Chicago and the Paradise Garage in New York. (1993, p. 41)

Although what counts as 'house' has changed over time and in different social contexts, Rietveld states elsewhere that:

'house music' was used to indicate a kind of urban DIY electronic disco music, incorporating a rich African-American cultural tradition which can be traced back to jazz, funk, soul music and gospel, mixed with European styles like electronic trance and electronic pop. (1997, pp. 106–7)

Acid house comprised an eclectic mix of musical styles with an underlying baseline tempo at around 120–140 beats per minute (bpm), within a 4/4 pattern, using 'sequencers, synthesizers' and 'samplers' (ibid.). *Hip-hop* has a baseline beat of around 100 bpm (Sommer, 2001) and *techno*, which has connections to German electro-pop music, works with the faster tempo of 120–160 bpm (Gore, 1997). The vocals in house music, unlike traditional popular music, are not as important as the sounds.

Rave, as the above quotations from Rietveld suggest, borrowed from many cultural practices and forms. Redhead (1993a), for example, points to the influence of 1970s northern soul, with its all-night and all-day parties, its mixing of musical styles inspired by rhythm and blues and its drug culture. Redhead argues that contrary to the CCCS's interpretation of British youth subcultures since the mid-1940s as 'an unfolding progression of one youth style upon another' (1993a, p. 4), rave and acid house were 'notorious for mixing all kinds of styles on the same dance floor and for attracting a range of previously opposed subcultures from football hooligans to New Age hippies'. McRobbie (1993, p. 417) cites the grafting of particular aspects of black cultural practices in Britain and the USA onto rave, such as 'the dance party and the pre-eminent role of the DJ' (see Brewster and Broughton, 1999, for a detailed historical survey of the impact of black Americans on the rise and the development of DJing). Gore (1997, pp. 52–6) points to links with 1960s hippie culture such as the 'feel good factor', experimentation, drugs and the 'multi-media participatory event of the 1960s, the happening'. The word 'acid' was a synonym for LSD, the psychedelic drug of the 1960s flower-power era. Rietveld suggests that the strobe lighting, dry ice and 'psychedelic imagery' which featured extensively in rave parties 'seem to be derived from the Acid Test parties in California in the 1960s' (1993, p. 42). These extra-musical features were revived in London clubs in 1987, along with a 'Balearic "mishmash" of musical styles' (ibid.).

Traditionally, the practice of 'going dancing' has involved dressing up, particularly for women. While mainstream nightclubbers put on the style to go dancing in 'Thatcherite Britain's designer 1980s', the men and women ravers, at least in the initial stages of the movement, dressed down. They wore brightly coloured clothing (stimulated by images of holidays in Ibiza); loose-fitting, cheap, baggy T-shirts, shorts or tracksuit bottoms, bandanas and shoes that had some bounce in them, such as sneakers or trainers. The ravers' approach to dressing was in line with what Polhemus and Proctor (1984) and subculturalist theorists have labelled 'anti-fashion'. Rietveld (1993) argues that the clothing worn by the participants was not so much determined by a conscious counter-hegemonic politics of style, but by a lack of financial means. The freedom to 'shop until you drop' which underscored the consumer-oriented 1980s was not available to all. The sparkling images and representations in the mass media and the high street and the idea of the good life that accompanied them provided a sharp contrast to the grinding realities of unemployment and poverty of significant portions of the population. As Britain began to creep into recession in the last half of the decade, youth unemployment increased (Featherstone, 1991a). One DJ reported that he had to 'dress down' to be accepted by the clubbers in particular venues in Manchester in the late 1980s because many of the young people attending the event could not afford expensive clothes (Rietveld, 1993).

Two other key features of the rave event itself influenced the approach to dress: the use of Ecstasy (MDMA) or 'E' as a 'recreational' drug and 'intensive' dancing. The combination of the two meant that people sweated a great deal and therefore 'baggy clothing was the most comfortable to wear' (Rietveld, 1993, p. 53.). Indeed, as Rietveld (1993) and McRobbie (1993) among others have noted, there was a childlike quality to the style of dress of the raving 'day-glo warriors', which was heightened by the presence of signifiers such as babies' dummies and whistles hanging round their necks. The ice lollies, Lucozade and 'designer' water (instead of alcohol), which the party-goers consumed to 'chill out' and keep the body from dehydrating from the effects of Ecstasy and the continuous dancing, also added weight to this image. Cultural commentators such as McRobbie (1993), Rietveld (1993) and Reynolds (1998) equated the childlike imagery and trappings of rave culture with the pre-Oedipal phase articulated in Freudian psychoanalytic theory. Cultural analysis of rave culture is awash with speculative notions such as this which are seldom tested out or indeed argued through in a systematic manner. McRobbie (1993, p. 419) at least qualified this dubious supposition by acknowledging that this is a 'drug culture that *masquerades* its innocence in the language of childhood' (emphasis added).

Ecstasy is a 'designer' or manufactured drug which was made an illegal Class A substance in Britain in 1977 (Redhead, 1993b). Although it was first discovered in 1912 in Germany, it was shelved for many years (Collin, 1998). MDMA was developed in the USA in the 1960s and by the mid-1970s was used for therapeutic purposes. By the mid-1980s, Ecstasy's 'euphoria inducing effects' became a popular 'legal high' in the club scene across the USA (Reynolds, 1998, p. xxiii). It received a one-year ban in 1985 and was classified as a Schedule 1 drug by the Federal Court of Appeals in 1987. Ecstasy had been imported into Britain in small quantities since the beginning of the 1980s and manufactured in Britain from around the middle of the decade (Redhead, 1993b). Its first widespread use 'throughout major cities in Britain' (ibid., p. 9) was in the summer of 1987. Since 1988, in particular, which has been referred to as the 'second summer of love' (a nostalgic echo of the first one which took place in 1967), E has been connected with nightclubs in different parts of the country where house or rave culture music was being played (ibid.). Ecstasy and rave, then, seem to go together in the minds of most observers, commentators and participants; it is commonly called the 'dance-drug' (Collin, 1998).

The British press was initially friendly to this emergent form of acid house entertainment with its youthful (almost childlike), happy participants dressed in bright, baggy clothes, with the 'smiley' face insignia emblazoned on their T-shirts. But this was very short-lived and a moral panic soon ensued. At the beginning of October 1988, *The Sun* described acid house as 'cool and groovy'. Just over two weeks later that friendly, low-key depiction of rave had given way to the 'EVIL OF ECSTASY' (cited in Redhead, 1990, p. 2). The pathologising and demonising of acid house, and with it the young people who participated in events and those who organised them, continued apace. Towards the end of October, *The Sun*'s headline spoke of 'DRUG CRAZED ACID HOUSE FANS' and on the last day of the month, the heading read 'GIRL 21 DROPS DEAD AT ACID DISCO' (ibid.). The other tabloids joined in too, as did television, to pass 'comment on the state of the nation's youth' (ibid.).

Rave was characterised as an 'evil cult' with its 'Acid Pied Pipers' and the 'Mr Bigs...– unscrupulous drug dealers and warehouse party organisers...in a seduction of the innocent' (ibid.). Ecstasy was equated with opiates such as heroin and with LSD. At first, it was young people in general who were deemed to be most at risk from the acid house cult but soon it was young women who were seen as being in the most danger. Reports indicated that young girls were smoking cannabis and taking LSD. Ecstasy was depicted as a 'sex drug', with men lying in wait to spike the drinks of women so that they could rape them later on when the drug had taken effect. The threat of violation that underpinned talk of 'sex orgies' at raves was made explicit. 'Women', as Redhead (ibid.) noted, 'were thus established as the victims of deviance within the Acid House scene'. The idea that the women were in potential moral danger and in need of protection was not new. It was already well-established in nineteenth-century literature, particularly with regard to middle-class women, as indicated in Chapter 2. Moreover, dancing, particularly 'mixed dancing', since the Puritans' numerous attempts to ban it from the seventeenth century onward, through to the ballroom and rock 'n' roll, has been viewed as an activity which, if left unchecked, can lead to licentious behaviour resulting in a threat to standards of morality and common decency, particularly of women. At the same time, as was noted in the brief summary of the development of professional ballet in Chapter 4, training in the 'noble art' of dancing was considered essential to the development of civility and distinction, particularly for the aristocracy, until the late nineteenth century. A sound training in the social dances of the day, under the tutelage of a recognised 'dancing master', assisted the cultivation of fine manners, upright posture and grace of movement. These tropes of bodily civility marked the individual with social distinction and rank, as the litany of manuals on dancing and social etiquette published over four centuries (for example, Aldrich, 1991) amply testify. Thus, dancing, on the one hand, has been treated as dangerous through its association with the Dionysian and, on the other, it has been elevated through its connection with the Apollonian. In the context of the western tradition of thought, the fear and suppression of the Dionysian has generally had the upper hand. Taking these factors into consideration, we can begin to understand why some feminist critics and cultural commentators have recently come to use the word 'dance' or 'dancing' as a metaphor for resistance, freedom and transgression.[6]

The negative media attention on acid house and the emergent rave scene became the focus of a new moral panic. Rave culture, like most postwar youth subcultures, was inextricably linked with 'sex 'n' drugs 'n' rock 'n' roll' (Gilbert and Pearson, 1999), with the drugs in particular becoming more important since the 1960s (McRobbie, 1993). The mass media, according to Rietveld, 'gave attention to something that just had been good dancing parties' (1993, p. 46). The result was that 'youngsters were alerted: they wanted in on the action' (ibid.). What had formally been an underground, marginal activity became a national pastime for a significant and growing number of British youth. Thus, as Sarah Thornton's analysis of club cultures demonstrates, far from being incidental to the development of rave culture, the mass media were there from the very beginning and were 'integral to youth's social and ideological formations' (1995, p. 117).

Licensed nightclubs in the cities that included acid house or rave music soon came under the scrutiny of the police and the local licensing authorities and were subjected to spot checks (Redhead, 1993b). Some had their licences taken away. As the city clubs, licensed and unlicensed, were attracting an increasing amount of attention from the authorities, the rave events moved from the urban centres to more remote, inconspicuous locations in the suburbs positioned around the M25 (London's orbital motorway) and the countryside. Events were held in disused factories, warehouses, aircraft hangars, car parks and farmers' fields and were attended by thousands of young people. In June 1989, *The Sun* reported that '11,000 youngsters go drug crazy in Britain's biggest-ever Acid Party' (cited in Rietveld, 1993, p. 46).

It is difficult to be precise about the number of young people who participated in raves or indeed just how many took drugs, although there appears to be an inextricable link between rave and recreational drug use and statistical data seem to support this. Given its illegal status as a Class A drug, it would not be surprising if users of Ecstasy were disinclined to reveal the fact to 'official' sources. Nonetheless, evidence indicates that there was a relentless upward rise in drug seizures from 1988 to 1995, 'compared with the years leading up to acid house' (Collin, 1998, p. 284). The drug economy in those seven years 'grew by over 500 per cent – particularly the amounts of Ecstasy, amphetamines, cannabis and LSD' (ibid.). Matthew Collin (ibid.) points out that although 'a causative link is difficult to prove, the year that acid house turned Ecstasy into a dance drug, drug consumption exploded'. A range of surveys undertaken in the mid-1990s, as Collin demonstrates, indicate that around 50 per cent of young people in Britain 'have tried illegal substances' (p. 306). Jeremy Gilbert and Ewan Pearson, drawing on a 1996 Parliamentary Office of Science and

Technology report, also note that 'the rise of dance culture in the UK has occurred simultaneously with an exponential rise in the numbers of people who regularly take drugs' (1999, p. 138). Drugs, in effect, they argue, drawing on Collin's ideas (1998), may be treated 'as a form of technology' (ibid.). It is 'an indisputable fact that "drugs" are central to contemporary dance culture' and that since the 1960s 'they have played an important part in most dance-oriented cultures' (ibid.).

The death of a young, white, middle-class woman in 1995, Leah Betts, as a result of taking Ecstasy at her eighteenth birthday party at which her parents were present, brought home the fact that drug-taking was not just a feature of the problem inner-city areas or the housing estates in Scotland, it had also reached into the suburbs and countryside of 'middle England' (see Collin, 1998, pp. 299–306). Drug usage is no longer a marginal activity among young people, as Gilbert and Pearson (1999) point out. Rather, they argue, it has become 'an unremarkable feature of the everyday life of many people' (pp. 139–40). Nevertheless, it is only certain kinds of drugs that become 'normalised' in given cultural contexts. *The British Crime Survey*, published by the Home Office in 1996, indicated that lifestyle is a good indication of 'likely drug usage'. The report states:

> Clubbers are more likely to take drugs whatever their age, with between 80 and 90 per cent having ever taken drugs. (http://www.statistics.gov.uk/ StatBase/xsdataset.asp?vlnk=872&More=Y)

The question of what counts as rave as opposed to other dance music events/nightclubs is also not very clear-cut. The commercial surveys on nightclubs and discothèques by Mintel, which are updated every two years, are concerned with 'the nightclubbing industry as a whole'. Therefore, it would be impossible to extrapolate figures for raves or the more '*Time Out*'-style of clubs from this source (Malbon, 1999, p. 7). Moreover, rave parties could be organised on a commercial basis or on a private basis and could be either licensed or unlicensed. Clearly, it would be more difficult to track with any degree of accuracy the numbers and the frequency of private and illegal events. Furthermore, the fact that information regarding where and when a rave was going to be held was mostly filtered though unofficial 'secret' channels such as 'fly posters', telephone or by word of mouth, in order to prevent the event coming to the attention of the authorities, also presents difficulties in generating accurate figures. Nevertheless, research conducted by the Henley Centre for Forecast in 1993 indicated that 'more than one million young people attended raves each week' (Ward, 1997, p. 4).

It was also suggested that participation in raves was likely to be greater than this as the research only included legal events. Clearly, then, this was not a minor subcultural activity, but a significant 'social movement', although, perhaps not in the strict macro-political sense that cultural critics generally associate with social movements (see Reynolds, 1998).

The fact that large numbers of young people were travelling across the city streets, the suburbs and the countryside in the dead of night, often in convoys of cars, to congregate *en masse* at some unknown location in order to dance the night or weekend away to loud music pounding out of huge PA systems, with laser lights sweeping across the dance space, and (in all probability) take drugs was viewed as a potential threat to social order. There were also concerns about fire and safety hazards and the increased drug trafficking and extortion by criminal organisations at unlicensed events (Reynolds, 1998, p. 67). The sheer size of the M25 orbital events was staggering. In 1989, '25,000 people attended an Energy mega-rave', much to the amazement of the Brooklyn DJ Frankie Bones, who made his debut at the event. Bones normally worked in clubs in the USA, with a capacity for a few hundred people (p. 63). The Entertainments (Increased Penalties) Act of 1991 (sponsored by Graham Bright, the Conservative MP for Luton South) made the staging of large-scale unlicensed rave events and warehouse parties illegal. The Bright Bill, according to Rietveld, effectively criminalised 'a whole section of the youth population as the hedonistic search for the "right to party" inevitably continued into the illegal sector' (1993, p. 47).

Although rave culture continued, 'it was mostly forced back into the clubs again' (p. 49). The local licensing authorities began to take a more liberal attitude towards commercial promoters and licensing hours were extended, 'allowing for the growth of rave-style clubs' (Reynolds, 1998, p. 68) where participants could party all night until six o'clock in the morning or even later, although regional variations remained. Thus, the rave scene crossed the dance floor and merged with the club scene again. It also seems that young people, with little disposable income, became 'disenchanted' with spending money and time getting to an event, only to find it had been moved to a different location, or that the police had stopped it taking place, or the event itself did not live up to its promotional promises (p. 66).

The Criminal Justice and Public Order Act of 1994 placed further restrictions on rave culture. The legislation targeted 'problem' alternative cultural groups such as New Age travellers, squatters and direct action protesters involved in 'the occupation of land, hunt sabotage and outdoor free parties' (Gilbert and Pearson, 1999, p. 150). Section 63 of the Act specifically mentions rave by name. It gave the police the power 'to remove persons attending or preparing for a rave' (cited in Gilbert and Pearson, 1999, p. 51). A rave is defined as 'a gathering on land in the open air (including a place partly open to the air) of 100 or more persons (whether or not trespassers), at which amplified music is played during the night (with or without intermissions)' (ibid.). The Act makes reference to the bpm that underscore house music in stating that ' "music" includes sounds wholly characterised by the emission of a succession of repetitive beats' (ibid.).

Although large-scale rave events and house parties diminished as a consequence of such legislation, the range of musical styles that rave spawned has continued to grow (Bennett, 2000). A number of cultural analysts have commented on the rapid and increasing fragmentation of the urban dance music scene into discernible sub-genres in the 1990s (Thornton, 1995; Redhead *et al.*, 1998; Rietveld, 1998; Gilbert and Pearson, 1999; Malbon, 1999; Bennett, 2000). Indeed, Andy Bennett argues that rave as a term became redundant in the early 1990s:

> Contemporary urban dance music now includes forms such as *techno, garage, ambient* and *jungle* in addition to house, which itself became fragmented into a range of different forms including *deep house, piano house, happy house* and *hard house*. (2000, p. 75)

Moreover, while Britain might have been the hub of rave in the late 1980s and early 1990s, it was almost simultaneously transported across the globe to other urban centres, where the various styles were further transformed and fragmented. Just as the Argentine tango, as indicated in the previous chapter, was 'sold' back to its source after it was transformed in Europe, so house was exported back as rave to its major source, the USA, in the early 1990s. From this point on, the story of rave in the major USA urban centres is strikingly similar to that in Britain in the late 1980s and early 1990s. US raves became 'large-scale mainstream dance events with massive gatherings in the thousands' which 'could take place in legitimate clubs or in moveable "secret" outdoor or indoor venues whose locations were broadcast through an underground network of phone numbers and the Internet that everybody seemed able to access' (Sommer, 2001, p. 78). Although the media were initially friendly to the rave parties, they soon began to link rave with Ecstasy and warn of the dangers of the new 'dance craze'. A crackdown on the clubs in New York City, licensed and unlicensed, followed in 2000/1 and a number of venues were closed (ibid.). As a reaction against the closures and the expensive mainstream clubs, clubbers wanted to experience a return to the sentiments and identifications of 'house roots'. This nostalgia for 'old house' contains a major contradiction, as Sommer notes. This is a dance culture that is at once enthralled by the 'futuristic', while displaying a nostalgic longing for the past 'underground house'.

Dance culture, youth culture and subculture

One of the most interesting features from the point of view of this book is the fact that dancing for long periods at a time was central to the rave event and contemporary clubbing. Those cultural analysts (for example, Redhead, 1990, 1993c; Saunders, 1995) who did address this extraordinary mass youth rave culture 'movement' that swept the country in the late 1980s and early 1990s, with perhaps the exception of Angela McRobbie (1993), paid scant attention to the activity of dancing itself. Neither did they address the participants' experiences of dancing nor the meanings that they associated with the activity (see Thrift, 1997; Ward, 1997; and Malbon, 1999, for critiques of the literature in this area). For example, as Andrew Ward (1997, p. 5) points out, although Steve Redhead's (1993c) collection mentions the word 'dance' or 'dancing' at least fifty times, 'there is no sustained address of dance per se'.[7] When the word 'dance' is used in this volume, it is 'usually as a descriptor or qualifier as in "dance drug", "dance craze", "Indie Dance crossover", "groovy dance single", "psychedelic dance hall" etc.' (ibid.). These couplings, like the linking of dance with difference discussed in the previous chapter, effectively displace the attention away from dance. Ward notes that even when dance is addressed, as in the penultimate chapter of the Redhead collection (Russell, 1993), it surfaces as an incidental response to other primary factors. The argument that Russell puts forward is that because the musical genres were 'derived from unlicensed and under-age clubs in ghettos, where alcohol was not sold', an 'open market' was made 'for punters who had *no other option* than to dance' (cited in Ward, 1997, p. 5). Ward considers that this kind of argumentation, which typifies the approach to dance in the Redhead collection, means that 'dance is glossed over and its importance and centrality to raves is effectively ignored' (ibid.). I would also suggest that this kind of analysis may be treated as a contemporary equivalent to nineteenth-century anthropological evolutionary approaches which assumed that when 'other' (non-western, pre-literate) societies could not understand something because they lacked or had not yet developed 'reason', they simply danced!

The history of social dancing from the 1960s, as indicated earlier, has been largely bound up with specific youth cultures and their identification with certain music styles, groups or individual vocalists. In the previous chapter, it was argued that the feminisation of dance within the western theatrical tradition contributed to dance's marginal status within the academy. The peripheral status of theatre dance in social and cultural studies has been reflected in the scant attention paid to dancing in subcultural analysis (see McRobbie, 1990; Ward, 1993; Thomas, 1995), despite the importance placed on dance by successive subcultures, as a symbol of their particular subcultural style, if not always as the central practice (Gore, 1997).

The dance hall, from the 1950s in particular, has been connected with concerns over the behaviour of urban, working-class youth (Chambers, 1985). Indeed, it has played a key role in working-class leisure since the 1920s, as Paul Cressey's (1968 [1932]) classic Chicago school study of the taxi-dance hall revealed. Cressey linked the emergence of the 'dime a dance' taxi-dance hall in Chicago and other major US urban centres in the late 1920s with the increasing 'commercialisation of stimulation' in the recreational activities of city life and to promiscuity, which he defined as 'intimate behaviour upon the basis of casual association' (1968, author's preface). In the taxi-dance hall, which often masqueraded under the title of 'dancing academy' or 'school of dancing instruction', the all-male patrons paid the women- and girls-only 'dancing instructors' to dance with them. The women were not allowed to refuse to dance with any man, hence the title 'taxi-dancer'. The takings were usually divided between the proprietors and the dancers on a fifty-fifty basis (p. 3).

Cressey's study was based on data gleaned from social agencies in Chicago such as the Juvenile Protective Association, from social workers and a team of observers and researchers. The 'official' data, however, were scanty and unreliable. Moreover, the owners, customers and dancers were unwilling to cooperate with researchers on a formal interview basis once they had revealed the purpose of their inquiries. As a consequence, a team of 'observers' were sent into the taxi-dance hall establishments as 'anonymous strangers and acquaintances', with instructions 'to mingle with the others and become as much a part of this social world as ethically possible' (1968, author's preface).

In this early example of a 'covert' participant observation study, Cressey argued that the opportunity for promiscuity stemmed from the anonymity of city life, where it is difficult to form friendships, particularly for those who fall out of the mainstream of American life such as foreigners, displaced individuals and disabled people. The taxi-dance hall, according to Cressey, highlighted the problems that helped 'to shape behaviour in all public dance halls' (ibid.). The problems of city life were magnified in these places of dancing. In the taxi-dance hall and public dance hall in general, 'can be found in bold relief the impersonality of the city, the absence of restraints, the loneliness of individual adjustment and distraction characteristic of the life of many in the urban environment' (ibid.).

The taxi-dance hall, like the public dance hall some years before, came under the scrutiny of the police and social workers. The taxi-dance hall was suspected of harbouring 'immorality and prostitution' (p. 262). Plans were put into place by the Chicago Juvenile Protection Association to try to 'control and supervise' the institution, 'wherever possible' (p. 270), including forcing the taxi-dance halls to apply for amusement licences, similar to those held by the commercial dance halls in the city. The 'Chicago Plan', which had proved successful in establishing standards and codes of practices in the city's dance palaces, through the cooperation of the authorities with the proprietors of the dance halls, based on mutual interest, was later applied to the taxi-dance halls, but with varying degrees of success. Cressey concluded that even if it were completely regulated, the taxi-dance hall 'can never be a substitute for normal social life. For both taxi-dancer and patrons the institution ... can never be entirely free from moral danger and the hazards involved in promiscuous acquaintanceships' (p. 293). Thus, the taxi-dance hall in particular, and the dance hall in general, constituted sites of potential moral danger for young people.

As I have noted elsewhere, the democratisation of ballroom dancing reached its peak in the 1920s, with the introduction and the spread of the sumptuous dance halls, with their big bands, specially created for a mass public (Thomas and Miller, 1997, pp. 102–3). With the rise to prominence of ragtime music through the work of black composers such as Scott Joplin and the subsequent development of 'rag dances' in the first decade of the twentieth century, the actual steps or the movement of social dances became less important than before. Instead the impetus for the new 'rag dances' such as the *turkey trot* and *chicken reel*, as Julie Malnig's (1995) study of the development of exhibition dancing demonstrates, came from ragtime's syncopated rhythm. New ballroom dances were created out of 'a fusion of syncopated rags with traditional-European based social dances' (Malnig, 1995, p. 7) such as the *hesitation waltz*, where the couple pause or hover on the second and third counts. Moreover, the uniformity that had characterised ballroom dancing before this period gave way to an increasing emphasis on individuality and freedom in dancing and the popularity of solo dancing in the 1920s like the *charleston*, the *shimmy* and the *black bottom*. Thus, solo social dancing was popular long before the advent of dance crazes in the 1960s like the *twist*, *shake* and the *bluebeat*, which was inspired by Jamaican dance music (Brewster and Broughton, 1999).

While some authorities on dancing in England in the early 1920s welcomed the new jazz-inspired vernacular dances as innovative and exciting, others equated them with 'artistic bolshevism' (Richardson, 1948, pp. 42–3). Moves to regulate and standardise ballroom dancing were set into motion in the 1920s and by the end of the decade, the highly individualistic dancing of the jazz era was codified into what later became known as the 'English style'. Implicit in the codification of dancing and the regulation of the dance halls is the management of the masses, particularly of young people, and a de-emphasis or erasure of the influence of black music and black dance practices on the development of western dance music cultures.[8]

There is evidence to suggest that young people have been the object of their elders' criticisms as far back as the eighteenth century (Malbon, 1999). The construct of youth as a sociological category emerged in the 1920s and can be traced to the work of the Chicago school. Cressey's study of the taxi-dance hall exemplifies a concern with the relationship between deviant youth and leisure in the context of the changing social structures through the development and the fragmentation of the city. For the Chicago school sociologists, delinquent behaviour was a 'normal' response that was rooted in cultural norms, not in individual pathology. The 'youth as a social problem industry' began to develop in Britain after the end of World War II around the time when the concept of 'the teenager' became dominant. The overriding view of the delinquent was that of a bored youth who had too much money and time to spend it on hedonistic pursuits. In reality, as Simon Frith was to point out much later in *The Sociology of Rock* (1978), wages were low and, contrary to prevailing ideas about embourgeoisement, class divisions were strong and consumption was restricted.

The term 'subculture' initially referred to a subsection of the national culture (Brake, 1985). The concept of culture employed in subcultural analysis stems from the anthropological view of culture 'as a way of life'. This horizontal view of culture encompasses a wider framework than the vertical (hierarchical) concept of culture, which derives from the culture and civilisation tradition in which culture is defined as 'the best that has been thought and said'. The former approach allows for extra-materialist considerations, such as the values, ideas, symbols and so on that enable people to recognise themselves as members of a group and which help to keep the group together, to be taken into account. These wider considerations were activated by subcultural theory in the 1970s. Mike Brake (1985, pp. 58–9) categorises the development of subcultural theory from the 1950s to the late 1970s into four main approaches. First, there were 'the early social ecology [approaches] of the late 1950s and early 1960s'. Second, there were the 'studies related to the sociology of education', which analysed 'the relation between youth, leisure and youth culture'. Third, the 1970s 'neighbourhood studies' examined 'local youth groups in the context of social reaction and labelling'. Finally, there was the work of the Birmingham-based CCCS, which 'was influenced by the new criminology of the National Deviancy Conferences' and which utilised 'a combination of theories of culture, structuralism, Marxist theory and theories of ideology, in particular Gramsci's view of hegemony'.

Youth became a major focus of the members of the CCCS in the 1970s. The interdisciplinary approach which the CCCS adopted moved away from the study of youth gangs and towards the analysis of the styles of specific spectacular youth cultures such as the teddy boys, mods, rockers and skinheads, which since the end of World War II had become a feature of British social life. The publication in 1975 of a collection of papers from the CCCS, *Resistance through Rituals* (Hall and Jefferson, 1976) constituted an important marker in this development. Subcultural analysis examined the relationship of youth subculture to the parent culture (notably the working class in the case of the CCCS) and the dominant culture (mainstream youth). Working-class youth subcultures were seen to arise to resolve 'magically' the contradictions in the material and economic forms that were also experienced in the parent culture. The term 'magical' was derived from Althusser's (1969) structuralist Marxist approach to the concept of ideology, which implies an imaginary relation of individuals to their 'real' conditions of social existence. Subcultures, within this framework, can never resolve structural problems; rather they can only 'appear' to do so, or to divert them from their 'true' nature.

Marxist perspectives were central to the work of the CCCS on subcultures. In *Policing the Crisis*, Hall *et al.* (1978) mobilised Gramsci's concept of the crisis in hegemony to examine the moral panics that arose in the 1970s around the black teenager, who emerged as the central problematic youth 'folk devil' of the time. Gramsci (1971) maintained that ruling elites in society have to exert authority over subordinate groups by not only winning but also by shaping consent (hegemony) to their authority. Ruling-class hegemony is never fixed or total but is constantly shifting and is caught up in an ongoing process of negotiation and struggle. In the Gramsci-inspired CCCS approach, subcultures were viewed as being engaged in a struggle over cultural 'space' (Brake, 1985). Their solutions, however, as indicated before, could only be 'imaginary'.

Lévi-Strauss's (1969) construct of bricolage was also employed to examine the symbolic elements of subcultural style in *Resistance and Rituals* (Hall and Jefferson, 1976). Here, everyday objects and symbols are taken from their original contexts and reordered to generate new meanings. The way in which a given subculture used commonplace commodities, according to Dick Hebdige (1979, p. 103), separated 'the subculture off from more orthodox formations'. Thus, the appropriation and transformation of the Edwardian Savile Row suit of the 1950s by working-class teddy boys, who were all dressed up and nowhere to go, could be treated as 'an act of bricolage' because the meanings associated with the 'original' style were subverted or erased by reordering the stylistic components into a different 'symbolic ensemble' (ibid.). 'Youth cultural style' in the CCCS approach, as Brake (1985, p. 68) argues, was 'treated as a text which can be read at a level beyond the verbal through the pattern of styles, argot and appearances'. Subcultural stylistic resistance, because of its deep-seated connection with the domain of leisure, offered a 'symbolic critique' of the dominant social order 'through a symbolic representation of social contradictions' (ibid.).

Certain members of the CCCS (for example, Hall and Jefferson, 1976; Willis, 1978) considered that stylistic resistance relied on a match or 'homology' (also borrowed from Lévi-Strauss) between 'certain types of style, artefacts and the group identity' (Brake, 1985, p. 68). Thus, all the elements of the subculture were put together to form a whole image that expressed the group's sense of identity and its difference from other groups. Hebdige (1979, p. 117), challenged the one-to-one relationship between sign and signifier in homological approaches to subcultural stylistic resistance. He argued that the construct of homology was overly simplistic and inadequate for making sense of, for example, the 'difficult and contradictory text of punk style'. In order to understand 'the seemingly endless, often apparently random, play of signifiers in evidence' in punk style, Hebdige adopted a 'polysemic' reading of punk's stylistic signifying practices, 'whereby each text is seen to generate an infinite number of meanings' (ibid.).[9] The recuperations of a subcultural style by younger age groups and by commercial culture, in the eyes of theorists from the CCCS, signalled the demise of the authentic subculture and the cue for the subcultural-ists to search out and appropriate different everyday symbols or create new ones and thus carry on the symbolic fight.

The work of the CCCS represented the first systematic analysis of style of spectacular youth cultures in Britain and it had a profound influ-ence on subsequent work in the area. As the 1970s gave way to the 1980s, subcultural theory was subjected to a number of criticisms (see Brake, 1985, p. 70). It was accused of romanticising working-class youth culture and of over-theorising. It was criticised for paying too lit-tle attention to 'raw' data (with perhaps the exception of Willis, who maintained a commitment to ethnographic work) and for not taking the subjective meanings of the subculturalists into account. By focusing on the 'card-carrying' members of subcultures (working-class, males), sub-cultural theory overlooked the fact that the majority of youth also engaged in the forms and the practices of subcultures (see Bennett, 2000, p. 22). It also assumed an all too unitary view of subcultures and thus did not take regional variations into account (ibid.). These criticisms, in time, along with changes in youth culture, led to a questioning of the term 'subculture' (Redhead, 1990; Thornton, 1995; Muggleton, 2000) and a shift away from class-based interpretations of youth in favour of different models based on 'lifestyle' (Chambers, 1985), 'grounded aesthetics' (Willis *et al.*, 1990) and the experiences of ethnic minorities (see Bennett, 2000, pp. 28–30). One of the most swingeing sociological criticisms of the CCCS approach to subcultural resistance and style came from Stanley Cohen in the second edition of his classic study of *Folk Devils and Moral Panics* (1980) which was first published in 1972.

Cohen (1980) argued that by decoding subcultural style in terms of resistance and opposition, subcultural theory glossed over those occa-sions when style might be highly conservative, with the group taking on the trappings of the dominant commercial culture. Moreover, Cohen challenged the notion that subcultural stylistic resistance arose spontaneously from within the group itself, with little input from the media and other cultural influences. This overlooked the fact that changes in youth culture have often been manufactured and dictated by consumer society and/or the media. Cohen's study, which drew on labelling theory and transactional analysis, set out to show how two subcultures, mods and rockers, came into visibility. For Cohen, it was their treatment in the mass media that led to these groups being designated 'folk devils', which, in turn, led to the creation of a 'moral panic'. Once these folk devils were identified, large numbers of British teenagers consciously took on these two deviant roles. The moral panic that ensued, underpinned by the fear of disruption to the social order, gave rise to indiscriminate arrests and calls for tighter controls and harsher punishments from the media and the moral guardians of society. Cultural analysts of rave and club culture, as indicated earlier (Redhead, 1990; Rietveld, 1993; Thornton, 1995), have also noted the importance of the media in alerting vast numbers of young people to the emergent rave party scene and the resulting moral panics that followed on soon after. Indeed, Thornton (1995) argues that subcultures are ultimately 'media constructions' and Redhead (1990) suggests that authentic subcultures are a construction of subcultural theories.

The subcultural studies of the CCCS paid scant attention to women. Postwar youth subcultures, as Brake (1985) has argued, have been both 'male dominated' and 'masculinist' in outlook. 'If subcultures are solutions to collectively experienced problems', he argues, 'then traditionally those have been the problems experienced by young men' (1985, p. 163). In subcultures, 'maleness' has been treated as a 'solution to identity otherwise undermined by structural features' (ibid.). In the late 1970s, McRobbie and Garber (1991) began to question the persistent absence of women and ethnic minorities in subcultural analysis of postwar youth cultures. She both built on and critiqued the pioneering work that emanated from the CCCS, where she had been an MA student (Hall and Jefferson, 1976; Willis, 1977, 1978; Hebdige, 1979). The 'invisible girl' in subcultural analysis, according to McRobbie and Garber (1991) and Brake (1985), was not only a consequence of subcultural members' attitudes towards femininity, but also of women's relation to production. The young women, according to McRobbie (1991), were not marginal to the subcultural groupings. Rather, they occupied a structurally different position to the men. Because they were engaged in a different range of activities (which centred around the private sphere), young women were pushed to the margins of successive subcultures by male dominance. Part of the problem may be laid at the feet of the male researchers who identified with the males in subcultures and who colluded with the subjects under study to remove girls from their view (McRobbie, 1991). Dancing, in McRobbie's (1990) view, is an activity that traditionally has provided girls with 'the fantasy of achievement', 'bodily self-expression' and control, even if this were only for the limited amount of time they remained on the dance floor. The importance of dancing to young women is reiterated in a more recent article on rave culture:

Dance is where girls were always found in subcultures. It was their only entitlement. Now in rave it becomes the motivating force for the entire subculture. (McRobbie, 1993, p. 419)

The centrality of dance in rave, McRobbie argues, 'gives girls a new found confidence and prominence' (ibid.). In rave and club culture, 'girls are highly sexual in their dress and appearance' in their 'aerobic' outfits of 'bra tops, leggings and trainers'. In a post-AIDS world, however, a tension in rave arises for girls between 'remaining in control, and at the same time losing themselves in dance and music'. 'Losing it' on the dance floor has to be balanced against 'the exercise in control of sex' (ibid.). McRobbie suggests that one way round this problem might lie 'in cultivating a hyper-sexual appearance' which nevertheless is sealed off by incorporating (pre-sexual) childhood objects like the dummy or the ice lolly into the body picture. The suggestion that young women ravers surround their bodies with symbols and rituals to ward off potential danger or invasion from outside forces resonates to some extent with Douglas's (1970, 1973) analysis of bodily symbolism in periods of societal 'risk', which was discussed in Chapter 1.[10]

Although dancing was and is central to rave, women themselves have not been at the centre of the production processes. For example, the shamans of rave and club culture, the DJs, are overwhelmingly male. Indeed, throughout their substantial history of the rise of the DJ, Brewster and Broughton (1999) purposefully refer to the disc jockey as 'he': 'In DJing's 94 years', they note, 'women have been largely frozen out of the picture with very few exceptions' (p. 405). They also suggest that acid house culture opened up the possibility for at least some women to enter into what was traditionally the 'boys' club of the popular music world' (ibid.).

In general, the advances that women have made in the division of labour since the sexual revolution have not been replicated in the field of dance music production, despite the centrality of dance in rave culture and their presence on the dance floor. Indeed, just as academic feminism has all but ignored theatre dance, so it has also failed to take account of the claims of women ravers 'regarding the apparent ability of rave to dissolve social divisions based upon sex, sexuality, age, race and class' (Pini, 1997a, p. 118) on the dance floor, if not off it. Maria Pini's (2001) study sets out to investigate female subjectivities in rave and club culture, to reinstate the women's dancing experiences back into the frame of dance culture and feminism.

Ward (1997) argues that part of the problem of dance being 'every-where' and yet 'nowhere' in society, from the perspective of cultural analysts and feminists alike, lies in the fact that dance is associated with the 'non-rational'. In order to understand the meanings of dance, Ward suggests that it is necessary to go directly to the sites where dance takes place and ask the participants what dance means for *them*. Whilst I would agree with this, it is also worth noting that the problem of translation from sentient movement to (verbal) meaning, as discussed in the previous chapter, presents difficulties for cultural analysts, although these may not be intractable. There is also evidence to suggest that some respondents find it difficult to give voice to their under-standings of what dance means for them (Thomas, 1993b; Malbon, 1999). It may be the case that cultural analysts do not 'know' how to 'look' or write about movement. Redhead, for example, speaks of acid house as 'a dance which required "no expertise" whatsoever' (1990, p. 6). This implies that any movement will do, which clearly is not the case. There is a sociality at work in the way that people use their bodies in solo 'expressive' dancing, just as there is in ballroom dancing and, as demonstrated in Chapters 1 and 2, in the everyday world outside of the dance event.

Individuals do make distinctions between what is good dancing and what is not, either in regard to themselves or others, as Malbon (1999) points out, although they may not be able to articulate these in the lan-guage of critical aesthetics. For example, *circa* 1980s disco dance style, incorporating stepping, turning, arms gesturing into space and gyrating hips 'playing the rhythm' would be considered very 'un-cool' in the con-text of contemporary rave or clubbing, where the virtuoso performance and stepping or moving into general space are not noticeably the order of the day. The virtuoso dancing performances of the jivers described earlier in the 1950s story would be viewed as similarly 'un-hip', unless, of course, it was a 1950s theme night. But even here, the dancing would be somewhat different from that in the earlier period. The techniques of the body associated with social dancing have changed over time and, with the increasing fragmentation of the club scene, may also take on certain local characteristics (see Bennett, 2000, on this point). This is not to imply that there is a 'fixed way' to dance disco or jive or that dancers do not individualise their dancing. I would want to argue that there are some observable patterns or stylistic elements to social danc-ing in particular contexts which are known and shared by co-present dancers, although these may be localised rather than global and depen-dent on differences in age, gender, race and experience.

I encountered an example of this at a recent college Christmas ball, which was attended by people of different ages, from about 20 to 50+

years old. As I looked around the dance floor, I was struck by the fact that even when the younger men and women danced to 1980s disco sounds, they moved very differently from the older people on the floor, who had danced to sounds of disco the first time round. In contrast to the older dancers whose front and eye focus changed through stepping and turning and whose gestures inhabited the space around the body, the younger people danced on the spot, with their feet, moving subtly, keeping a distinctive light (pulse-like) bounce. Focusing to the front, to their co-dancers, their arms moved lightly up and down in the space in front of and to the side of the upper body in a sinewy and flowing manner with subtle, almost imperceptible, isolated movements in the upper body providing the impulse for the shaping movements of the arms. Both age groups were dancing to the same music at the same time and in the same space but the techniques of the body employed in the dancing were observably different and, at least in this instance, these appeared to be age-related, no matter how good or bad the performance. It was also evident that the younger people found their elders' dancing very funny and 'out of date', while the latter seemed blissfully unaware that they were doing something different from the younger dancers. I suspect that they would not care very much in any case, as they were dancing to music of their (past) time.[11]

This is not to deny that clubbers, as Malbon (1999) points out, dance in an individualised way, even when copying others. Although 'an individual clubber will dance quite differently according to the stage of the night, the type of night, whether they have consumed drugs or alcohol', where and with whom they are dancing and so on, 'there are, nevertheless, very well-established "ways of doing" dancing' (1999, p. 98). In other words, just as a clubber has to conduct certain negotiations in order to get through the door of the club in the first instance, so there are certain interactional dancing codes of practice that a clubber has to learn to be accepted as a co-clubber (see Goffman, 1959). Clubbers may learn to dance by watching others dance and copying them and through absorbing, making bodily sense of and going with the music. The manner in which individuals learn to dance and the levels of competency they achieve will depend on a range of factors: age, race, gender, experience, musicality, aptitude and so on. If the individual is in any doubt as to how to proceed, they can always consult the myriad of dance videos or the articles that appear in clubbing magazines and books, which offer 'relatively accurate diagrams and descriptions of dance clubbers' (Malbon, 1999, p. 98). These published transcriptions, which transform three-dimensional dance actions, such as those of disco or clubbing genres, into two-dimensional diagrammatic representations showing 'a series of footmarks traced on the page', according to Gilbert and Pearson (1999, p. 12), are not without fault. In general, they combine 'apparently democratic motives with a ruthlessly commercial agenda' (ibid.). The publication of a profusion of books on how to dance at certain points in time, for example, in the late 1970s when disco emerged out of the gay black scene in New York and entered the global mainstream, testifies to the popularity of dancing during such periods. The books and articles may help to draw in 'a broader demographic of dancer' who may not have accumulated the cultural capital to dance in an appropriate manner in the context of, say, disco or contemporary clubbing genres. The underside of this, for Gilbert and Pearson, is that in the drive to sell more and more copies to a broader public, the forms themselves may become ossified and 'reduced to strictly ordered set of moves' (p. 13). The problems of creating a living movement form from a notated score alone were addressed in the chapter on dance reconstruction. However, 'how to' dancing manuals, as suggested earlier, are by no means a recent phenomenon, nor do they simply depict footprints on a page, although there are conventions for doing just that. Moreover, as indicated above, people learn to dance in a variety of ways and not just through 'dancing by numbers'. Even when individual moves are restricted in a highly codified form, individuality in some way will find its way out onto the dance floor. In modern sequence dancing, for example, the floor patterns and steps are set within a repeated 16-bar phrase and the couples, one in front of the other, move in unison round the dance floor. I have observed time and time again the idiosyncratic movements of couples and individuals: a little flick of a hand movement here, a lingering backward tilt too far there,[12] despite the fact that they were concerned to perform the same steps and moves at the same time as everyone else.

From subcultures to club cultures

Academic interest in youth club cultures has grown considerably since the mid-1990s. There has been a shift of interest from subcultures to club cultures in cultural criticism, which is evidenced in the increasing numbers of articles, books and PhD projects on aspects of dance music cultures and youth.[13] According to Pini, 'rave appears to have had some quite fundamental effects in altering the traditional relations between Left scholarship and social dance cultures' (2001, p. 24). The academic left's concern with resistance, as discussed earlier, rested uneasily with rave culture's emphasis on physicality, its pursuit of pleasure and partying. Popular dance music cultures, like disco in the 1970s or rave in the early 1990s, were generally characterised as inauthentic, conformist and consumerist in contrast to punk, whose oppositional stance towards consumer capitalism became, in effect, the yardstick by which subsequent subcultures came to be measured (Redhead, 1993a; Pini, 2001). Maria Pini argues that the continuing and growing appeal of rave to diverse groups of youth and the politicisation of the 'right to party' in the face of legislation to curtail and contain rave culture have made rave 'more difficult to ignore as a highly significant cultural phenomenon' (2001, p. 28). The fragmentation and segmentation of rave's musical genres and sub-genres and the concomitant 'technological developments which have made for important changes within the sphere of musical production' (ibid.) have also generated academic interest. Moreover, the questioning of the constructs of subculture and resistance within critical academic thinking opened up the possibility of 'a more sophisticated view of the relations between cultural practice, subjectivity and "politics" ' (ibid.). As discussed in Chapters 2 and 3, with developments in feminism, postmodernism and poststructuralist thinking in the 1980s and 1990s, the dualistic thinking which had dominated the western humanist tradition of thought was increasingly called into question. Once the hierarchical distinction between authentic/inauthentic is abandoned or called into question, then mass cultural forms and practices, such as pop music and dance cultures, which were formerly treated as passive and conventional, can be examined in a more considered light.

Sarah Thornton's (1995) study of *Club Cultures* made an important contribution to the development of this emergent field. She moved away from the more speculative statements regarding the significance of rave by the few cultural commentators who addressed the movement in the early 1990s such as Redhead and McRobbie. Redhead proposed that the 'changes in youth culture' brought about by acid house and rave 'are at the cutting edge of a "politics of deviance" ' (1993a, p. 5). McRobbie considered that 'rave seems to overturn many of the expectations and assumptions we might now have about youth subcultures' (1993, p. 418). Thornton provides a sustained account of club cultures as 'taste cultures'. She begins from the position that:

> Club crowds generally congregate on the basis of their shared taste in music, their consumption of common media and ... their preference for

people like themselves. Crucially, club cultures embrace their own hierarchies of what is authentic and legitimate in popular culture – embodied understanding of what can make one 'hip'. These distinctions – their socio-cultural logics, their economic roots – are the main subject of this book. (1995, p. 3)

Thornton adopts the vertical model of culture, which is concerned with aesthetic values and judgements, as opposed to the horizontal 'culture as a way of life' approach which studies in popular culture have generally employed. She draws on Bourdieu's analysis of 'cultural capital' and 'distinction', which was outlined briefly in Chapter 2, to make sense of 'the hierarchies of club culture' (1995, p. 11). Thornton defines her approach as 'post-Birmingham', which means that her work is both indebted to it and distinguishes itself from it. She rejects the definition of subcultures offered by the CCCS 'as empirically unworkable' (p. 8). Instead, the term 'subcultural' is adopted to identify 'the practices that clubbers call "underground"', while the term 'subcultures' is employed 'to identify those taste cultures which are labelled by the media as subcultures' (ibid.). Thus, Thornton is concerned with the empirical study of 'social groups' as opposed to 'an elaboration of theory' (ibid.). As such, she identifies her approach with that of the Chicago school. She adopts an ethnographic survey method of approach: participant observation, with observation taking precedence over participation, a historical survey of the development of recorded musical 'authenticities' since the end of World War II and a textual analysis of the media.

In examining the taste cultures of clubbing, Thornton distinguishes between the sphere of the 'mainstream' and that of the 'hip' or 'cool'. 'The mainstream', she argues, 'is the entity against which the majority of clubbers define themselves' (p. 5). 'Hipness' is a form of subcultural capital. It confers on its owner the marks of distinction and taste that separate him or her off from the mainstream, the crowd or the mass, in the eyes of others. Subcultural capital, as indicated in the quotation cited above, can be 'objectified or embodied'. 'It is objectified in the form of fashionable haircuts and well-assembled record collections' (p. 11) and is embodied in the knowingness of subcultural style and argot. That is, individuals have to demonstrate that they know just how to dress, that they know the right amount of and kind of slang to use and that they can perform the latest dance styles so that it looks as if their dancing is as natural to them as walking. These practices should be integral to their bodily habitus, to use Bourdieu's term. Thornton's study, as indicated earlier, provides evidence that youth cultures do not simply emerge through an act of will in isolation from other social and cultural influences; rather these forces, including the media, are integral to the formation and practices of youth cultures.

Despite noting the importance of Thornton's study to this emergent field of research, Malbon (1999) argues that she fails to attend to the experience of clubbing itself. He also points out, like Ward (1997), that this neglect is evidenced in other recent work, such as Redhead *et al.*'s (1998) reader on *Clubcultures*. Pini, on the other hand, suggests that Thornton's study colludes in the 'tendency to double raving women's invisibility' (2001, p. 31). The central focus of the study, subcultural capital, Pini argues, is directed principally towards the preserve of men. The construct of the mainstream that Thornton employs is associated with the feminine and the mass (see Huyssen, 1986, on this relation) and is set against the continually redefining 'insider' underground position. Thornton, of course, is aware of the hierarchy of gender at work in the game of subcultural capital. Women, she notes, 'often opt out of the game of "hipness", refusing to compete and conceding defeat' (Thornton, cited in Pini, 2001, p. 32). Women's subject positions in relation to the hierarchy of taste in club cultures, as Pini argues, are limited to admitting defeat on the one hand, or differentiating themselves from 'Sharon and Tracy' on the other, by aligning themselves with the 'cool' (the masculine). Pini's research on women ravers in London suggests that relations between mainstream and underground 'might signify differently for men and women' (p. 33). She argues that other factors, such as feeling (sexually) safe going to and within a dance event, are important to women, which suggests rather different meanings to the mainstream/hip distinction articulated in Thornton's study. In such instances, the mainstream signifies potentially annoying male behaviour towards the women for whom 'rave's major appeal lies in its provision of the opportunities for taking drugs, going "mental" and dancing through the night without sexual harassment' (p. 34). The notion of 'cool', here, 'is about testing the limits of traditionally "appropriate" femininity' (ibid.).

Pini's analysis of female subjectivities in rave and post-rave dance cultures, like that of McRobbie (1993) and other researchers discussed in the preceding chapter, emphasises the liberatory potential of dance. Andy Bennett's (2000) study of music youth cultures in Newcastle in the north-east of England also indicates that the women who attend the weekly Pigbag Club are particularly enthusiastic about this alternative clubbing event, precisely because they can dance without encountering unwanted male attention. This is contrary to their perceptions of traditional city nightclubs. For the clubbers at this event and other similar 'urban dance music events', it is dancing above all else which is important, according to Bennett (2000, p. 93). The importance of dancing is signalled by the fact that the 'normal spatial divisions between the dance floor and non-dance areas merge together'. Although the dancers appropriate non-dance spaces, there is an unspoken code of practice whereby others who wish to occupy the non-dance spaces give priority to the dancers by not crossing into the latter's personal space. If bodily contact occurs, then the non-dancers offer an 'excuse-me' to the dancers who are occupying the non-dance space.[14] This kind of bodily sensibility, according to Bennett, re-emphasises the non-sexist atmosphere 'that prevails at urban dance music events and their special appeal for female enthusiasts' (ibid.). Malbon (1999) is more cautious and argues that it might be more accurate to say that *some* women experience this kind of freedom but it is not necessarily the case for all women clubbers. Contrary to the general claims of McRobbie and Pini, Malbon's research into clubbing in London found that 'some women clubbers experience clubbing as involving a level of often heightened sexualisation or sexual display' (1999, p. 45). In agreement with Pini though, he suggests that this display of sexuality may not be about getting a partner as such, but rather about the women constructing a sexuality of expression for themselves, in a way that is not open to them in other 'ordinary' areas of their lives. This interpretation resonates with Miller's (1991) reading of female wining in the Trinidadian carnival, which was discussed in the previous chapter. The female winers, according to Miller, invoked a sexuality that was not dependent on men, an auto-sexuality, which momentarily inverted the cross-gender relations they experienced in everyday life. Whilst Malbon does not evoke the notion of auto-sexuality or the construct of absolute freedom, he nevertheless agrees that dance can be liberatory for 'some' women in particular contexts. He suggests that in such cases, the women do not become de-sexualised, but, rather, that 'their sexuality becomes *differently* important' (1999, p. 45).

Despite differences between the studies of Pini (2001), Bennett (2000) and Malbon (1999), they share a number of features in common. To begin with, these studies primarily focus on the local, micro-sociological level and, for the most part, do not make grand claims about the applicability of their findings to the global level, although this is perhaps less so in Pini's work. The relations between space, place and time are important. Nevertheless, as indicated above, the connection between dance and liberation is never very far away from the surface. Emphasis is placed on the partial and empirical as opposed to invoking the sweeping narratives of postmodern theorising which characterised some earlier accounts of rave and club culture (for example, Rietveld, 1993; Melchi, 1993), in which rave was interpreted as a kind of 'mass disappearance', which signified 'a death of meaning', a 'depthlessness'. These three studies are concerned with the experience of clubbing from the participants' point of view and unlike Thornton's study, for example, ethnographic methods are central to these clubbing accounts.[15] In Bennett's and Malbon's work, the influence of the Chicago school studies of micro-social interactions within the urban environments is strong, and all three studies draw on ethnographic interviews and participant observation to develop their analyses. All three studies emphasise the sociality of dance music cultures. But it is not the sense of the social that may be gleaned from earlier functionalist analysis, which drew heavily on Durkheim's idea of society as a social fact (see Chapter 1). Rather the sense of sociality that emerges in these three studies is much more fluid, transient and fragmented. Pini (2001), for example, draws on Rosie Braidotti's (1994) corporeal feminist idea of 'nomadic subjects' and Donna Haraway's (1991) construct of the 'cyborg' as a way of understanding the new shifting modes of female inter-subjectivities which the women in her study claim that they experience in rave culture. Malbon[16] and Bennett, on the other hand, draw critically on Michel Maffesoli's (1996) concepts of 'neo-tribe' and 'sociality' as a background to their discussions of the practices of sociality and identifications in clubbing and dance music cultures. Sociality, according to Maffesoli, is important in contemporary consumer-oriented societies. The notion of tribe he employs is not the fixed, static version that characterised earlier anthropological studies. Rather, Maffesoli's construct of neo-tribe describes the shifting nature of collective associations and affiliations in postmodern consumer cultures based on shared interests, as opposed to political ideologies (Bennett, 2000). Sociality constitutes a range of often taken-for-granted everyday practices that underpin social life: the glue that binds social existence (Malbon, 1999, p. 24). Although the individual's sense of identification with the clubbing crowd in the urban environment may ebb and flow throughout the evening, the forms of sociality that are invoked are generally viewed in the affirmative, although sometimes qualified by acknowledgements of social distinction and exclusivity in club culture. The positive, affective, transient sense of the social among friends, strangers and casual acquaintances in the analysis of contemporary social dance cultures stands in sharp contrast to Cressey's (1932) view of the dance hall generally and the taxi-dance hall in particular in the expanding 'anonymous' city life of the 1920s.

Both the shifting, transient socialities which feature in the analyses of club cultures and the expression of 'anomie' which Cressey identified in the early dance halls are rather different from the strong sense of communitas which many of the older 'social' dancers in the south-east London and Essex study expressed (Thomas and Cooper, 2002). This was particularly evident in modern sequence dancing, where couples, one in front of the other, perform the same steps at the same time in a circle (see McNeill, 1995, on the historical significance of 'moving together in time'). For the over-60s participants in the study, sequence dancing evokes a different time when social solidarity, rather like Durkheim's organic solidarity, appeared to them to be more important than the cult of the individual or the 'me' generation of today. A strong sense of bonding and coming together of the group was also expressed by older individuals who preferred a mixture of ballroom and sequence and those who preferred creative dance. An important element of this project involved filming the dancing, the people and the venues. Nine edited videos with details of the project are available for viewing at http://dance.gold.ac.uk, and instead of giving further details of the sense of community which the participants expressed through their dancing, I invite the reader to explore this further with reference to the videos.

Subjectivities, as Thornton (1995), Pini (2001), Bennett (2000) and Malbon (1999) note, are embodied and one of the key ways in which these subjectivities and inter-subjectivities are articulated in club cultures is through dancing. Only Malbon offers a sustained discussion of the practices of clubbing, which includes a careful address of 'embodied understanding' and the relations of individual identities and identifications with the crowd through dancing. Malbon merges Goffman's (1959) approach to performativity with that of Judith Butler (1990a), which, he argues, 'can improve our understandings of how the consuming experience of the crowd can be simultaneously expressive (Goffmanian) and constructive (Butlerian) of the self' (1999, p. 29).

Dancing in contemporary club cultures, as Malbon notes, can mean different things to different people and can thus be interpreted in a range of ways:

> Dancing within clubbing might be interpreted as an expressive form of thinking, sensing, feeling and processing which may be constituted through, as well as reflecting, strong relationships between a clubber and

the clubbing crowd, and in turn between the clubbing crowd and the society of which it is a part... Dancing within clubbing can be about fun, pleasure and escape, about being together or being apart, about sexual interaction and display, about listening to the music, and even a form of embodied resistance and source of personal and social vitality. (pp. 86–7)

Ultimately, for Malbon, it is the 'social centrality' of dancing in the lives of many clubbers, which has been 'glossed over' by cultural analysts, that necessitates an investigation into the 'socio-spatio-temporalities of dancing in clubbing' (p. 86). This entails asking 'how' questions rather than 'why' questions: 'How is dancing performed and how might we start to conceptualise its practices?' (ibid.). In so doing, Malbon propels the activity of dancing to the centre of the study of club cultures.

Conclusion

This book aimed to achieve several ends. The overarching aim was to demonstrate that dance forms and practices offer a rich set of resources for exploring the possibilities and the limitations of the study of the body in society, a topic which, in the wake of the 'turn to culture' in the 1980s, has preoccupied much social and cultural criticism. It also sought to make a contribution to the area of study by giving 'the body' an empirical focus, by adopting a dance case studies approach and by drawing on the tools of dance analysis. In order to do this, it was first necessary to situate the chosen dance case studies against the backdrop of a number of key themes and issues that have emerged out of the study of the body in social and cultural theory. The dance case studies gave rise to a number of methodological and theoretical issues which, in turn, aimed to shed light on debates in contemporary cultural theory.

The interest in 'body studies', as shown in Chapters 1 and 2, has been evidenced in a range of sub-disciplines of the social sciences. Post-positivist developments in social and cultural theory (feminism, psychoanalysis, poststructuralism and social philosophy) have had a considerable impact in moving 'the body' centre stage in the social science arena. As demonstrated in Chapter 1, initially theorists argued that the body had been absent or at least had occupied a marginal position in sociology and anthropology as a consequence of the concern within the dominant canon of these disciplines to demonstrate the cultural aspects of human existence over natural or non-social features. More recent accounts, however, drawing on the insights of contemporary theoretical approaches, have shown that with a careful rereading of the sociological canon, for example, 'the body' may not have been quite so absent in the classical tradition of sociology as was previously thought. In addition, as shown in Chapter 1, a concern for understanding the role of the body in culture surfaced at other points in twentieth-century social science prior to the 1980s. These, in turn, contributed to the subsequent dominance of social constructionist approaches in contemporary social and cultural studies. Social constructionist perspectives, as discussed in Chapter 2, sought to lift the body out of the domain of the natural or the biological and into the textual, symbolic or discursive realms by theorising the body as an unfinished entity, which is shaped and constructed in and invented by society. The 'story' of the body in social science, before and after the establishment of body studies, circled around the shifts and nuances in perspectives of the debate between social constructionism and foundationalism. The dualisms inherent in western social thought were never far from the surface. Because the social sciences and cultural studies are inherently critical, recent developments in and approaches to the study of the body have also been subject to debate and critique, as shown in Chapter 2.

One of the major criticisms of recent body studies is that there has been an over-attention to theory at the expense of empirical analysis. That is, body studies on the whole fail to offer concrete evidence to substantiate or develop the theoretical stances adopted. Another is that body studies tend to use the body as a focus for studying something else (for example, consumer culture, gender, race and ethnicity, risk, health and illness, technologies of the body), with the result that the body simply disappears as it is brought into discourse. It may be that 'writing' about the body, in the first instance, is always going to miss the mark of a cultural practice that is not linguistically based. However, as shown in Chapters 1, 2, 4 and 6, the body is not situated in some pre-discursive universe. Rather, the body in dance and culture is firmly rooted and implicated in the social. For example, the professional dancer's body in western theatre dance, trained to be flexible and strong and to move in ways that 'ordinary' humans can only wonder at, can reveal the infinite possibilities of the body in movement and stillness. This could be the social constructionist's dream case study. At the same time, however, the mostly young, finely honed, fit dancer encounters physical limitations and bodily recalcitrance on a daily basis, which, in turn, throws a dark shadow over the social constructionist's standpoint. Yet another criticism is that the dominant image of the body that emerges from body studies is static and immobile, a frozen entity locked in space and time. Moreover, while body studies researchers sought to overcome the dualisms in western thought, they have also been criticised for shoring them up. By choosing dance as a topic and resource of bodily inquiry, this book aimed to explore and counter these tendencies.

The body in western theatre dance and social dance is generally a key mode of expression and representation. The body, therefore, is almost always implicated in the choreographic forms and the analyst is forced to pay attention to bodily relationalities. That is, it is almost impossible to escape the dynamic, living, presence of the body in movement and stillness, for both the performer and the analyst. As argued in Chapter 3, dancing constitutes a form of cultural knowledge that is articulated through the 'bodily endeavours' of dancing subjects and not through the 'power of the word'. In dancing, as the case studies in this book hopefully show, individual embodied subjects/subjectivities enact and 'comment' on a variety of taken-for-granted social and cultural bodily relationalities:[1] gender and sexuality, identity and difference, individuality and community, mind and body and so on. As such, close attention to dancing can provide the social and cultural analyst with layers of insights into culturally contingent relations and practices which have hitherto gone largely unnoticed or unexamined (see also Ness, 2003, on this). For example, as demonstrated in Chapter 3, the ethnographic field is an embodied field and yet few ethnographers outside of dance studies have explored this aspect in any depth. From an examination of recent ethnographic research on specific social and ritual dance genres in Chapters 3[2] and 6, which employed 'embodied', participatory methodologies, it was argued that close analysis of dance forms, practices and events raises challenges to disembodied participant observation studies and offers a more focused, empirical approach to body studies. Employing a movement of choreographic ethnography, it should be emphasised, will not generate cultural truths. Rather, by offering a relatively unexplored and now you see it, now you don't 'forest of symbols' (Turner, 1974) to explore the multivocal, these movement ethnography case studies (in both Chapters 3 and 6) offer a new perspective on cultural symbols and embodied modes of interpretation and the opportunity of overcoming the mind/body dualisms which have shadowed much of the work in body studies.

A close reading of dance forms, content, traditions and bodily regimes can reveal the ways in which particular aesthetic bodily practices can also underscore and reflect the dualisms inherent in western cultural traditions. This was demonstrated in Chapter 4 through a close examination of the prioritising of the senses of sight in classical ballet and touch in contact improvisation, from the performers' and spectators' viewpoints. I also reflected back on the notion that 'bodies have histories' (outlined in Chapter 2) through exploring the attempts of two groups of contemporary modern dance students to learn and perform Doris Humphrey's early modern dance *Water Study* (1930). The (body) politics of reconstructing dances of the past was explored further in Chapter 6 through a range of theoretical and practical issues which underpinned the complex interrelations of authenticity and interpretivity.

Although social and cultural critics have seldom paid 'close' attention to dance, feminist scholarship and debates on the body in social and cultural theory have had a significant impact on recent studies in dance history. As indicated in Chapter 6, this is hardly surprising given the centrality of the body in western dance and the fact that the majority of performers are women. This led to a consideration of the ways in which representations of women and sexuality in dance have been analysed in recent studies in dance history, by initially using, then developing and critiquing the theory of the male gaze. Daly's (1995) study of Isadora Duncan's dance practice revealed not one but five interrelated shifting bodies, thus challenging the idea that the body is a fixed 'limited edition'. Daly's study also took on board the impossibility of separating gender from other aspects of culture by considering the relationalities of body/dancer/gender/sexuality/race/nation. While some theatrical dance forms such as ballet are almost always viewed as retrogressive by feminist dance scholars, others, particularly post-modern dance, are viewed as potentially transgressive. The idea that dance can equal liberation was explored further in relation to feminist and poststructuralist invocations of 'choreographing difference'. The theme of dance and liberation was further explored in the final case study on rave and club cultures, the discourses on which generally conjure up an image of emergent (postmodern) shifting modes of sociality, where sexual and racial differences are given over to the ecstasies of moving on the dance floor.

In this book, I have shifted across a range of dance practices, not wishing to privilege theatrical (art) dance over social dance forms. I have also moved back and forth between social and cultural theory, body studies and dance studies. The case studies were chosen on the basis of my research interests and knowledge base. As indicated at various stages of the book, it is difficult (although by no means impossible) to conduct this kind of work at a bodily distance. There are many more dance cases waiting to be excavated and explored. I hope that this text will point others in this direction too.

Notes

Introduction

1. I am not going to rehearse why dance has been a neglected topic of social and cultural inquiry in the past as, along with others (for example, Desmond, 1997; Foster, 1997), I have discussed this elsewhere (Thomas, 1995).

1 The Body in Culture: Before the Body Project

1. In other places I taught, such as one particular art school, student antagonisms to the lecture course I gave on 'The Body as Symbol' were not only directed towards the teacher but also towards other students. However, in the two dance courses and fashion courses I taught on in other institutions, the response to 'body work' was quite different. Chapter 5 begins with a discussion of the dance students' responses.
2. I am indebted to Jamilah Ahmed for pointing this out to me.
3. Weber's analysis of the 'disenchantment of the world', as Turner (1992) notes, converges with aspects of Michel Foucault's later, influential analysis of the disciplinary technologies of power/knowledge, which is discussed in the next chapter.
4. The term 'Labanotation' is employed in the USA while 'kinetography Laban' is generally used in the UK and Europe.
5. See Chapter 4, note 9, for an outline of the main components of Labanotation or kinetography Laban and the system of movement analysis Laban developed to analyse movement qualities.

2 The Body in Culture: The Body Project

1. These recent feminist critiques will be elaborated on at various points in subsequent chapters. Some feminists, like Donna Haraway (1991), for example, celebrate new technologies and see the cyborg as a means of transcending the problems located in the situated practices of gender identification by reinventing 'nature'. Other scholars consider that the construct of feminism is itself outmoded, that it does not speak to women

today because we are living in a 'postfeminist' culture (Brooks, 1997). Cyberfeminism and postmodernism will be touched upon again in Chapter 7.

2. I found this approach particularly helpful for making sense of certain discussions about the body, dance and dancers that emerged in the second phase of an ethnographic study of a youth and community dance group (Thomas, 1997). Gilman's (1992) historical analysis of traditional and pervasive images of black sexuality, and particularly black female sexuality in western culture, was illuminating. It helped me to make sense of a range of images that a group of young black men and women dancers invoked in regard to what they perceived to be dominant perceptions of male/female, black/white, black male/black female dancers, which, to a certain extent, they shared.

3. In his fascinating essay on Cézanne in the 'Eye and the Mind', Merleau-Ponty (1968) writes in terms of apperception as opposed to perception, in order to move away from a dualistic approach to seeing or looking. He is concerned to convey the sense that we do not simply see an object or the other in our mind, but that we grasp the object or the other at the very same moment that the object or other grasps us.

3   Ethnography Dances Back

1. Hermeneutics is the science of interpretation. Geertz is concerned with interpreting cultural meanings and practices.

2. See Chapter 4, note 9 for a summary of this system of notation.

3. See Chapter 4, note 9 for a synopsis of this approach to analysing the qualitative aspects of movement.

4. Chapter 5 also contains a discussion of 'authenticity' and tradition in relation to the problems associated with reconstructing past dances belonging to the western theatre dance tradition of modern dance.

5. See the section on the Cuban rumba and the Argentine tango in Chapter 6 for a further discussion of, in this case, African Spanish diasporic dance practices and the differences between the male and female movement styles in these forms.

6. This terminology is drawn from LMA. See Chapter 4, note 9.

4   The Body in Dance

1. Sally Banes's influential study of the development of post-modern dance in the 1960s and 1970s, *Terpsichore in Sneakers*, made its first appearance in 1980 in Britain. Banes adopted the hyphenated word because the practitioners used this term to describe their work. 'Post-modern' dance, for Banes (1987), is a descriptive term that refers to the work of a particular group of choreographers at a particular point in time. In this book, I use

'post-modern' dance when specifically referring to Banes's work, otherwise I adopt the more common usage 'postmodern' dance. On the front cover of Banes's book is a side-on photograph of Douglas Dunn, a leading figure in post-modern dance, in full (but controlled) flight, wearing a long-sleeved shirt, tracksuit bottoms and sneakers. The celebration of everyday movement was a key feature of post-modern dance (see also Sheets-Johnstone, 1979). The spring of 1977 witnessed the publication of the first issue of *New Dance* magazine in Britain. Over the eleven years of its existence *New Dance* offered a platform for a growing and diverse experimental dance movement in Britain. The magazine came out of the X6 Collective, a dance cooperative, which, according to Stephanie Jordan (1992, p. 58), 'spearheaded a kind of movement and thinking' about alternative dance modes and their relation to politics and art that lasted well into the 1980s. The late 1970s in Britain witnessed the expansion of independent dance companies and audience expansion. Innovative post-modern choreographers from the USA, such as Douglas Dunn, Sara Rudner and Steve Paxton, presented their work at the early Dance Umbrella festivals. Dance Umbrella was first launched in 1978. It was initially conceived as a (selective) showcase for contemporary British dance but it also aimed to expose artists and audiences to outside influences, particularly dance innovators from the USA, where there was a much longer tradition of contemporary dance (see Jordan, 1992, pp. 95–102).

2. Cynthia Jean Cohen Bull was a brilliant dancer and a trained anthropologist. She died in 1996. Most of her work, including her extraordinary ethnographic study of contact improvisation (1990) was published under the name of Cynthia Novack. In her paper on the senses of dance, Bull (1997) includes a third dance form, Ghanaian dance, which I do not discuss. She argues that Ghanaian dance privileges the primacy of hearing over touch and sight and that the dancing is oriented towards the group as opposed to the individual.

3. A fuller discussion of these two frameworks is set out in *Dance, Modernity and Culture* (Thomas, 1995). I initially envisioned the extrinsic and the intrinsic methods of approach as binary opposites that could be mediated through a detailed examination of a particular dance work, in an attempt to reveal both the refractive and reflective qualities of dance. With hindsight, I now prefer to see them in a continuum so that the analyst can oscillate back and forth depending on the task at hand.

4. Bull draws on Paul Stollar's (1989) notions of 'sensibility' and 'intelligibility' in his book *The Taste of Ethnographic Things: Senses of Anthropology*.

5. Elsewhere, Bull defines kinaesthetic sense as the 'perception of movement in the body' (Novack, 1990, p. 159).

6. See *Chambers Twentieth Century Dictionary*, edited by A.M. Macdonald (1975), Edinburgh: Chambers, p. 909.

7. This will be taken up again in the chapter after next in regard to feminist critiques of the female dancing body in western theatrical dance.

8. When the movement attempts to mimic the music bar for bar, it is called 'mickey mousing'.

9. Laban analysis is concerned with analysing the qualitative aspects of movement. It was founded on the movement theories of Rudolf Laban (1879–1958) and was further developed and refined by other colleagues and followers. What follows is a minimalist and rudimentary summary of the main thrust of this system of analysis. For a more detailed discussion see Bartenieff and Lewis (1980). Laban analysis takes into consideration 'a configuration of three components ... body, effort and space' (Lepczyk, 1989, pp. 46–7) and within each of these components qualitative distinctions are considered. The body component refers to the 'orchestration of the body'. Here, the concern is to examine which parts of the body are activated, how the weight of the body is supported and how the body shapes are created.

The effort component refers to the dancer's attitude towards the 'four motion factors' of 'weight, space, time and flow', each of which is 'subdivided into extremes': the weight factor ranges from strong to light movement; the space factor from direct to flexible; the time factor from sustained to quick, and the flow factor from bound to free. These are treated as qualities, not quantities, of movement. For example, rather than measuring weight in terms of kilos or time in terms of minutes, effort actions gauge qualities or attitudes of 'resisting' or 'giving' into weight, or 'indulging' or 'fighting' against time. When two or more effort factors are combined simultaneously they are called 'states' and where three or more are combined at once they are termed 'drives'.

The spatial component of the analysis developed out of Laban's study of 'choreutics', which investigated 'spatial relationships of movement and dance' (Maletic, 2000, p. 8). The body is a three-dimensional structure which 'occupies space and is surrounded by it' (Laban, 1966, p. 10). There are three movement axes or planes in which the body moves: the vertical, horizontal and saggital. Each of these planes has two directions: up/down (vertical axis), left/right (horizontal axis) and forward/backward (saggital axis). There is an imaginary sphere around the body which Laban terms the 'kinesphere', the periphery of which can be reached easily by extending the limbs, without moving out of 'place'. When we move, we take our kinesphere or personal space with us to our new place. The space component of Laban analysis examines the manner in which the dancer moves or carves out shapes in space, and the 'spatial pathways', relationships or 'tensions' that the dancer creates as they reach out within the space immediately surrounding the body (the kinesphere).

The 'postural and gestural' aspects of the analysis, according to Lepczyk (1990, p. 72) 'are used to qualify the variables of effort, shape and spatial tension'. 'Postural' means that the movement quality is carried through the whole body, while 'gestural' signifies that it comes from 'one area or part' (ibid.). Proponents of the system view the various components of effort/shape as interrelated.

As well as generating a vocabulary for analysing movement qualities that focus on the 'how' of movement, Laban also created a system for notating dances that describes the structure of the 'what, where and when' of body movement. The latter is called Labanotation (USA) or kinetography Laban (Europe). It uses a vertical staff to represent the body with a line going down the middle to delineate the left- and right-hand sides of the body. The line is 'partitioned by bar strokes' to record timing. The system uses 'directional signs and shape symbols' to show the dancer 'moving in space' (Thornton, 1971, p. 62). The vertical staff also allows for 'continuity of movement' and by lengthening or shortening the movement symbols, the 'exact duration of any action' (Hutchinson, 1977, p. 3) is recorded. Kinetography has been largely used to record dances. As with a musical score, qualitative aspects of movement can be indicated at the side of the score.

10. In her ethnographic study of contact improvisation conducted over a period of ten years, Bull (Novack, 1990) stresses the fact that contact improvisation grew out of a number of sources, including the social and political movements of the 1960s. It can also be traced back to the dance experiments of a new generation of dancers such as the members of the Judson group in the early 1960s and the Grand Union collective (1970–6), whose critiques of established contemporary dance practices were infused with the ideals of the new political movements and developments in theatre and art. Paxton, a former dancer in the Cunningham Company, was an original member of the collective whose workshops and performances were held at the Judson Church in New York. Yvonne Rainer, Trisha Brown and David Gordon among others were also members of this group. He was also one of nine performers/dance-makers of the Grand Union collective. The collective 'made group improvisations embracing dance, theatre, and theatrics in an ongoing investigation into the nature of dance and performance' (Banes, 1980, p. 204).

11. Paxton and others have acknowledged the difficulty of maintaining the principle of a non-hierarchical organisation (see Novack, 1990, pp. 207–10).

12. The consequences and contradictions of gendering in ballet, as indicated earlier, will be taken up in Chapter 6.

13. Bourne, with the company he co-founded, Adventures in Motion Pictures (AMP), has choreographed other modern dance works from the ballet repertoire, such as *The Nutcracker* (1992) and *Highland Fling* (1992), based on the nineteenth-century romantic ballet *La Sylphide*.

14. Parts of the discussion that follows were taken from a paper I gave at the 'Preservation Politics: Dance Revisited, Reconstructed, Remade' conference at Roehampton Institute in 1997. This was subsequently published

in the conference proceedings as 'Reproducing the Dance: In Search of the Aura' (Thomas, 2000).

15. I am grateful to Lesley Main and the two groups of students at Middlesex University for allowing me to interview them and observe the rehearsals. Main has a company that is devoted to bringing works by Doris Humphrey to contemporary audiences. Ernestine Stodelle, who was a member of Humphrey's early company in from 1929 to 1935, taught Main. Main's approach to recreating or directing Humphrey's work is discussed more fully in the next chapter.

16. In a footnote, Siegel (1979, p. 27) states that her analysis of *Water Study* is based on Ernestine Stodelle's 1976 reconstruction for students at New York University.

17. Cohen's (1972) chronology of Humphrey's dances indicates that sixteen dancers originally performed *Water Study*, but it can be and has been performed with smaller numbers. In *The Art of Making Dances* (1959, p. 142), Humphrey states that the dance was composed for fourteen women.

18. Parts of this section on *Water Study* have been published in conference proceedings (see note 14 above).

19. I am familiar with a number of versions of this dance through video recordings (housed in the Dance Collection, New York Public Library) and a live performance. Humphrey believed that choreography is a craft that could and should be taught. She was supportive of efforts to promote dance literacy, as is her son Charles Woodford, who is in charge of her estate. There are two Labanotation scores of *Water Study* and several other works have been notated over the years. I should point out that although I examined the scores, mainly to compare and contrast them, my knowledge of Labanotation is fairly rudimentary. I have also drawn on two Laban movement analyses of *Water Study* (Davies and Schmais, 1967; Kagan, 1978), and although I could not call myself an expert in this area either, I studied and used 'effort' in teaching dance. I also drew on it implicitly for the analysis of Graham's 1944 masterpiece, *Appalachian Spring* (Thomas, 1995).

5 Reconstructing the Dance: In Search of Authenticity?

1. The notion of a 'usable past' was borrowed from the writer Van Wicks Brooks by a group of young American composers in the 1920s, who included Aaron Copland, Roy Harris and Virgil Thomson. They were trying to search out past 'lost' American composers to assist them in their task of developing a serious American musical style. See Copland (1953, pp. 96–110) for his discussion of this search for a usable past.

2. Lesley Main is completing a PhD on Humphrey's work which involves theoretical and practical aspects. I am an external supervisor for her

project. The direction of Lesley's work and its aims are somewhat different from what I am trying to do here, and therefore I would hope that
I am not impinging on the important contribution to knowledge in the
field that I anticipate her thesis will make. Lesley has read and commented on this chapter and sections of the previous chapter.

3. The Foundation's goals are directed towards 'theatrical and educational
concerns relating to the creation and performance opportunities for
Humphrey dances, and the growing number of young professionals
working in this field' (Main, 1995, p. 14).

4. The performances took place in the foyer of the Royal Festival Hall in
London, Roehampton Institute and Middlesex University. Lesley Main
also performed one of the solo pieces in 'The Singular Voice of Woman'
programme at the Place Theatre, London in 1997.

5. The terms dance 'reconstruction' and 'reconstructor' are generally used
by Labanotation practitioners (Van Zile, 1985–6). See Valerie Preston-
Dunlop (1995) for definitions of reconstruction from a variety of
sources. Hutchinson Guest (2000) provides another set of definitions on
reconstruction, recreation and so on.

6. In his illuminating study of Walter Benjamin, Howard Caygill (1998)
uses a similar translation to Foster: 'The Work of Art in the Epoch of its
Technical Reproducibility'. Caygill points out that although the essay
has been highly influential, it has also been greatly misunderstood.

7. Norman Denzin (Denzin and Lincoln 1994), who is an advocate of
post-positive sociology, also refers to qualitative interviewing as a kind of
'conversation' between the researcher and the researched.

8. In 1989, students at the Juilliard School in New York took part in an experiment to 'read the Labonotation transcription of Nijinsky's score of *L'Aprés-
Midi d'un Faune*' which was first performed in 1912 (Beck, 1991, p. 45).
The dancers in the Juilliard reconstruction learnt their individual parts
from the score, much like the musicians in an orchestra. The 'dance director' (Jill Beck) worked with the dancers in a similar way to a conductor.

9. Elizabeth Kendall (1979) also makes this point in her study of the emergence of women on the stage in the USA around the turn of the twentieth century.

10. It was that notion of the star image of the choreographer/artist that
Yvonne Rainer railed against in her manifesto in the 1960s (Banes, 1980).

11. For a discussion of the transnational world of ballet, see Helena Wulff's
(1998) ethnographic study of the culture of the contemporary ballet world.

12. The idea of the co-authoring of an artwork is the position that
R.G. Collingwood advocated in *The Principles of Art*, first published in
1938.

13. A video recording of the Dance Conduit Company performing *Dawn
in New York* was made in 1990. The recording also contains
rehearsal footage and a discussion on the problems and challenges of

reconstructing this work with Ray Cook and Ann Vachon, the company director. It is available for viewing at the Dance Collection in New York Public Library.

14. In their search for the 'original', Archer and Hodson seek to distinguish between 'what was conceived and what was realized' in the first performance (1994, p. 103). If a recovered lost ballet remains in the repertoire for some time, it will inevitably undergo some changes, mostly through changes in costumes and casts. In this instance, according to Archer and Hodson, the dance takes on the character of the second original, because that is the version that is best known. Archer and Hodson go on to talk about a third type of original, which is twice removed but which remains authoritative because of its connection to the first and second original.

15. This dance is sometimes called *Passacaglia in C Minor* or *Passacaglia and Fugue in C Minor* (see Mueller, 1974, p. 25).

16. Choreographed to Bach's *Passacaglia and Fugue in C Minor*, Humphrey's *Passacaglia* received a qualified critical reception when it was first performed (see Cohen, 1972, pp. 149–50), but later on tour it achieved critical acclaim. It went out of the repertory in 1941 and was revived by Humphrey in 1955 for a repertory class at the Juilliard School. Lucy Venable and Joan Gainer created a Labanotation score of the dance at the time of this revival. Venable staged a revival of the dance in 1965 using the score with the short-lived American Dance Theater. A film was made of the dance at this time and is included in the National Education Television Production, *Dance: The Four Pioneers* (1965). The score has also been used by succeeding generations of college dance groups to learn and perform the work.

17. This is akin to the idea of reproduction and production contained within the concept of the habitus, which was discussed in Chapters 1 and 2.

6 Dance and Difference: Performing/Representing/ Rewriting the Body

1. In the mid-1990s, feminist-inspired dance critics also began to explore the interrelations between gender, race and nation in their accounts of dance history (see Daly, 1995; Franko, 1995; Koritz, 1995; Thomas, 1997; Burt, 1998).

2. Daniel (1995) also points to the melding of indigenous, Spanish and African influences in the rumba.

3. Browning does not elaborate on how she gives up her literary voice. It is rather left up to the reader's imagination. In traditional anthropological terms, she seems to have 'gone native'. See the note immediately following this one.

4. Although Browning raises these questions, she does so with little self-reflexivity. She does not seem to consider, for example, that she, as a western academic 'slumming it', literally may be part of the problem.

I suspect that insider/outsider distinctions become blurred because she identifies so strongly with the culture and the dance.

5. These two edited collections, *Choreographing History* (1995) and *Corporealities* (1996b), emerged out of a conference held in 1992 and dialogic research seminars on 'Choreographing History', sponsored by the University of California Humanities Research Institute. Savigliano teaches at UC Riverside and she contributed to the 1996 collection.

6. For a critical and informative discussion of experimental, reflexive approaches in qualitative research, see *The Quality of Qualitative Research* (1999, pp. 159–88), by Clive Seale.

7. Savigliano situates herself and Argentina as 'exotic others' struggling against the colonised gaze of western imperialism in this tale of tango, as Grau's (1997) insightful critique of the work shows. In so doing, she 'glosses over other, less savoury, aspects of reality' (p. 86). For example, she does not explore the possibility of interconnecting links between, say, Germany, Japan and Argentina in the 1940s. While Argentina remained neutral throughout World War II, as Savigliano states, it is widely recognised that it became a stopping place for a number of Nazi criminals after the war. Moreover, although she notes that Western music was outlawed in Japan at the beginning of the war, there is no exploration as to why tango was permitted along with German and Italian classics. This is despite the fact that, as indicated in the text, Savigliano does mention Italian immigrant influences on the early development of tango in Argentina in the nineteenth century.

8. In *Bodies that Matter* (1993, p. 117), Judith Butler writes, 'How is race lived in the modality of sexuality? How is gender lived in the modality of race? How do colonial and neo-colonial nation states rehearse gender relations in the consolidation of state power?'

9. See, for example, Adair (1992), Manning (1993a), Thomas (1993a), Brown (1994), Burt (1995), Daly (1995), Franko (1995), Koritz (1995), Foster (1995, 1996b), Goellner and Murphy (1995), Morris (1996a), Cooper Albright (1997), Desmond (1997, 2001), Banes (1998), Briginshaw (2001).

10. I am grateful to Stacey Prickett for bringing this to my attention and indeed for downloading the relevant newspaper files from SF Gate, San Francisco, California, and sending them to me.

11. Foster draws on Hal Foster's (1983, p. xii) definition of 'reactionary' and 'resistive' postmodernism.

12. In this discussion, I draw heavily from a book review I wrote for the journal *Body & Society*, 1998b, 4, 3, pp. 115–18.

13. Daly does not discuss Kristeva's (1984) theory of signifying practice and the process of subjectivity in any depth in her book, although she does outline why she thinks it is useful to dance studies in an earlier paper (Daly, 1992). Daly does this intentionally because she does not want her study of Duncan to be 'about theory'. Rather, it informs and supports

her analysis. I offer an all too brief summary of Kristeva's complex position for the sake of clarity.

14. The notion of the feminine, here, does not refer to Woman as female essence. Kristeva's construct of the feminine is non-sex-specific and as such feminine signification can by embodied by either men or women.

15. Daly's ideas on the reproduction of class differences in Duncan's practice and rhetoric are informed by Bourdieu's (1984) construct of 'distinction', while Toni Morrison's (1992) construct of ' "American" literature as a rejoinder to designations of Africanism' (Daly, 1995, p. xii), informs her analysis of the interrelationship between class and race differences in Duncan's work.

16. As noted in Chapter 3, there is no universally applicable concept as to what constitutes dance.

7   Dancing the Night Away: Rave/Club Culture

1. Malbon (1999, pp. 7–9) gives a very useful summary of two major sources of data: the 1996 survey on *Nightclubs and Discotheques* by Mintel, the Market Intelligence International Group Ltd, and the 1997 *Release Drugs and Dance Survey: An Insight to Culture*. Here, he points out some of the difficulties with using the data gleaned from the two surveys. Mintel, for example, covers 'all kinds of discotheques and nightclub establishments', whereas the Release Survey is concerned specifically with clubbing events. The figures presented in my text are taken from Malbon's summary. I have used this as most of the research I discuss in this chapter was undertaken either just before or around this period.

2. This is based on a personal email communication from the University of Nottingham Students Union Ballroom Dancing Society.

3. This one-year qualitative study, *Dancing into the Third Age: Social Dance as Cultural Text*, was funded by the Arts and Humanities Research Board (AHRB). I would like to express my gratitude to the AHRB for supporting the research. Helen Thomas and Lesley Cooper conducted the study. I would also like to thank Lesley Cooper for being such a terrific Research Associate.

4. I am grateful to Theresa Buckland for alerting me to Owe Ronström's (1989) methodological discussion of the concept of the dance event, which draws on Goffman's ideas on the interaction ritual (1959) and the framing of a performance (1974).

5. Cooper and Thomas refer to this in 'Growing Old Disgracefully: Social Dance in the Third Age' (*Ageing and Society*, 22, 2002, pp. 689–708).

6. This issue was discussed in the previous chapter.

7. The very idea that there can be such a thing as dance *per se* is in itself problematic. Global definitions of dance do not work, despite previous attempts to generate a cross-cultural perspective (see Hanna, 1980). As indicated in Chapter 3, an activity that is associated with dancing in

one culture will not necessarily carry the same association in another. In this context, however, we are referring specifically to developments in the western dance tradition and for 'all practical purposes' (Garfinkel, 1984) there is an intersubjective understanding as to what counts as dance movement in general as opposed to everyday movement within that framework (Thomas, 1995).

8. The systematic erasure of the importance of race from the development of 'colonising' cultural forms was also noted in the previous chapter in regard to the samba, rumba and tango, and in the development of modern dance.

9. Hebdige adopted these concepts from the French Tel Quel group's approach to film and literary texts. Julia Kristeva, whose theory of signifying practice was set out briefly in the previous chapter, was a member of the Tel Quel group.

10. McRobbie, it must be said, does not make this connection.

11. Many of the dancers interviewed in the Dancing into the Third Age project mentioned above indicated that when the music of their youth is played in the tea dance events they attend, it brings back strong memories of when they were young. One 79-year-old woman talked with great affection of how her memories of dancing the charleston in the 1940s, wearing a black-beaded dress and high heels, were activated when she heard the music played at the weekly tea dance she attends. Although she can no longer perform the movements with vigour and ease as she had done in her youth, she nevertheless thought about these things with pleasure as she shadow-dances the steps in the tea dance each week.

12. Part of the Dancing into the Third Age project included video-recording the dancers in action. Although the modern sequence dancers move at the same time and dance the same steps, they also display their individuality as dancers in the videos.

13. See, for example, Jordan (1995), Saunders (1995, 1997), Thornton (1995), Gore (1997), Ward (1997), Pini (1997a, b, 2001), Collin (1998), Redhead *et al.* (ed.) (1998), Rietveld (1998), Reynolds (1998), Brewster and Broughton (1999), Gilbert and Pearson (1999), Malbon (1999), Bennett (2000), Muggleton (2000), Sommer (2001). The publications by Thornton, Pini, Malbon, Bennett, Gilbert and Muggleton are derived from their PhD studies. Some of this work (Brewster and Broughton, Reynolds, Collin), like that of Hebdige (1979), works across the divide of academia and journalism.

14. See the discussion of Goffman's ideas on social and personal space in Chapter 2.

15. The main aims, methods and problems of ethnographic research are examined in Chapter 3.

16. Malbon takes Maffesoli to task for being overly theoretical. He also considers that Maffesoli's view of neo-tribes as openly accessible is utopian. Like Thornton (1995), Malbon argues that 'access to clubbing crowds is clearly "not open to all" '.

Conclusion

1. The term 'relationalities' is used to denote contingent relational processes as opposed to the relatively 'fixed' sense of social relations which is characteristic of traditional sociological approaches. Here, I draw on Simon Carter and Mike Michael's (2003) fascinating article on the 'sociology of the sun'.

2. Deidre Sklar's extended study of the annual Tortugas fiesta, *Dancing with the Virgin*, was published in 2001, just after I had completed the final draft of Chapter 3. I have not included a discussion of it here. The methodology in the book shifted the embodied methodology proposed in the 1991 article further down the near/far continuum towards auto-ethnography. As indicated in Chapters 3, 4 and 6, auto-ethnography, like some philosophical phenomenological approaches to dance, has been criticised for concentrating on revealing rather more about the (reflexive) researcher than about the significant 'others' in the study.

References

Abu-Lughod, L. (1990) 'Can There Be a Feminist Ethnography?', *Women & Performance*, 5, 1, pp. 7–27.

Adair, C. (1992) *Women and Dance: Sylphs and Sirens*, London: Macmillan – now Palgrave Macmillan.

Adams, L. (1992) 'The Value of Dance', *Dance Connection*, 10, 3, pp. 24–6.

Alderson, E. (1987) 'Ballet as Ideology: Giselle, Act II', *Dance Chronicle*, 10, 3, pp. 290–304.

Aldrich, E. (1991) *From the Ballroom to Hell: Grace and Folly in Nineteenth-Century Dance*, Evanston, Ill.: Northwestern University Press.

Althusser, L. (1969) *For Marx* (translated by B. Brewster), London: Allen Lane.

Appadurai, A. (1988) 'Putting Hierarchy in its Place', *Cultural Anthropology*, 3, pp. 36–49.

Archer, K. and Hodson, M. (1994) 'Ballets Lost and Found: Restoring the Twentieth-Century Repertoire', in J. Adshead and J. Layson (eds), *Dance History: A Methodology for Study*, 2nd edn, London: Routledge.

Argyle, M. (1975) *Bodily Communication*, London: Methuen.

Atkinson, P. (1990) *The Ethnographic Imagination*, London: Routledge.

Auslander, P. (1988) 'Embodiment: The Politics of Postmodern Dance (Review of Susan Leigh Foster's *Reading Dancing*)', *The Drama Review*, 32, 4, pp. 7–23.

Back, L. (1997) 'Nazism and the Call of the Jitterbug', in H. Thomas (ed.), *Dance in the City*, London: Macmillan – now Palgrave Macmillan.

Bakhtin, M.M. (1968) *Rabalais and his World*, London: MIT Press.

Banes, S. (1998) *Dancing Women: Female Bodies on Stage*, London: Routledge.

—— (1987) *Terpsichore in Sneakers: Post-Modern Dance*, Boston, Mass.: Houghton Mifflin.

—— (1980) *Terpsichore in Sneakers: Post-modern Dance*, Boston, Mass.: Houghton Mifflin.

Barrett, M. (1988) *Women's Oppression Today: The Marxist/Feminist Encounter*, 2nd edn, London: Verso.

Bartenieff, I. and Lewis, D. (1980) *Body Movement: Coping with the Environment*, London: Gordon & Breach.

Bateson, G. (1972) *Steps to an Ecology of Mind*, New York: Ballantine Books.

Bateson, G. and Mead, M. (1942) *Balinese Character: A Photographic Analysis*, vol. 2, New York: Special Publications of the New York Academy of Sciences.

Baudrillard, J. (1987) *Forget Foucault, Forget Baudrillard*, New York: Semiotext(e).

de Beauvoir, S. (1972) *The Second Sex*, Harmondsworth: Penguin Books (first published in 1949).

Beck, J. (1991) 'Recalled to Life: Techniques and Perspectives on Reviving Nijinsky's Faune', *Choreography and Dance*, 1, pp. 45–79.

Beck, U. (1992) *Risk Societies: Towards a New Modernity*, London: Sage.

Benjamin, W. (1973) 'The Work of Art in the Age of Mechanical Reproduction', in *Illuminations* (translated by Suhrkamp Verlag, Frankfurt-am-Main in 1955), Glasgow: Fontana/Collins.

Bennett, A. (2000) *Popular Music and Youth Culture: Music, Identity and Place*, Basingstoke: Palgrave Macmillan.

Benthall, J. (1975) 'A Prospectus as Published in Studio International July 1972', in J. Benthall and T. Polhemus (eds), *The Body as a Medium of Expression*, London: Allen Lane.

Benthall, J. and Polhemus, T. (1975) *The Body as a Medium of Expression*, London: Allen Lane.

Bentley, T. (1982) *Winter Season*, New York: Vantage Books.

Berg, S. (1993) 'The Real Thing: Authenticity and Dance at the Approach of the Millennium', in 'Dance Reconstructed: Modern Dance Art, Past, Present, Future', *Proceedings of Society of Dance History Scholars Sixteenth Annual Conference*, 1992, Rutgers University, New Brunswick: Society of Dance History Scholars, pp. 109–26.

Berger, J. (1980) *About Looking*, London: Writers and Readers Publishing Cooperative.

—— (1972) *Ways of Seeing*, London and Harmondsworth: BBC and Penguin Books.

Bernstein, B. (1971) *Class, Codes and Control*, vol. 1, *Theoretical Studies towards a Sociology of Language*, London: Routledge & Kegan Paul.

Betterton, R. (1996) *Intimate Distance*, London: Routledge.

—— (ed.) (1987) *Looking On: Images of Femininity in the Visual Arts and Media*, London: Pandora Press.

Birdwhistell, R. (1973) *Kinesics in Context: Essays in Body–Notion Communication*, Harmondsworth: Penguin University Books.

—— (1953) *Introduction to Kinesics*, Louisville: University of Louisville.

Blacking, J. (ed.) (1977) *The Anthropology of the Body*, ASA Monograph 15, London: Academic Press.

Booth, C. (1902–3) *Life and Labour of the People of London*, London: Macmillan – now Palgrave Macmillan.

Bordo, S. (1993) *Unbearable Weight: Feminism, Western Culture and the Body*, Berkeley: University of California Press.

—— (1990a) 'Feminism, Postmodernism and Gender-Scepticism', in L.J. Nicholson (ed.), *Feminism/Postmodernism*, London: Routledge.

—— (1990b) 'Reading the Slender Body', in M. Jacobson, M.F. Keller and S. Shuttleworth (eds), *Body/Politics: Women and the Discourses of Science*, New York: Routledge.

Bourdieu, P. (1993) *Sociology in Question* (translated by Richard Nice), London: Sage.

—— (1991) *Language and Symbolic Power* (edited and introduced by J.B. Thompson, translated by G. Raymond and M. Adamson), Cambridge, Mass.: Harvard University Press.

—— (1990a) *In Other Words: Essays Towards a Reflexive Sociology* (translated by M. Adamson), Cambridge: Polity Press.

—— (1990b) *The Logic of Practice* (translated by R. Nice), Cambridge: Polity Press.

—— (1984) *Distinction: A Social Critique of the Judgement of Taste* (translated by R. Nice), London: Routledge & Kegan Paul.

—— (1977) *Outline of a Theory of Practice* (translated by R. Nice), Cambridge: Cambridge University Press.

Boyce, J., Daly, A., Jones, B.T. and Martin, C. (1988) 'Movement and Gender: A Roundtable Discussion', *The Drama Review*, 32, 4, pp. 82–101.

Boyne, R. (1999) 'Citation and Subjectivity: Towards a Return of the Embodied Will', *Body & Society*, 5, 2–3, pp. 209–25.

Boyne, R. and Rattansi, A. (eds) (1990) *Postmodernism and Society*, London: Macmillan – now Palgrave Macmillan.

Braidotti, R. (1994) *Nomadic Subjects: Embodiment and Sexual Difference in Contemporary Feminist Theory*, New York: Columbia University Press.

Brake, M. (1985) *Comparative Youth Culture*, London: Routledge & Kegan Paul.

Braverman, H. (1974) *Labor and Monopoly Capitalism: The Degradation of Work in the Twentieth Century*, New York: Monthly Review Press.

Brewer, J.D. (1994) 'The Ethnographic Critique of Ethnography: Sectarianism in the RUC', *Sociology*, 28, 1, pp. 231–44.

Brewster, B. and Broughton, F. (1999) *Last Night a DJ Saved my Life*, London: Headline Book Publishing.

Briginshaw, V.A. (2001) *Dance, Space and Subjectivity*, Basingstoke: Palgrave Macmillan.

Broadhurst, S. (1999) 'The (Im)mediate Body: A Transvaluation of Corporeality', *Body & Society*, 5, 1, pp. 17–29.

Brooks, A. (1997) *Postfeminisms: Feminism, Cultural Theory and Cultural Forms*, London: Routledge.

Brooks, V. (1993) 'Movement in Fixed Space and Time: Film, Choreographers, and the Audience', *Ballett International*, 3, pp. 25–7.

Brown, C. (1994) 'Re-Tracing our Steps: The Possibilities for Feminist Dance Histories', in J. Adshead-Lansdale and J. Layson (eds), *Dance History: An Introduction*, London: Routledge.

Browning, B. (1995) *Samba: Resistance in Motion*, Bloomington: Indiana University Press.

Buckland, T.J. (ed.) (1999) *Dance in the Field: Theory, Methods and Issues in Dance Ethnography*, London: Macmillan – now Palgrave Macmillan.

Bull, C.J.C. (1997) 'Sense, Meaning, and Perception in Three Dance Cultures', in J.C. Desmond (ed.), *Meaning in Motion: New Cultural Studies of Dance*, Durham and London: Duke University Press.

Burkitt, I. (1999) *Bodies of Thought: Embodiment, Identity and Modernity*, London: Sage.

Burt, R. (1998) *Alien Bodies: Representations of Modernity, 'Race' and Nation in Early Modern Dance*, London: Routledge.

—— (1995) *The Male Dancer: Bodies, Spectacle and Sexuality*, London: Routledge.

Butler, J. (1993) *Bodies that Matter: On the Discursive Limits of 'Sex'*, London: Routledge.

—— (1990a) *Gender Trouble: Feminism and the Subversion of Identity*, London: Routledge.

—— (1990b) 'Performative Acts and Gender Constitution: An Essay in Phenomenology and Feminist Theory', in S.-E. Case (ed.), *Performing Feminisms: Feminist Critical Theory and Theatre*, Baltimore, Md.: Johns Hopkins University Press.

Caplan, P. (1988) 'Engendering Knowledge: The Politics of Ethnography (Pt. I)', *Anthropology Today*, 14, 5, pp. 8–12.

Carter, A. (1999) 'Staring Back, Mindfully: Reinstating the Dancer – and the Dance – In Feminist Ballet Historiography', in *Proceedings of Society of Dance History Scholars Twenty-Second Annual Conference*, 10–13 June, University of New Mexico: Albuquerque, New Mexico: Society of Dance History Scholars, pp. 227–32.

—— (1998) 'Feminist Strategies for the Study of Dance', in L. Goodman with J. de Gay (eds), *The Routledge Reader in Gender and Performance*, London: Routledge.

Carter, S. and Michael, M. (2003) 'Here comes the Sun: Shedding Light on the Cultural Body', in H. Thomas and J. Ahmed (eds), *Cultural Bodies: Ethnography and Theory*, Oxford: Blackwell.

Case, S.-E., Brett, P. and Foster, S.L. (eds) (1995) *Cruising the Performative: Interventions into the Representation of Ethnicity, Nationality and Sexuality*, Bloomington and Indianapolis: Indiana University Press.

Caygill, H. (1998) *Walter Benjamin: The Colour of Experience*, London: Routledge.

Chambers, I. (1985) *Urban Rhythms: Pop Music and Popular Culture*, London: Macmillan – now Palgrave Macmillan.

Chambers Twentieth-Century Dictionary (1972), Edinburgh: W. & R. Chambers Ltd.

Chanter, T. (1999) 'Beyond Sex and Gender', in D. Welton (ed.), *The Body*, Oxford: Blackwell.

Chernin, K. (1986) *The Hungry Self: Women, Eating and Identity*, London: Virago.

—— *The Obsession: Reflections of the Tyranny of Slenderness*, New York: Harper & Row.

Cixous, H. (1981) 'The Laugh of Medusa', in E. Marks and I. de Courtrivon (eds), *New French Feminisms*, New York: Schocken Books.

Clarke, M. and Crisp, C. (1973) *Ballet: An Illustrated History*, London: A. & C. Black Ltd.

Clifford, J. (1988) *The Predicament of Culture: Twentieth-Century Ethnography, Literature, and Art*, Cambridge, Mass.: Harvard University Press.

—— (1983) 'Power and Dialogue in Ethnography: Marcel Griaule's Initiation', in G. Stocking (ed.), *Observers Observed: Essays in Ethnographic Fieldwork*, Madison: University of Wisconsin Press.

Clifford, J. and Marcus, G.E. (eds) (1986) *Writing Culture: The Poetics and Politics of Ethnography*, Berkeley: University of California Press.

Coffey, A. (1999) *The Ethnographic Self: Fieldwork and the Representation of Identity*, London: Sage Publications.

Cohen, S. (1980) *Folk Devils and Moral Panics: The Creation of the Mods and Rockers*, 2nd edn, Oxford: Martin Robinson (first published in 1972).

Cohen, S.J. (1993) 'Dance Reconstructed', *Dance Research Journal*, 25, 2 (Fall), pp. 54–5.

—— (ed.) (1972) *Doris Humphrey: An Artist First* (A Dance Horizons Book), Pennington, NJ: Princeton Book Company.

Collin, M. and with contributions by Godfrey, J. (1998) *Altered State: The Story of Ecstasy Culture and Acid House*, 2nd edn, London: Serpent's Tail.

Collingwood, R.G. (1958) *The Principles of Art*, Oxford: Oxford University Press.

Cook, R. (1990) 'Dawn in New York: Researching a Lost Masterpiece', in *Proceedings of 5th Hong Kong International Dance Conference: International Congress on Movement Notation*, 4, Hong Kong: The Hong Kong Academy for Performing Arts, pp. 44–52.

Cooley, C.H. (1956) *Human Nature and the Social Order*, Glencoe, Ill.: The Free Press.

Cooper, L. and Thomas, H. (2002) 'Growing Old Gracefully: Social Dance in the Third Age', *Ageing and Society*, 22, pp. 689–708.

Cooper Albright, A. (1999) 'A Particular History: Contact Improvisation at Oberlin College', in *Proceedings of Society of Dance History Scholars Twenty-Second Annual Conference*, Albuquerque, 10–13 June, University of New Mexico, Wisconsin: Society of Dance History Scholars, pp. 51–4.

—— (1997) *Choreographing Difference: The Body and Identity in Contemporary Dance*, Hanover, NH: Wesleyan University Press.

Copeland, R. (1994) 'Reflections on Revival and Reconstruction', *Dance Theatre Journal*, 11, 3, pp. 18–20.

—— (1993a) 'Dance, Feminism and the Critique of the Visual', in H. Thomas (ed.), *Dance, Gender and Culture*, London: Macmillan – now Palgrave Macmillan.

—— (1993b) 'Perspectives in Reconstruction (Keynote Panel)', in 'Dance Reconstructed: Modern Dance Art, Past, Present, Future', in *Proceedings of*

Society of Dance History Scholars Sixteenth Annual Conference, Rutgers University, New Brunswick, Wis.: Society of Dance History Scholars, pp. 11–26.

Copland, A. (1953) *Music and Imagination*, Cambridge, Mass.: Harvard University Press.

Cowan, J. (1990) *Dance and the Body Politic in Northern Greece*, Princeton, NJ: Princeton University Press.

Coward, R. (1984) *Female Desire*, London: Paladin Grafton Books.

Cressey, P.G. (1968) *The Taxi-Dance Hall: A Sociological Study in Commercialized Recreation and City Life*, New York: Greenwood Press (first published in 1932).

Croce, A. (1977) *Afterimages*, New York: Knopf.

Crossley, N. (1996a) 'Body–Subject/Body–Power: Agency, Inscription and Control in Foucault and Merleau-Ponty', *Body & Society*, 2, 2, pp. 99–116.

—— (1996b) *Intersubjectivity: The Fabric of Social Becoming*, London: Sage.

—— (1995a) 'Body Techniques, Agency and Intercorporeality: On Goffman's Relations in Public', *Sociology*, 29, 1, pp. 133–49.

—— (1995b) 'Merleau-Ponty, the Elusive Body and Carnal Sociology', *Body & Society*, 1, 1, pp. 43–62.

—— (1994) *The Politics of Subjectivity: Between Foucault and Merleau-Ponty*, Aldershot: Avebury.

Csordas, T.J. (ed.) (1994a) *Embodiment and Experience: The Existential Ground of Culture and Self*, Cambridge: Cambridge University Press.

—— (1994b) 'Introduction: The Body as Representation and Being-in-the-World', in T. Csordas (ed.), *Embodiment and Experience: The Existential Ground of Culture and Self*, Cambridge: Cambridge University Press.

—— (1993) 'Somatic Modes of Attention', *Cultural Anthropology*, 8, 2, pp. 135–56.

Culler, J. (1983) *On Deconstruction*, London: Routledge & Kegan Paul.

—— (1976) *Saussure*, Glasgow: Fontana Paperbacks.

Cunningham, M. (in conversation with J. Lesschaeve) (1985) *The Dancer and the Dance*, New York: Marian Boyars.

Curti, L. (1998) *Female Stories, Female Bodies: Narrative, Identity and Representation*, London: Macmillan – now Palgrave Macmillan.

Daly, A. (1995) *Done into Dance: Isadora Duncan in America*, Bloomington: Indiana University Press.

—— (1992) 'Dance History and Feminist Theory: Isadora Duncan and the Male Gaze', in L. Senelick (ed.), *Gender in Performance*, Hanover, NH: Tufts University Press.

—— (1991) 'Unlimited Partnership: Dance and Feminist Analysis', *Dance Research Journal*, 23, 1 (Spring), pp. 2–3.

—— (1988) 'Movement Analysis: Piecing Together the Puzzle', *The Drama Review*, 32, 4, pp. 40–51.

—— (1987/88) 'Classical Ballet: A Discourse of Difference', *Women & Performance*, 3, 2, pp. 57–66.

—— (1987) 'The Balanchine Woman: Of Hummingbirds and Channel Swimmers', *The Drama Review*, 31, 1, pp. 8–21.

Daly, M. (1978) *Gyn/Ecology: The Metaethics of Radical Feminism*, Boston, Mass.: Beacon Press.

Daniel, Y.P. (1995) *Rumba: Dance and Social Change in Contemporary Cuba*, Bloomington and Indianapolis: Indiana University Press.

Daniel, Y.P. (1991) 'Changing Values in Cuban Rumba, A Lower Class Black Dance Appropriated by the Cuban Revolution', *Dance Research Journal*, 23, 2, pp. 1–10.

Darwin, C. (1969) *The Expression of the Emotions in Man and Animals*, Chicago, Ill.: Chicago University Press (first published in 1872).

Davies, M. and Schmais, C. (1967) 'An Analysis of the Style and Composition of "Water Study"', *CORD Research Annual*, 1, pp. 105–13.

DeFrantz, T. (ed.) (2002) *Dancing Many Drums: Excavations in African American Dance*, Madison: University of Winconsin Press.

Deleuze, G. and Guattari, F. (1982) *A Thousand Plateaus: Capitalism and Schizophrenia*, London: Athlone Press.

Dempster, E. (1988) 'Women Writing the Body: Let's Watch a Little How She Dances', in S. Sheridan (ed.), *Grafts: Feminist Cultural Criticism*, London: Verso.

Denzin, N.K. (1997) *Interpretive Ethnography*, London: Sage.

Denzin, N.K. and Lincoln, Y.S. (eds) (1994) *Handbook of Qualitative Research*, Newbury Park: Sage.

Derrida, J. and McDonald, C.V. (1995) 'Choreographies', in E.W. Goellner and J. Shea Murphy (eds), *Bodies of the Text: Dance as Theory, Literature as Dance*, New Brunswick, NJ: Rutgers University Press.

Desmond, J.C. (ed.) (2001) *Dancing Desires: Choreographing Sexualities on and off the Stage*, Madison: University of Wisconsin Press.

—— (1998) 'Embodying Differences: Dance and Cultural Studies', in A. Carter (ed.), *The Routledge Dance Studies Reader*, London: Routledge.

—— (ed.) (1997) *Meaning in Motion: New Cultural Studies of Dance*, Durham and London: Duke University Press.

Dils, A. (1993) 'Performance Practice and Humphrey Reconstruction', in 'Dance Reconstructed: Past, Present, Future', *Proceedings of Society of Dance History Scholars Sixteenth Annual Conference*, Rutgers University, New Brunswick, Wisconsin: Society of Dance History Scholars, pp. 223–7.

Dingwall, R. (1997) 'Accounts, Interviews and Conversations', in G. Miller and R. Dingwall (eds), *Context and Method in Qualitative Research*, London: Sage.

Doane, M.A. (1987) *The Desire to Desire: The Woman's Film of the 1940s*, London: Macmillan – now Palgrave Macmillan.

Douglas, M. (1975a) 'Do Dogs Laugh?: A Cross-Cultural Approach to Body Symbolism', in *Implicit Meanings: Essays in Anthropology*, London: Routledge & Kegan Paul.

—— (1975b) *Implicit Meanings: Essays in Anthropology*, London: Routledge & Kegan Paul.

Douglas, M. (1973) *Natural Symbols*, Harmondsworth: Penguin.

—— (1970) *Purity and Danger: An Analysis of Concepts of Pollution and Taboo*, Harmondsworth: Penguin.

Drama Review (1984) 'Reconstruction Issue', 28, 3, pp. 2–98.

Duncan, I. (1983) 'The Dance of the Future', in R. Copeland and M. Cohen (eds), *What is Dance?*, Oxford: Oxford University Press.

Durkheim, É. (1976) *The Elementary Forms of Religious Life* (translated by J.W. Swain), 2nd edn, London: Allen & Unwin (first published in 1915).

Eckert, C. (1990) 'The Carole Lombard in Macy's Window', in J. Gaines and C. Herzog (eds), *Fabrications: Costume and the Female Body*, New York: Routledge.

Efron, D. (1972) *Gesture, Race and Culture*, The Hague: Mouton.

Eibl-Eibesfeldt, I. (1972) 'Similarities and Differences between Cultures in Expressive Movements', in R.A. Hinde (ed.), *Non-Verbal Communication*, Cambridge: Cambridge University Press.

Ekman, P. (1977) 'Biological and Cultural Contributions to Body and Facial Movement', in J. Blacking (ed.), *The Anthropology of the Body*, ASA Monograph 15, London: Academic Press.

Elias, N. (1978) *The Civilizing Process*, Vol. 1, *The History of Manners*, Oxford: Basil Blackwell (first published in 1939).

Elton, H. (1992) 'Reconstruction: The Archaeology of Dance: In Conversation with Five Choreographers', *Dance Connection*, 10, 3, pp. 22–35.

Emery, L.F. (1988) *Black Dance from 1619 to Today*, 2nd edn, London: Dance Books (first published in 1972).

Enslin, E. (1994) 'Beyond Writing: Feminist Practice and the Limitations of Ethnography', *Cultural Anthropology*, 9, 4, pp. 537–68.

Everett, P. (1986) *You'll Never be 16 Again: An Illustrated Guide to the British Teenager*, London: BBC Publications.

Falk, P. (1994) *The Consuming Body*, London: Sage Publications.

Farnell, B. (1999) 'It Goes Without Saying – But Not Always', in T. Buckland (ed.), *Dance in the Field: Theories, Methods and Issues in Dance Ethnography*, London: Macmillan – now Palgrave Macmillan.

—— (1994) 'Ethno-Graphics and the Moving Body', *MAN*, 29, pp. 929–74.

Fast, J. (1970) *Body Language*, London: Pan Books.

Featherstone, M. (1991a) 'The Body in Consumer Culture', in M. Featherstone, M. Hepworth and B.S. Turner (eds), *The Body: Social Processes and Cultural Theory*, London: Sage Publications (paper first published in 1982).

—— (1991b) *Consumer Culture & Postmodernism*, London: Sage.

Featherstone, M., Hepworth, M. and Turner, B.S. (eds) (1991) *The Body: Social Processes and Cultural Theory*, London: Sage.

Felföldi, L. (1999) 'Folk Dance Research in Hungary: Relations among Theory, Fieldwork and the Archive', in T.J. Buckland (ed.), *Dance in the Field: Theory, Methods and Issues in Dance Ethnography*, London: Macmillan – now Palgrave Macmillan.

Filmer, P., Phillipson, M., Silverman, D. and Walsh, D. (eds) (1972) *New Directions in Sociological Theory*, London: Collier-Macmillan.

Firestone, S. (1970) *The Dialectic of Sex*, New York: Bantam.

Forster, W. (1990) 'Report of International Movement Notation Alliance Conference (New York 8 June 1990)', *Dance Research Journal*, 22, 2, pp. 49–51.

Foster, H. (1996) *The Return of the Real: the Avant-Garde the End of the Century*, Cambridge: MIT Press.

—— (ed.) (1983) *Anti-Aesthetic: Essays on Post-Modern Culture*, Port Townsend, Wash.: Bay Press.

Foster, S.L. (1998) 'Choreographies of Gender', *Signs: Journal of Women in Culture and Society*, 24, 1, pp. 1–33.

—— (1997) 'Dancing Bodies', in J.C. Desmond (ed.), *Meaning in Motion: New Cultural Studies of Dance*, Durham: Duke University Press.

—— (1996a) 'The Ballerina's Phallic Pointe', in S.L. Foster (ed.), *Corporealities: Dancing Knowledge, Culture and Power*, London: Routledge.

—— (ed.) (1996b) *Corporealities: Dancing Knowledge, Culture and Power*, London: Routledge.

—— (ed.) (1995) *Choreographing History*, Bloomington: Indiana University Press.

—— (1986) *Reading Dancing: Bodies and Subjects in Contemporary American Dance*, Berkeley: University of California Press.

Foucault, M. (1986) 'Neitzche, Genealogy, History', in P. Rabinow (ed.), *The Foucault Reader*, Harmondsworth: Penguin Books.

—— (1984) *The History of Sexuality*, vol. 1, *An Introduction*, Harmondsworth: Peregrine Books.

—— (1980) *Power/Knowledge: Selected Interviews and Other Writings 1972–1977* (ed. C. Gordon), London: Harvester Press.

—— (1977) *Discipline and Punish: The Birth of the Prison*, Harmondsworth: Peregrine Books.

—— (1973) *The Birth of the Clinic*, London: Tavistock.

Fraleigh, S. (1991) 'A Vulnerable Glance: Seeing Dance through Phenomenology', *Dance Research Journal*, 23, 1, pp. 11–16.

Frank, A.W. (1991) 'For a Sociology of the Body: An Analytical Review', in M. Featherstone, M. Hepworth and B.S. Turner (eds), *The Body: Social Processes and Cultural Theory*, London: Sage Publications.

Franko, M. (1995) *Dancing Modernism/Performing Politics*, Bloomington: Indiana University Press.

—— (1993) *Dance as Text: Ideologies of the Baroque Body*, Cambridge: Cambridge University Press.

—— (1989) 'Repeatability, Reconstruction and Beyond', *Theatre Journal*, 41, 1, pp. 56–74.

Fraser, M. (2000) 'Classing Queer', in V. Bell (ed.), *Performativity and Belonging*, London: Sage Publications.

Frith, S. (1996) *Performing Rites: On the Value of Popular Music*, Oxford: Oxford University Press.

—— (1978) *The Sociology of Rock*, London: Constable & Co.

Gaines, J. and Herzog, C. (eds) (1990) *Fabrications: Costume and the Female Body*, London: Routledge.

Gallagher, C. and Laqueur, T. (eds) (1987) *The Making of the Modern Body: Sexuality and Society in the Nineteenth Century*, Berkeley: University of California Press.

Gamman, L. and Makinen, M. (1994) *Female Fetishism: A New Look*, London: Lawrence & Wishart.

Gamson, A. (1993) 'Reflections on the Re-Creation and the Interpretation of the Dances of Duncan, Wigman, and King', in 'Dance Reconstructed: Modern Dance Art, Past, Present, Future', *Proceedings of the Society of Dance History Scholars Sixteenth Annual Conference*, Rutgers University, New Brunswick, Wis.: Society of Dance History Scholars, pp. 263–5.

Garafola, L. (1993) 'Book Review: "Martha: The Life and Work of Martha Graham" by Agnes de Mille. New York: Random House 1991; "Blood Memory: An Autobiography" by Martha Graham. New York, Doubleday, 1991; "The Techniques of Martha Graham" by Alice Helpern. *Studies in Dance History*, 2, no. 2 (Spring/Summer 1991); "Martha Graham: The Evolution of her Dance Theory and Training 1926–1991". Edited by Marian Horosko. Pennington, NJ: A Capella Books, 1991; "Louis Horst: Musician in a Dancer's World" by Janet Mansfield Soares. Durham: Duke University Press, 1992"', *The Drama Review*, 37, 1, pp. 167–72.

Garber, M. (1992) *Vested Interests: Cross-Dressing and Cultural Anxiety*, London: Routledge.

Garfinkel, H. (1984 [1967]) *Studies in Ethnomethodology*, Cambridge: Polity Press.

Gatens, M. (1996) *Imaginary Bodies: Ethics, Power and Corporeality*, London: Routledge.

Geertz, C. (1989) *Works and Lives: The Anthropologist as Author*, Cambridge and Oxford: Polity Press in association with Basil Blackwell.

—— (1975) *The Interpretation of Cultures*, London: Hutchinson & Co.

Gellner, E. (1992) *Postmodernism, Reason and Religion*, London: Routledge.

Giddens, A. (1991) *Modernity and Self-Identity*, Cambridge and Oxford: Polity Press in association with Blackwell Publishers.

Gilbert, J. and Pearson, E. (1999) *Discographies: Dance Music, Culture and the Politics of Sound*, London: Routledge.

Gilman, S. (1995) *Health and Illness: Images of Difference*, London: Reaktion Books.

—— (1992) 'Black Bodies, White Bodies: Towards an Iconography of Female Sexuality in Late Nineteenth Century Art, Medicine and Literature', in J. Donald and A. Rattansi (eds), *'Race', Culture and Difference*, London: Sage.

Goellner, E.W. and Murphy, J.S. (eds) (1995) *Bodies of the Text: Dance as Theory, Literature as Dance*, New Brunswick, NJ: Rutgers.

Goffman, E. (1979) *Gender Advertisements*, London: Macmillan – now Palgrave Macmillan.

—— (1974) *Frame Analysis: An Essay on the Organization of Experience*, New York: Harper & Row.

—— (1972) *Relations in Public: Microstudies of the Public Order*, Harmondsworth: Penguin Books.

—— (1971) *The Presentation of Self in Everyday Life*, Harmondsworth: Penguin Books.

—— (1959) *Interactional Ritual: Essays on Face-to-Face Behaviour*, Garden City, NY: Anchor Books.

Goldberg, M. (1987/88) 'Ballerinas and Ball Passing', *Women & Performance*, 3, 2, pp. 7–31.

Goldstein, L. (ed.) (1991) *The Female Body: Figures, Styles, Speculations*, Ann Arbor: University of Michigan Press.

Gore, G. (1999) 'Textual Fields: Representation in Dance Ethnography', in T. Buckland (ed.), *Dance in the Field: Theory, Methods and Issues in Dance Ethnography*, London: Macmillan – now Palgrave Macmillan.

—— (1997) 'The Beat Goes On: Trance, Dance and Tribalism in Rave Culture', in H. Thomas (ed.), *Dance in the City*, London: Macmillan – now Palgrave Macmillan.

Gramsci, A. (1971) *Selections from the Prison Notebooks* (edited and translated by Q. Hoare and G.N. Smith), London: Lawrence & Wishart.

Grau, A. (1997) 'Book Review: Rumba: Dance and Social Change in Contemporary Cuba by Yvonne Daniel; Samba: Resistance in Motion, by Barbara Browning; Tango and the Political Economy of Passion, by Marta Savigliano', *Dance Research*, 15, 1, pp. 79–88.

—— (1993) 'John Blacking and the Development of Dance Anthropology in the UK', *Dance Research*, 25, 2, pp. 21–32.

Griffin, S. (1978) *Women and Nature: The Roaring Inside Her*, New York: Harper & Row.

Grosz, E. (1994) *Volatile Bodies: Towards a Corporeal Feminism*, Bloomington and Indianapolis: Indiana University Press.

Grosz, E. and Probyn, E. (eds) (1995) *Sexy Bodies: The Strange Carnalities of Feminism*, London: Routledge.

Hall, E.T. (1969) *The Hidden Dimension*, Garden City, NY: Anchor Books.

—— (1955) 'The Anthropology of Manners', *Scientific American*, 194, 4, pp. 84–90.

Hall, S., Critcher, C., Jefferson, T. and Roberts, B. (eds) (1978) *Policing the Crisis*, London: Macmillan – now Palgrave Macmillan.

Hall, S. and Jefferson, T. (eds) (1976) *Resistance through Rituals: Youth Subcultures in Post-War Britain*, London: Hutchinson (first published in 1975 as *Working Papers in Cultural Studies*).

Hammersley, M. (1992) *What's Wrong with Ethnography*, London: Routledge.

—— (1991) 'A Myth of a Myth? An Assessment of Two Ethnographic Studies of Option Choice Schemes', *British Journal of Sociology*, 42, 1, pp. 61–94.

—— (1990) 'What's Wrong with Ethnography? The Myth of Theoretical Description', *Sociology*, 24, 4, pp. 597–615.

Hammersley, M. and Atkinson, P. (1995) *Ethnography: Principles in Practice*, 2nd edn, London: Routledge.

Hanna, J.L. (1987) *Dance, Sex and Gender: Signs of Identity, Dominance, Defiance, and Desire*, Chicago, Ill. and London: University of Chicago Press.

—— (1980) *To Dance is Human*, Austin: Texas University Press.

Haraway, D.J. (1988) 'Situated Knowledges: The Science Question in Feminism and the Privilege of Partial Perspective', *Feminist Studies*, 14, 3, pp. 575–99.

—— (1991) *Simians, Cyborgs and Women: The Reinvention of Nature*, London: Free Association Books.

Harding, S. (ed.) (1987) *Feminism and Methodology*, Bloomington, Indiana and Milton Keynes: Indiana University Press and Open University Press.

Hartsock, N. (1987) 'Rethinking Modernism: Minority and Majority Theories', *Cultural Critique*, 7, pp. 187–206.

Harvey, D. (1989) *The Condition of Postmodernity*, Oxford: Basil Blackwell.

Hastrup, K. (1992) 'Out of Anthropology: The Anthropologist as an Object of Dramatic Representation', *Cultural Anthropology*, 7, 3, pp. 327–45.

Hebdige, D. (1979) *Subcultures: The Meaning of Style*, London: Methuen.

Henley, N.M. (1977) *Body Politics: Power, Sex and Nonverbal Communication*, Englewood Cliffs, NJ: Prentice-Hall.

Hertz, R. (1973) 'The Pre-Eminence of the Right Hand: A Study in Religious Polarity', in R. Needham (ed.), *Right and Left*, Chicago, Ill.: Chicago University Press (first published in 1909).

Hirst, P. and Woolley, P. (1982) *Social Relations and Human Attributes*, London: Tavistock.

Holland, J., Ramazanoglu, C., Sharpe, S. and Thomson, R. (1998) *The Male in the Head: Young People, Heterosexuality and Power*, London: Tufnell Press.

hooks, b. (1992) *Black Looks: Race and Representation*, London: Turnaround Press.

Horton, R. (1971) 'African Traditional Thought and Western Science', in M.F.D. Young (ed.), *Knowledge and Control: New Directions for the Sociology of Education*, London: Collier-Macmillan.

Humphrey, D. (1959) *The Art of Making Dances*, London: Dance Books.

Hunter, I. and Saunders, D. (1995) 'Walks of Life: Mauss on the Human Gymnasium', *Body & Society*, 1, 2, pp. 65–81.

Husserl, E. (1965) *Phenomenology and the Crisis in Philosophy*, New York: Harper & Row.

Hutchinson, A. (1977) *Labanotation, or Kinetography Laban: The System of Analysing and Recording Movement* (ed. and illustrated by D. Anderson), New York: Theatre Arts Books.

Hutchinson Guest, A. (2000) 'Is Authenticity to be had?', in S. Jordan (ed.), *Preservation Politics: Dance Revived, Reconstructed, Remade*, London: Dance Books, pp. 65–71.

—— (1991) 'Nijinsky's Faune', *Choreography and Dance*, 1, pp. 3–34.

—— (1984) *Dance Notation: The Process of Recording Movement on Paper*, London: Dance Books.

Huyssen, A. (1986) *After the Great Divide: Modernism, Mass Culture, Modernism*, London: Macmillan – now Palgrave Macmillan.

Irigaray, L. (1985) *This Sex Which is not One* (translated by C. Porter and C. Burke), Ithaca, NY: Cornell University Press.

James, A., Hockey, J. and Dawson, A. (eds) (1997) *After Writing Culture: Ethnography and Praxis in Contemporary Anthropology*, London: Routledge.

Jay, M. (1999) 'Returning the Gaze: The American Response to the French Critique of Ocularcentrism', in G. Weiss and H.F. Faber (eds), *Perspectives on Embodiment: The Intersections of Nature and Culture*, London: Routledge.

Jenkins, R. (1992) *Pierre Bourdieu*, London: Routledge.

Johnston, L. (1998) 'Reading the Sexed Bodies and Spaces of the Gym', in H.J. Nast and S. Pile (eds), *Places through the Body*, London: Routledge.

Jordan, S. (2000) *Moving Music: Dialogues with Music in Twentieth-Century Ballet*, London: Dance Books.

—— (1993) 'The Musical Key to Reconstruction', in 'Dance Reconstructed: Past, Present, Future', *Proceedings of Society of Dance History Scholars Sixteenth Annual Conference*, Rutgers University, New Brunswick, Wis.: Society of Dance History Scholars, pp. 185–90.

—— (1992) *Striding Out: Aspects of Contemporary and New Dance in Britain*, London: Dance Books.

Jordan, S. and Thomas, H. (1994) 'Dance and Gender: Formalism and Semiotics Reconsidered', *Dance Research*, 12, 2, pp. 3–14.

Jordan, T. (1995) 'Collective Bodies: Raving and the Politics of Gilles Deleuze and Felix Guattari', *Body & Society*, 1, 1, pp. 125–44.

Jowitt, D. (1988) *Time and the Dancing Image*, New York: William Morrow & Co.

Jung, H.Y. (1996) 'Phenomenology and Body Politics', *Body & Society*, 2, 2, pp. 1–22.

Kaeppler, A. (1999) 'The Mystique of Fieldwork', in T. Buckland (ed.), *Dance in the Field: Theory, Methods and Issues in Dance Ethnography*, London: Macmillan – now Palgrave Macmillan.

—— (1991) 'American Approaches to the Study of Dance', *Yearbook of Traditional Music*, 23, pp. 11–21.

—— (1985) 'Structured Movement Systems in Tonga', in P. Spencer (ed.), *Society and the Dance*, Cambridge: Cambridge University Press.

—— (1972) 'Method and Theory in Analyzing Dance Structure with an Analysis of Tongan Dance', *Ethnomusicology*, 16, 2, pp. 173–217.

Kagan, E. (1978) 'Towards the Analysis of a Score: A Comparative Study of *Three Epitaphs* by Paul Taylor and *Water Study* by Doris Humphrey', *Dance Research Annual*, IX, pp. 75–92.

Kaplan, E.A. (1983) 'Is the Gaze Male?', in E.A. Kaplan (ed.), *Women and Film: Both Sides of the Camera*, New York: Methuen.

Kealiinohomoku, J. (1989) 'Variables that Affect Gender Actions and Re-Actions in Dance Ethnology', *Journal of Dance Ethnology*, 13, pp. 48–53.

Kealiinohomoku, J. (1979) 'Cultural Change: Functional and Dysfunctional Expressions of Dance, a Form of Affective Culture', in J. Blacking and J. Kealiinohomoku (eds), *The Performing Arts*, The Hague: Mouton.

—— (1970) 'An Anthropologist Looks at Ballet as a Form of Ethnic Dance', in *Impulse 1970*, San Francisco: Impulse Publications.

Kendall, E. (1979) *Where She Danced*, New York: Arnold A. Knopf.

Kenyon, N. (1988) *Authenticity and Early Music: A Symposium*, Oxford: Oxford University Press.

Kirkland, G. with Lawrence, G. (1987) *Dancing on My Grave*, New York: Jove Books.

Kirstein, L. (1983) 'Classical Ballet: Aria of the Aerial', in R. Copeland and M. Cohen (eds), *What is Dance?*, Oxford: Oxford University Press.

—— (1971) *Movement and Metaphor: Four Centuries of Ballet*, London: Pitman Publishing.

Kivy, P. (1995) *Authenticities: Philosophical Reflections on Musical Performance*, Ithaca, NY: Cornell University Press.

—— (1993) *The Fine Art of Repetition: Essays in the Philosophy of Music*, Cambridge: Cambridge University Press.

Koritz, A. (1995) *Gendering Bodies/Performing Art: Dance and Literature in Early Twentieth Century British Culture*, Ann Arbor: University of Michigan Press.

Koutsouba, M. (1999) 'The "Outsider" in an "Inside" World, or Dance Ethnography at Home', in T. Buckland (ed.), *Dance in the Field: Theories, Methods and Issues in Dance Ethnography*, London: Macmillan – now Palgrave Macmillan.

Kozel, S. (1997) ' "The Story is Told as a History of the Body": Strategies of Mimesis in the Work of Irigaray and Bausch', in J.C. Desmond (ed.), *Meaning in Motion: New Cultural Studies of Dance*, Durham and London: Duke University Press.

Kriegsman, S.A. (1993) 'Dance Reconstructed: Modern Dance Art, Present and Future', *Ballett International*, 6, pp. 15–17.

Kristeva, J. (1984) *Revolution and Poetic Language* (translated by M. Waller), New York: Columbia University Press.

—— (1982) *Powers of Horrors: An Essay on Abjection*, New York: Columbia University Press.

—— (1978) 'Gesture: Practice or Communication', in T. Polhemus (ed.), *Social Aspects of the Human Body*, Harmondsworth: Penguin Books (first published in 1969).

Kroeber, A. (1952) *The Nature of Culture*, Chicago, Ill.: Chicago University Press.

Kuhn, T.S. (1962) *The Structure of Scientific Revolutions*, Chicago, Ill.: University of Chicago Press.

Laban, R. (1966) *Choreutics* (annotated and edited by L. Ullmann), London: Macdonald & Evans.

La Barre, W. (1978) 'The Cultural Basis of Emotions and Gestures', in T. Polhemus (ed.), *Social Aspects of the Human Body*, Harmondsworth: Penguin.

Lange, R. (1980) 'The Development of Anthropological Dance Research', *Dance Studies*, 4, pp. 1–23. Jersey/Centre for Dance Studies.

Langer, S.K. (1953) *Feeling and Form*, New York: Scribner.

—— (1942) *Philosophy in a New Key*, Cambridge, Mass.: Harvard University Press.

Laqueur, T. (1987) 'Organism, Generation, and the Politics of Reproductive Biology', in C. Gallagher and T. Laqueur (eds), *The Making of the Modern Body: Sexuality and Society in the Nineteenth Century*, Berkeley: University of California Press.

de Lauretis, T. (1987) *Technologies of Gender*, Bloomington: Indiana University Press.

—— (1984) *Alice Doesn't: Feminism, Semiotics, Cinema*, Bloomington: Indiana University Press.

Laver, J. and Hutcheson, S. (eds) (1972) *Communication in Face to Face Interaction*, Harmondsworth: Penguin Books.

Lepczyk, B.F. (1990) 'A Contrastive Study of Movement Style in Dance through the Laban Perspective', *Proceedings of the 5th Hong Kong International Dance Conference, Conference Papers*, 2, Hong Kong: Hong Kong Academy For Performing Arts, pp. 66–86.

—— (1989) 'Martha Graham's Movement Invention Viewed through Laban Analysis', *Dance: Current Selected Research*, 1, pp. 45–62.

—— (1987) 'Towards a Quantitative Analysis of Classic Ballet: The Upper Body Technique viewed through Choreutics', *Progress and Possibilities: 20 Years of Dance Research CORD Annual Conference Papers* October, New York: Congress on Research in Dance, pp. 43–64.

Lévi-Strauss, C. (1978) *Structural Anthropology*, vol. 2, Harmondsworth: Penguin Books.

—— (1969) *The Savage Mind*, London: Weidenfeld & Nicolson.

Lewis, J.L. (1995) 'Genre and Embodiment: From Brazilian Capoeira to the Ethnology of Human Movement', *Cultural Anthropology*, 10, 2, pp. 221–43.

Lloyd, M. (1974) *The Borzoi Book of Modern Dance*, New York: Dance Horizons (first published in 1949).

Lyon, M.L. and Barbalet, J.M. (1994) 'Society's Body: Emotion and "Somatization" of Social Theory', in T. Csordas (ed.), *Embodiment and Experience: The Essential Ground of Culture and Self*, Cambridge: Cambridge University Press.

Lyon, M.L. (1997) 'The Material Body, Social Processes and Emotion', *Body & Society*, 3, 1, pp. 1–7.

Macpherson, C.B. (1964) *The Political Theory of Possessive Individualism: Hobbes to Locke*, Oxford: Oxford University Press.

MacSween, M. (1993) *Anorexic Bodies: A Feminist and Sociological Perspective on Anorexia*, London: Routledge.

Maffesoli, M. (1996) *The Time of the Tribes: The Decline of Individualism in Mass Society* (translated by D. Smith), London: Sage Publications.

Main, L. (1995) 'Preserved and Illuminated', *Dance Theatre Journal*, 12, 2, pp. 14–15.

Malbon, B. (1999) *Clubbing: Dancing, Ecstasy and Vitality*, London: Routledge.

Maletic, V. (2000) *Workbook for Effort Dance Dynamics: Phrasing*, Ohio: Vera Maletic.

Malnig, J. (1995) *Dancing Till Dawn*, New York: New York University Press.

Manning, S.A. (1997) 'The Female Dancer and the Male Gaze', in J.C. Desmond (ed.), *Meaning in Motion: New Cultural Studies of Dance*, Durham and London: Duke University Press.

—— (1996) 'American Document and American Minstrelsy', in G. Morris (ed.), *Moving Words: Re-Writing Dance*, London and New York: Routledge.

—— (1993a) *Ecstasy and the Demon: Feminism and Nationalism in the Dances of Mary Wigman*, Berkeley: University of California Press.

—— (1993b) 'Perspectives in Reconstruction (Keynote Panel)', in 'Dance Reconstructed: Modern Dance Art, Past, Present, Future', *Proceedings of Society of Dance History Scholars Sixteenth Annual Conference 1992*, Rutgers University, New Brunswick: Society of Dance History Scholars, pp. 11–26.

Marcus, G.E. and Fischer, M.J. (1986) *Anthropology as Cultural Critique: An Experimental Moment in the Social Sciences*, Chicago, Ill. and London: Chicago University Press.

Marion, S. (1990) 'Authorship and Intention in Re-Created and Notated Dances', *Proceedings of 5th Hong Kong International Dance Conference: International Congress on Movement Notation*, 4, Hong Kong: Hong Kong Academy For Performing Arts, pp. 107–22.

Martin, E. (1987) *The Woman in the Body*, Milton Keynes: Open University Press.

Martin, J. (1965) *The Modern Dance*, New York: Dance Horizons (first published in 1933).

Marx, K. (1959) *Economic and Philosophical Manuscripts of 1844*, London: Lawrence & Wishart (first published in 1844).

Mauss, M. (1979) *Sociology and Psychology*, London: Routledge & Kegan Paul.

—— (1973) 'The Techniques of the Body' (translated by B. Brewster), *Economy and Society*, 2, 1, pp. 70–88 (first published in 1934).

Mayhew, H. (1861) *London Labour and the London Poor*, London: Griffin Bohn.

McGuigan, J. (ed.) (1997) *Cultural Methodologies*, London: Sage.

McNay, L. (1999) 'Gender, Habitus and the Field: Pierre Bourdieu and the Limits of Reflexivity', *Theory, Culture and Society*, 16, 1, pp. 95–117.

—— (1992) *Foucault and Feminism*, Oxford: Polity Press.

McNeill, W.H. (1995) *Keeping Together in Time: Dance and Drill in Human History*, Cambridge, Mass.: Harvard University Press.

McRobbie, A. (ed.) (1997) *Back to Reality?: Social Experience and Cultural Studies*, Manchester: Manchester University Press.

—— (1993) 'Shut up and Dance: Youth Culture and Changing Modes of Femininity', *Cultural Studies*, 7, 3, pp. 406–26.

—— (1992) 'The 'Passagenwerk and the Place of Walter Benjamin in Cultural Studies', *Cultural Studies*, 6, 2, pp. 147–69.

—— (1991) 'Settling Accounts with Subcultures: A Feminist Critique', in *Feminism and Youth Culture: From Jackie to Just Seventeen*, London: Macmillan – now Palgrave Macmillan (first published in 1980).

—— (1990) '*Fame, Flash Dance* and Fantasies of Achievement', in J. Gaines and C. Herzog (eds), *Fabrications: Costumes and the Female Body*, London: Routledge.

McRobbie, A. and Garber, J. (1991) 'Girls and Subcultures', in A. McRobbie, *Feminism and Youth Culture: From Jackie to Just Seventeen*, London: Macmillan – now Palgrave Macmillan (first published in 1978).

Mead, G.H. (1934) *Mind, Self and Society*, Chicago, Ill.: Chicago University Press.

Meduri, A. (1996) 'Nation, Woman, Representation: The Saturated History of Devadasi and Her Dance', PhD dissertation, New York University, New York.

—— (1988) 'Baratha Natyam – What are You?', *Asian Theatre Journal*, 5, pp. 1–22.

Melchi, A. (1993) 'The Ecstasy of Disappearance', in S. Redhead (ed.), *Rave Off: Politics and Deviance in Contemporary Youth Culture*, Aldershot: Avebury.

Merleau-Ponty, M. (1978) 'The Philosopher and Sociology', in T. Luckmann (ed.), *Phenomenology and Sociology*, Harmondsworth: Penguin.

—— (1968) *The Primacy of Perception*, Evanston, Ill.: Northwestern University Press.

—— (1965) *The Structure of Behaviour*, London: Methuen.

—— (1962) *Phenomenology of Perception*, London: Routledge & Kegan Paul.

Miller, D. (1995) 'Introduction: Anthropology, Modernity and Consumption', in *Worlds Apart: Modernity Through the Prism of the Local*, London: Routledge.

—— (1991) 'Absolute Freedom in Trinidad', *MAN*, 26, pp. 323–41.

Miner, H. (1956) 'Body Ritual among the Nacirema', *American Anthropologist*, 58, pp. 503–7.

Mitchell, J. and Rose, J. (eds) (1982) *Feminine Sexuality: Jacques Lacan & the École Freudienne*, London: Macmillan – now Palgrave Macmillan.

Moi, T. (1986a) 'Introduction', in T. Moi (ed.), *The Kristeva Reader*, Oxford: Basil Blackwell.

—— (ed.) (1986b) *The Kristeva Reader*, Oxford: Basil Blackwell.

—— (1985) *Sexual/Textual Politics*, London: Methuen.

Morris, D. (1979) *Intimate Behaviour*, St Albans, Hertfordshire: Panther Books.

Morris, G. (2001, Winter) 'Bourdieu: The Body and Graham's Post-War Dance', *Dance Research*, 19, 2, pp. 52–82.

—— (1996a) *Moving Words: Re-Writing Dance*, London: Routledge.

—— (1996b) ' "Styles of the Flesh": Gender in the Dances of Mark Morris', in G. Morris (ed.), *Moving Words: Re-Writing Dance*, London and New York: Routledge.

—— (1993) 'The Reappearance of the Past', *Dance Ink*, (Spring), 4, 1, pp. 34–8.

Morrison, T. (1992) *Playing in the Dark: Whiteness and the Literary Imagination*, Cambridge, Mass.: Harvard University Press.

Mueller, J. (1974) *Films on Ballet and Modern Dance: Notes and a Directory*, New York: American Dance Guild.

Muggleton, D. (2000) *Inside Subculture: The Postmodern Meaning of Style*, Oxford: Berg.

Mulvey, L. (1989) 'Afterthoughts on "Visual Pleasure and Narrative Cinema" Inspired by King Vidor's Duel in the Sun', in M. Mulvey (ed.), *Visual and Other Pleasures*, London: Macmillan – now Palgrave Macmillan.

—— (1975) 'Visual Pleasure and Narrative Cinema', *Screen*, 16, 3, pp. 6–18.

Nast, H.J. and Pile, S. (eds) (1998) *Places through the Body*, London: Routledge.

Nead, L. (1992) *The Female Nude: Art, Obscenity and Sexuality*, London: Routledge.

Needham, R. (ed.) (1973) *Right and Left: Essays on Symbolic Classification*, Chicago, Ill.: Chicago University Press.

Ness, S.A. (2003) 'Being a Body in a Cultural Way: Understanding the Culture in the Embodiment of Dance', in H. Thomas and J. Ahmed (eds), *Cultural Bodies: Ethnography and Theory*, Oxford: Blackwell Publishers.

—— (1997) 'Originality in Postcolony: Choreographing the Neoethnic Body of Philippine Ballet', *Cultural Anthropology*, 12, 1, pp. 64–108.

—— (1996) 'Observing the Evidence Fail: Difference Arising from Objectifications in Cross-Cultural Studies of Dance', in G. Morris (ed.), *Moving Words: Re-Writing Dance*, New York: Routledge.

—— (1992) *Body, Movement and Culture: Kinesthetic and Visual Symbolism in a Philippine Community*, Philadelphia: University of Pennsylvania Press.

Nicholson, L.J. (ed.) (1990) *Feminism/Postmodernism*, London: Routledge.

Nixon, S. (1992) 'Have You got the Look? Masculinities and Shopping Spectacle', in R. Shields (ed.), *Lifestyle Shopping: The Subject of Consumption*, London: Routledge.

Novack, C. (1993) 'Ballet, Gender and Cultural Power', in H. Thomas (ed.), *Dance, Gender and Culture*, London: Macmillan – now Palgrave Macmillan.

—— (1990) *Sharing the Dance: Contact Improvisation and American Culture*, Madison: University of Wisconsin Press.

Oakley, A. (1974) *Sex, Gender and Society*, London: Temple Smith.

O'Connor, B. (1997) 'Safe Sets: Dance and "Communitas" ', in H. Thomas (ed.), *Dance in the City*, London: Macmillan – now Palgrave Macmillan.

O'Neill, J. (1985) *Five Bodies: The Human Shape of Modern Society*, Ithaca, NY: Cornell University Press.

Orbach, S. (1986) *Hunger Strike: The Anorectic's Struggle as a Metaphor for our Age*, London: Faber & Faber.

—— (1978) *Fat is a Feminist Issue*, London: Arrow Books.

Ortner, S. (1974) 'Is Female to Male as Nature is to Culture?', in M. Rosaldo and L. Lamphere (eds), *Women, Culture and Society*, Stanford, Calif.: Stanford University Press.

Parker, R. and Pollock, G. (eds) (1987) *Framing Feminism*, London: Pandora.

—— (1981) *Old Mistresses*, London: Pandora.

Parsons, T. (1951) *The Social System*, New York: The Free Press.

Penny, P. (1999) 'Dance at the Interface of the Social and the Theatrical: Focus on the Participatory Patterns of Contemporary Ballroom Dancers in Britain', *Dance Research*, 17, 1, pp. 47–74.

Pernod, J. and Ginsberg, A. (1997) 'Dialogue: New Work and Reconstructed Work in the Context of Dance Repertory', *Dance Research Journal*, 29, 1, pp. 1–5.

Perpener, J.O. III (2001) *African-American Concert Dance: The Harlem Renaissance and Beyond*, Urbana and Chicago: University of Illinois Press.

Phelan, P. (1993) *Unmarked: The Politics of Performance*, London: Routledge.

Pini, M. (2001) *Club Cultures and Female Subjectivity: The Move from Home to House*, Basingstoke: Palgrave Macmillan.

—— (1997a) 'Cyborgs, Nomads and the Raving Feminine', in H. Thomas (ed.), *Dance in the City*, London: Macmillan – now Palgrave Macmillan.

—— (1997b) 'Women and the Early British Rave Scene', in A. McRobbie (ed.), *Back to Reality: Social Experience and Cultural Studies*, Manchester: Manchester University Press.

Polhemus, T. (ed.) (1978) *Social Aspects of the Human Body*, Harmondsworth: Penguin Books.

—— (1975) 'Social Bodies', in J. Benthall and T. Polhemus (eds), *The Body as a Medium of Expression*, London: Allen Lane.

Polhemus, T. and Proctor, L. (1984) *Pop Styles*, London: Vermillion.

Pollock, G. (1988) *Vision and Difference*, London: Routledge.

Poole, R. (1975) 'Objective Sign and Subjective Meaning', in J. Benthall and T. Polhemus (eds), *The Body as a Medium of Expression*, London: Allen Lane.

Preston-Dunlop, V. (1995) *Dance Words*, Chur: Harwood Academic Publishers.

Rabinow, P. (ed.) (1986a) *The Foucault Reader: An Introduction to Foucault's Thought*, London: Penguin Books.

—— (1986b) 'Introduction', in P. Rabinow (ed.), *The Foucault Reader: An Introduction to Foucault's Thought*, London: Penguin Books.

Redhead, S. (1993a) 'The End of the End-of-the-Century Party', in S. Redhead (ed.), *Rave Off: Politics and Deviance in Contemporary Youth Culture*, Aldershot: Avebury.

Redhead, S. (1993b) 'The Politics of Ecstasy', in S. Redhead (ed.), *Rave Off: Politics and Deviance in Contemporary Youth Culture*, Aldershot: Avebury.

—— (ed.) (1993c) *Rave Off: Politics and Deviance in Contemporary Youth Culture*, Aldershot: Avebury.

—— (1990) *The End-of-the-Century Party: Youth and Pop towards 2000*, Manchester: Manchester University Press.

Redhead, S. with Wynne, D. and O'Connor, J. (eds) (1998) *The Clubcultures Reader: Readings in Popular Cultural Studies*, Oxford: Blackwell Publishers.

Reed, S.A. (1998) 'The Politics and Poetics of Dance', *Annual Review of Anthropology*, 27, pp. 503–32.

Reynolds, S. (1998) *Energy Flash: A Journey through Rave Music and Dance Culture*, London: Picador.

—— (1997) 'Rave Culture: Living Dream or Living Death', in S. Redhead with D. Wynne and J. O'Connor (eds), *The Clubcultures Reader: Readings in Popular Cultural Studies*, Oxford: Blackwell Publishers.

Richardson, P.J.S. (1948) *A History of English Ballroom Dancing (1910–1945): The Story of the Development of the English Style*, London: Herbert Jenkins.

Rietveld, H. (1998) *This is Our House*, London: Arena.

—— (1997) 'The House Sound of Chicago', in S. Redhead with D. Wynne and J. O'Connor (eds), *The Clubcultures Reader: Readings in Popular Cultural Studies*, Oxford: Blackwell Publishers.

—— (1993) 'Living the Dream', in S. Redhead (ed.), *Rave On: The Politics of Ecstasy*, Aldershot: Avebury.

Ronström, O. (1989) 'The Dance Event: A Terminological and Methodological Discussion of the Concept', in L. Torp (ed.), *Proceedings of the 15th Symposium ICTM Study Group on Ethnochoreology*, Copenhagen: ICTM.

Royce, A.P. (1980) *The Anthropology of Dance*, Bloomington: Indiana University Press.

Rubidge, S. (1996) 'Does Authenticity Matter? The Case for and against Authenticity in the Performing Arts', in P. Campbell (ed.), *Analysing Performance*, Manchester: Manchester University Press.

Russell, K. (1993) 'Lysergia Suburbia', in S. Redhead (ed.), *Rave Off: Politics and Deviance in Contemporary Youth Culture*, Aldershot: Avebury.

Ruyter, N.L.C. (1979) *Reformers and Visionaries: The Americanization of the Art of Dance*, New York: Dance Horizons.

Ryman, R. (1992) ' "Writing It All Down" in Conversations with 5 Canadian Dance Professionals', *Dance Connection*, 10, 3, p. 29.

Said, E. (1979) *Orientalism*, New York: Vantage Books.

Sanchez-Colberg, A. (1993) ' "You put your left foot in, then you shake it all about..." Excursions and Incursions into Feminism and Bausch's Tanztheater', in H. Thomas (ed.), *Dance, Gender and Culture*, London: Macmillan – now Palgrave Macmillan.

Sandywell, B., Filmer, P., Phillipson, M. and Silverman, D. (eds) (1975) *Problems of Reflexivity and Dialectics in Sociological Inquiry*, London: Routledge & Kegan Paul.

Saunders, N. (ed.) (1997) *Ecstasy Reconsidered*, London: Neal's Yard Press.
—— (ed.) (1995) *Ecstasy and Dance Culture*, (with contributions by M.A. Wright and an annotated bibliography by A. Shulgin), London: Neal's Yard Press.
Savigliano, M.E. (1995) *Tango and the Political Economy of Passion*, Boulder, Col.: Westview Press.
Sayers, L.A. (1997) 'Madam Fudge, Some Fossils, and Other Missing Links: Unearthing the Ballet Class', in H. Thomas (ed.), *Dance in the City*, London: Macmillan – now Palgrave Macmillan.
Scheflen, A.E. (1964) 'The Significance of Posture in Communication Systems', *Psychiatry*, pp. 126–36.
Scheper-Hughes, N. and Lock, M. (1987) 'The Mindful Body: A Prolegomenon to Future Work in Medical Anthropology', *Medical Anthropology Quarterly*, 1, pp. 6–41.
Schiebinger, L. (1987) 'Skeletons in the Closet: Illustrations of the Female Skeleton in Eighteenth-Century Anatomy', in C. Gallagher and T. Laqueur (eds), *The Making of the Modern Body: Sexuality and Society in the Nineteenth Century*, Berkeley: University of California Press.
Schilder, P. (1950) *The Image and Appearance of the Human Body: Studies in the Constructive Energies of the Psyche*, New York: International Universities Press (first published in 1935).
Schmidt, J. (1988) 'The Weariness of the Dance World', *Ballett International*, 11, 6/7, pp. 28–33.
Schultze, L. (1990) 'On the Muscle', in J. Gaines and C. Herzog (eds), *Fabrications: Costume and the Female Body*, New York: Routledge.
Schutz, A. (1967) *Collected Papers 1: The Problem of Social Reality*, The Hague: Marinus Nijhoff.
Seale, C. (1999) *The Quality of Qualitative Research*, London: Sage.
Seymour, W. (1998) *Remaking the Body: Rehabilitation and Change*, London: Routledge.
Sheets-Johnstone, M. (ed.) (1984) *Illuminating Dance*, Cranbury, NJ: Associated University Presses.
—— (1979) *The Phenomenology of Dance*, 2nd edn, London: Dance Books.
Shelton, S. (1981) *Ruth St. Denis: A Biography of a Divine Dancer*, Austin: University of Texas Press.
Shilling, C. (1993) *The Body and Social Theory*, London: Sage.
—— (1991) 'Educating the Body: Physical Capital and the Production of Social Inequalities', *Sociology*, 25, 4, pp. 653–72.
Siegel, M.B. (1993) 'Translations', *Dance Ink*, 4, 1, pp. 20–9.
—— (1979) *The Shapes of Change*, Boston, Mass.: Houghton Mifflin.
—— (1968) *At the Vanishing Point. A Critic Looks at Dance*, New York: Saturday Review Press.
Sklar, D. (2001) *Dancing with the Virgin: Body and Faith in the Fiesta of the Tortugas, New Mexico*, Berkeley: University of California Press.

Sklar, D. (2000) 'Reprise: On Dance Ethnography', *Dance Research Journal*, 32, 1, pp. 70–7.

—— (1999) ' "All the Dances have Meaning to that Apparition": Felt Knowledge and the *Danzantes* of Tortugas', *Dance Research Journal*, 31, 2, pp. 14–33.

—— (1991) 'On Dance Ethnography', *Dance Research Journal*, 23, 1, pp. 6–10.

Slater, D. (1997) *Consumer Culture and Modernity*, Cambridge: Polity Press.

Sommer, S. (2001) ' "C'mon to my house": Underground House Dancing', *Dance Research Journal*, 33, 2, pp. 72–86.

Spencer, P. (ed.) (1985) *Society and the Dance: The Social Anthropology of Process and Performance*, Cambridge: Cambridge University Press.

Stacey, J. (1988) 'Can There be a Feminist Ethnography?', *Women's Studies International Forum*, 11, 1, pp. 21–7.

Stacey, J. and Thorne, B. (1985) 'The Missing Feminist Revolution in Sociology', *Social Problems*, 32, 4, pp. 301–16.

Stanley, L. (1990a) 'Doing Ethnography, Writing Ethnography: A Comment on Hammersley', *Sociology*, 24, 4, pp. 617–27.

—— (ed.) (1990b) *Feminist Practice*, London: Routledge.

Steinman, L. (1986) *The Knowing Body: Elements of Contemporary Performance & Dance*, Boston, Mass. and London: Shambhala.

Stokes, A. (1934) *Tonight the Ballet*, London: Faber & Faber.

Stollar, P. (1989) *The Taste of Ethnographic Things: The Senses of Anthropology*, Philadelphia: University of Pennsylvania Press.

Stone, R. (1982) *Let the Inside be Sweet: The Interpretation of Music Event among the Kpelle of Liberia*, Bloomington: Indiana University Press.

Strathern, M. (1987) 'An Awkward Relationship: The Case of Feminism and Anthropology', *Signs: Journal of Women in Culture and Society*, 2, 2, pp. 270–92.

Swingewood, A. (1998) *Cultural Theory and the Problem of Modernity*, London: Macmillan – now Palgrave Macmillan.

Sydie, R.A. (1987) *Natural Women, Cultured Men: A Feminist Perspective on Sociological Theory*, Milton Keynes: Open University Press.

Székely, E. (1988) *Never Too Thin*, London: The Women's Press.

Taruskin, R. (1995) *Text as Act: Essays on Performance*, Oxford: Oxford University Press.

Taylor, V. (1999) 'Respect, Antipathy and Tenderness: Why do Girls "Go to Ballet" ', *Proceedings of Society of Dance History Scholars Twenty-Second Annual Conference*, University of New Mexico: Albuquerque, New Mexico: Society of Dance History Scholars, pp. 177–84.

Terry, W. (1978) *I Was There: Selected Dance Reviews 1936–1976*, New York: Marcel Dekker.

Thomas, H. (2000) 'Dance Halls: Where Older People Come into Visibility in the City', in S. Pile and N. Thrift (eds), *City A–Z*, London: Routledge.

—— (1998a) 'Culture/Nature', in C. Jenks (ed.), *Core Sociological Dichotomies*, London: Sage.

—— (1998b) ' "Done into Dance: Isadora Duncan in America" by Ann Daly', *Body & Society*, 4, 3, pp. 115–18.

—— (1997) 'Dancing: Representation and Difference', in J. McGuigan (ed.), *Cultural Methodologies*, London: Sage.

—— (1996) 'Do You Want to Join the Dance: Postmodernism, Poststructuralism, the Body, and Dance', in G. Morris (ed.), *Moving Words: Re-Writing Dance*, London: Routledge.

—— (1995) *Dance, Modernity and Culture: Explorations in the Sociology of Dance*, London: Routledge.

—— (ed.) (1993a) *Dance, Gender and Culture*, London: Macmillan – now Palgrave Macmillan.

—— (1993b) 'An-Other Voice: Young Women Dancing and Talking', in H. Thomas (ed.), *Dance, Gender and Culture*, London: Macmillan – now Palgrave Macmillan.

—— (1986) 'Movement Modernism and Contemporary Culture: Issues for a Critical Sociology of Dance', PhD dissertation, The University of London.

Thomas, H. and Cooper, L. (2002) 'Dancing into the Third Age: Social Dance as Cultural Text – Research in Progress', *Dance Research*, 1, 2 pp. 54–80.

Thomas, H. and Miller, N. (1997) 'Ballroom Blitz', in H. Thomas (ed.), *Dance in the City*, London: Macmillan.

Thornton, Sam (1971) *A Movement Perspective of Rudolf Laban*, London: Macdonald & Evans.

Thornton, Sarah (1995) *Club Cultures: Music, Media and Subcultural Analysis*, Cambridge: Polity Press.

Thrift, N. (1997) 'The Still Point: Resistance, Expressive Embodiment and Dance', in S. Pile and M. Keith (eds), *Geographies of Resistance*, London: Routledge.

Todd, M.E. (1972) *The Thinking Body*, New York: Dance Horizons (first published in 1937).

Tomlinson, G. (1988) 'The Historian, The Performer, and Authentic Meaning in Music', in N. Kenyon (ed.), *Authenticity and Early Music: A Symposium*, Oxford: Oxford University Press.

Topaz, M. (1988) 'Issues and Answers Concerning Reconstruction', *Choreography and Dance*, 1, pp. 55–67.

Turner, B.S. (1992) *Regulating Bodies: Essays in Medical Sociology*, London: Routledge.

—— (1991) 'Recent Developments in the Theory of the Body', in M. Featherstone, M. Hepworth and B.S. Turner (eds), *The Body: Social Processes and Cultural Theory*, London: Sage Publications.

—— (1984) *The Body & Society*, Oxford: Basil Blackwell.

Turner, V. (1982) *From Ritual to Theatre*, New York: PAJ Publications.

—— (1974) *Dramas, Fields and Metaphors*, Ithaca, NY: Cornell University Press.

Ussher, J. (1989) *The Psychology of the Female Body*, London: Routledge.

Van Zile, J. (1985–6) 'What is the Dance? Implications for Dance Notation', *Dance Research Journal*, 17, 2 and 18, 1, pp. 41–7.

Vincent, L.M. (1979) *Competing with the Sylph*, New York: Andrews & McMeel.

Wacquant, L.J.D. (1995) 'Pugs at Work: Bodily Capital and Bodily Labour among Professional Boxers', *Body & Society*, 1, 1, pp. 65–94.

Walsh, D. (1972) 'Varieties of Positivism', in P. Filmer, M. Phillipson, D. Silverman and D. Walsh, *New Directions in Sociological Theory*, London: Collier-Macmillan.

Ward, A. (1997) 'Dancing around Meaning', in H. Thomas (ed.), *Dance in the City*, London: Macmillan – now Palgrave Macmillan.

—— (1993) 'Dancing in the Dark: Rationalism and the Neglect of Social Dance', in H. Thomas (ed.), *Dance, Gender and Culture*, London: Macmillan – now Palgrave Macmillan.

Weber, M. (1976) *The Protestant Ethic and the Spirit of Capitalism* (translated by T. Parsons), 2nd edn, London: George Allen & Unwin (first published in 1904–5).

Weiss, G. (1999) *Body Images: Embodiment as Corporeality*, New York: Routledge.

Weiss, G. and Haber, H.F. (eds) (1999) *Perspectives on Embodiment: The Intersection of Nature and Culture*, New York: Routledge.

Wild, S.A. (1987) 'Men as Women: Female Dance Symbolism in Walbiri Men's Ritual', *Journal for the Anthropological Study of Human Movement*, 4, 3, pp. 177–83.

Williams, D. (1999) 'Fieldwork', in T.J. Buckland (ed.), *Dance in the Field: Theory, Methods and Issues in Dance Ethnography*, London: Macmillan – now Palgrave Macmillan.

—— (1991) *Ten Lectures on Theories of the Dance*, Metuchen, NJ: Scarecrow Press.

—— (1977) 'The Nature of Dance: An Anthropological Perspective', *Dance Research Journal*, 9, 1, pp. 42–4.

—— (1976) 'An Exercise in Applied Personal Anthropology', *Dance Research Journal*, 9, 1, pp. 16–29.

Williams, R. (1981) *Culture*, London: Fontana.

Williams, S.J. and Bendelow, G. (1998) *The Lived Body: Sociological Themes, Embodied Issues*, London: Routledge.

Willis, P. (1978) *Profane Culture*, London: Routledge & Kegan Paul.

—— (1977) *Learning to Labour: How Working Class Kids get Working Class Jobs*, Farnborough: Saxon House.

Willis, P., with Jones, S., Canaan, J. and Hurd, G. (1990) *Common Culture*, Milton Keynes: Open University Press.

Wilson, B.R. (ed.) (1970) *Rationality*, Oxford: Basil Blackwell.

Wimsatt Jr, W.K. and Beardsley, M.C. (1946) 'The Intentional Fallacy', *Sewanee Review*, pp. 468–88.

Winch, P. (1958) *The Idea of a Social Science: And its Relation to Philosophy*, London: Routledge & Kegan Paul.

Wolf, M. (1992) *A Thrice-Told Tale: Feminism, Postmodernism and Ethnographic Responsibility*, Stanford, Calif.: Stanford University Press.

Wolff, J. (1995) 'Dance Criticism: Feminism, Theory and Choreography', in *Resident Alien: Feminist Cultural Criticism*, Cambridge: Polity Press.

—— (1990) 'Reinstating Corporeality: Feminism and Body Politics', in *Feminine Sentences: Essays in Women and Culture*, Oxford: Blackwell Publishers.

Woolgar, S. (1988) 'Reflexivity is the Ethnographer of the Text', in S. Woolgar (ed.), *Knowledge and Reflexivity: New Frontiers in the Sociology of Knowledge*, 1991 edn, London: Sage.

Wulff, H. (1998) *Ballet Across Borders*, Oxford: Berg.

Young, I.M. (1998a) 'Throwing Like a Girl', in D. Welton (ed.), *Body and Flesh: A Philosophical Reader*, Malden and Oxford: Blackwell (first published in 1980).

—— (1998b) ' "Throwing Like a Girl": Twenty Years Later', in D. Welton (ed.), *Body and Flesh: A Philosophical Reader*, Oxford: Blackwell.

Youngerman, S. (1974) 'Curt Sachs and his Heritage: a Critical Review of World History of Dance with a Survey of Recent Studies that Perpetuate his Ideas', *CORD News*, 6, 2, pp. 6–17.

World Wide Web references

http://dance.gold.ac.uk

http://www.sfgate.com/cgi-in/article.cg?file=/chronicle/archive/2000/12/08/DD15762.DTL

http://www.sfgate.com/cgi-in/article.cg?file=/chronicle/archive/2000/12/09/DD141289.DTL

http://www.sfgate.com/cgi-in/article.cg?file=/chronicle/archive/2000/12/13/DD133935.DTL

http://www.sfgate.com/cgi-in/article.cg?file=/chronicle/archive/2000/12/13/ED73230.DTL

http://www.sfgate.com/cgi-in/article.cg?file=/chronicle/archive/2000/12/19/DD12635.DTL

http://www.statistics.gov.uk.StatBase/xsdataset.asp?vlnk&More=Y

http://www.sfgate.com/cgi-in/article.cg?file=/chronicle/archive/2000/12/29/ED166641.DTL

Audio/visual references

Bird, B.: 'The Early Technique of Martha Graham', recorded interview with Helen Thomas, 1984.

Dawn in New York [choreographed by Doris Humphrey, 1956, as reconstructed by Ray Cook with additional choreography by Ray Cook] (videotape), performed by members of Ann Vachon/Dance Conduit Company, 30 and 31 March 1990.

Middlesex University dance students 'Learning *Water Study*', recorded group interview with Helen Thomas, 18 February 1997.

Main, L.: '*Water Study*: Doris Humphrey's Dances: Then and Now', recorded interview with Helen Thomas, 18 February 1997.

Water Study [choreographed by Doris Humphrey, 1928, as reconstructed by Eleanor King, directed by Ernestine Stodelle] (videotape), performed by students at NYU, the New York University Theatre, 11 August 1976.

Water Study [choreographed by Doris Humphrey, 1928, as reconstructed by Eleanor King, directed by Ernestine Stodelle in 1976] (videotape), National Doris Humphrey Association in collaboration with Princeton Book Company publishers, 1997.

Water Study [choreographed by Doris Humphrey, 1928] (motion picture), performed by Washington Dance Repertory Company, 1966.

Water Study [choreographed by Doris Humphrey, 1928, as reconstructed by Eleanor King, directed by Ernestine Stodelle in 1976] (Labanotation score), notated by Karen Barracuda, 1978–80, based on the Labanotation score by Michele Varon, 1976, 1978, revised by Karen Barracuda, 1999.

Water Study [choreographed by Doris Humphrey, 1928, as revived by Ruth Currier for the Washington Dance Repertory Theatre] (Labanotation score), Odette Blum, 1966, revised by Odette Blum, 1998.

Name Index

255

Subject Index

Printed in the United States
219780BV00001B/22/A

9 780333 724323